WOMEN AT WORK

WOMEN AT WORK

Tupperware,
Passion Parties,
and Beyond

L. Susan Williams
Michelle Bemiller

LYNNE
RIENNER
PUBLISHERS

BOULDER
LONDON

Published in the United States of America in 2011 by
Lynne Rienner Publishers, Inc.
1800 30th Street, Boulder, Colorado 80301
www.rienner.com

and in the United Kingdom by
Lynne Rienner Publishers, Inc.
3 Henrietta Street, Covent Garden, London WC2E 8LU

Library of Congress Cataloging-in-Publication Data
Williams, L. Susan.
Women at work : tupperware, passion parties, and beyond /
L. Susan Williams and Michelle Bemiller.
    p. cm.
  Includes bibliographical references and index.
  ISBN 978-1-58826-720-7 (alk. paper)
    1. Home parties (Marketing) 2. Women sales personnel
3. Direct selling. I. Bemiller, Michelle. II. Title.
HF5438.25W2987 2010
381'.14—dc22

                                   2010017261

British Cataloguing in Publication Data
A Cataloguing in Publication record for this book
is available from the British Library.

Printed and bound in the United States of America

The paper used in this publication meets the requirements
of the American National Standard for Permanence of
Paper for Printed Library Materials Z39.48-1992.

5 4 3 2 1

Contents

Tables and Figures

Tables

Figures

Case Studies

Acknowledgments

We recently heard a nice play on words (and on John Donne's famous quote): "No man is an island and no book is a solo." The words bring mindfulness about a few things—our social world's intractable insistence on male-gendered language, the transcending power of metaphors, and, for us, the steady, pulsing reminder that we were not, and are not, alone. This is our way of saying thank you to so many.

To Our Students

To the gender seminar students in 2007, thank you for inspiring me to peel back the layers of product parties and for giving me visuals of you, acting out at the now infamous Mary Kay party. Thank you to all my students, through all time, for giving me a reason to get up every day. Thank you for assuring me that my granddaughters and grandsons will have great, unruly leaders. —*Sue*

To my Sociology of Women students, thank you for providing me amazing insights about your gendered experiences and agreeing to serve as research participants for my field study. To all of my students, thank you for continuing to challenge me as a scholar and educator. —*Michelle*

To Our Mentors and Colleagues

Thank you, Myra, for your modeling of strength and insistence on getting it right, throughout my graduate school days and now; your guidance gave me vision for this book. Mangala, you are a great colleague and friend; thank you for your continuous support and faith in this book. I treasure all my fellow travelers from the University of Connecticut: Dena, Ruth, Julia, Denise, Loretta, Bandana, Marita, Nanette, and Rosie; and Joan, Idee, and many more from Louisiana State University; these are truly relationships that never end. —*Sue*

To my mentor, Kathy, thank you for all of your support throughout my graduate training and as I entered my first academic job. You have always served as a sounding board for my thoughts and ideas. It is much appreciated. To Jean-Anne, Rachel, Vicki, and Wendy—your continued support and friendship has carried me far beyond my dissertation days. I treasure you all. —*Michelle*

To Our Friends and Family

My mother passed away before the book was finished, but she contributed to it every day, as I remembered her words, her wisdom, and her life; thank you forever, Mom-mom. My family—Brent, Daralyn, and Kimber, and grandkids Kendra, Kyla, Justin, Kolton, and Jason—remain my rock of support, always. Perspective. That's what kids give you. Walt and Heidi, thank you for a million Sunday mornings, and for your friendship. Michelle, I'm eternally glad we have each other! —*Sue*

To Griffin, you are everything that I could hope for in a spouse, partner, friend, and coparent. Thank you for your support during this endeavor. To my daughter, Riley, and my son, Noah, I am so grateful for you both—you serve as a constant reminder of what matters in life, and why I get up in the morning. I hope that I serve as a positive role model for both of you throughout life's journey. To my parents, Deb and Steve; my grandparents, Joe and Irene; my brother, Shane, and his family (Tiffany and Jaedyn); and the Chance family (Aunt Roberta, Bryan, Nathaniel, Danielle, and Gabrielle)—thank you for your continued love and support as I pursue my personal and professional dreams. And last, but certainly not least, Sue. Thank you for including me on this project—it has been an amazing ride. I don't know what I would do without you in my life! —*Michelle*

To Our Team

Brett, your management of this project is without flaw; we appreciate your fine eye for detail and dedication to the project's spirit. Thank you. Leslie, though you came in at the final lap, your commitment, talent, and diligence are unparalleled. Kierston, David, Melissa, Caitlyn, Edward, Michael, Bradley—all of you played invaluable roles with good humor; we appreciate your work and your faithfulness.

You, our contributors, gave the book legs to stand with and wings to carry it forward. To work with you was our deep honor. Thank you beyond measure.

Finally, Andrew, thank you for believing in this project. You are simply the best.

We are none of us alone.

WOMEN AT WORK

1

The Gendering of Parties and Markets

Fun, Friends, and Flavors: This unique, interactive party is your opportunity to see, taste, and experience the new Tupperware lifestyle—amazing products, delicious recipes, and smart, simple solutions to improve your life. Plus, what a great opportunity to exchange ideas and make new friends. Whether you're a Consultant, a host, or a guest, there's a lot to enjoy at a Tupperware Party! It's party time! —*Party Inspiration Center, Tupperware.com*

Have you ever been to a Tupperware party (promoting airtight plastic containers) and a Passion Parties event (pushing plastic dildos named Jack Rabbit or Big Thriller) in the same week? The above excerpt from a Tupperware website leaves no doubt—a party is on! Now, picture a line of young women, poised before individual mirrored cosmetic cases the size of a lunch box (pink, of course), being carefully schooled in the (Mary Kay) art of sculpting and blending. Most at least pretend to take in the lesson; others giggle, and one yells out, "Hey look, I'm Bozo!" as she draws high eyebrows above her already rosy, rosy cheeks. Again, echoing from the Tupperware quote above, we are reminded that a product party is not *just* a party, it's a lifestyle.

This book is about gender parties: gatherings in which products are sold or made, while ideas about culturally appropriate male/female arrangements are constructed. And more.

Gender parties reside in all kinds of communities. Consider women milling around in home gatherings that feature flowing wine and fancy food, along with hundreds of designer handbags displayed on a staircase; then envision buying a handsome Louis Vuitton bag or a blue French leather Prada coin purse for $50— counterfeit replicas of bags that sell for hundreds or thousands of dollars. Excitement builds as more purses are ushered in, some in a familiar plaid, others with the Kate Spade logo or the Gucci G. Soon, the host (a woman) maneuvers an attendee (a woman) into the kitchen, where she explains the advantage of "joining" the multilevel marketing family; the solicitation phase has begun.

1

Yet all of these occasions are described not as work, but as a party.

The framework outlined in this book, together with its field studies, represents the first scholarly exploration of what we term the *party plan economy*.[1] As such, we refer to a loosely organized segment of a global informal economy, but we start by describing a mostly Westernized version of a multilevel marketing scheme in which a host (almost always a woman) invites friends into her home to purchase products shown by a company consultant (also usually a woman). The occasion is referred to as a party, complete with décor, food, drinks, games, and the chance to win free products. Another agenda, mostly subterranean, is to recruit other women into a pyramid-like structure in which graduated commissions are distributed hierarchically. Even this brief description reveals difficult-to-categorize facets of the party plan economy. Is it professional or personal? Hobby or hard work? Formal or informal work? Rule- or relationship-driven?

Certainly an air of fun permeates the party venue. But gender parties are about much more than the food and fun to which the word *party* alludes; parties are, in fact, work and networking, business and pleasure, public and private. The party plan economy, more than any other labor market segment, depends on roughly equal parts of economics and relationships. The problem is that traditional scholarship has neither language nor literature to deal with such a structure. Yet one underlying, largely unspoken and unacknowledged message comes through pretty clear: parties are what women do.

Not only are parties what women do, the term itself is gendered. On the one hand, the term *parties* conjures up feminine images such as social, ritual, celebration, decoration, fun, and festival. On the other hand, the term *markets* commands a masculine persona—market forces, stock market, bull markets, market data, competition. The concept and practice of gender accomplishes an almost complete (though artificial) segregation between the two terms: *market* is about serious work, clearly within a masculine domain, and *party* belongs to women and feminine venues.

Market portrays a degree of permanence and scope not attached to parties. To complement the economic structure of gender parties, we offer the concept *marketplaces of interaction*[2]—referring to a structure that is at once relational and utilitarian. It is this reference that situates *parties* in a more expansive context, while also retaining the concept of relations as critical to the party plan economy. By marketplaces of interaction, we refer to an organizational arrangement of relations that includes both professional and personal associations; these associations guide economic transactions but also incorporate friendship, reciprocity, and loosely structured social networks. The term also includes a culture of fun, though fun may not be primary or even present. Marketplaces of interaction can be related to physical locations, such as the home or streets or booths but also may reside in digital space (such as Facebook) and/or other interfaces such as organizations, clubs, or spaces for brief encounters.

The purpose of *Women at Work* is to bridge the traditionally male-modeled world of economics and the largely invisible work of relations, advancing the idea of a party plan economy that includes both formal and informal transactions. Recognizing the uniqueness of the party plan economy, wedged between formal labor and informal relationships, this book highlights overlapping circumstances of women's work and personal lives, whether participating in a cosmetic party in the United States or weaving a tapestry in Guatemala. These transactions are deeply gendered and distinct from male-centered arrangements, which have dominated labor market studies. To illustrate this idea, top scholars across several disciplines conducted original case studies specifically for this project, giving you a rare on-the-ground view of women's work in this part economic, part relational niche.

Twelve field studies illustrate intriguing facets of the party plan economy as they exist in somewhat dissimilar forms around the world. We expose two structures that are seemingly distinct—the party plan economy and marketplaces of interaction—and at once blur their boundaries; the two concepts are interdependent. Illustrating these two concepts through case studies, we tour women's experiences in a deeply gendered economy—from women vendors in the street markets of Brazil to piece workers in the Czech Republic to a comparative study of US party plan markets and "kitty parties" (a form of pooled resources) in India. Still other contributors' work yields situations as seemingly disparate as cloth weavers in Guatemala, African American book clubs, and drag queens gathering to sew costumes.

By situating the party plan economy within a global framework, we argue that women's experiences are marked by a common strand: individuals working within a mostly unregulated system that produces and sustains a deeply gendered system. In particular, women's informal work is often unacknowledged and/or trivialized (think about the party mode just described), yet it holds great promise for raising its members' group consciousness of themselves as women and, ultimately, as humanists, thus carrying potential for collective action.

How It All Began

As a professor of sociology, I (Sue) first became interested in the work/party phenomenon when listening to graduate students as they described themselves at a makeup party. In fact, the description of the Mary Kay scene at the beginning of this introduction came from these young students. They laughed at themselves as inept makeup artists, deliberated at seeming conflicts between being "girly" and being young feminists, and empathized (a little) with the party consultant, who obviously had no idea what to do with this group of young activists.

I could relate. Just previously, I had been to a Passion Parties gathering with a dozen or so of my colleagues. There must have been twelve PhDs in the room, and I can tell you it was not the demographic the Passion Parties consultant had been trained to manage. We laughed, made fun, tried on pink boas, and wondered aloud how our lesbian colleagues in the room felt about constant references to pleasing their "husbands." Poor consultant.

Intrigued, I took notice. It seemed that the party plan phenomenon was everywhere. My daughter in San Diego was invited to a shoe party that may have been as suspect as the illegal designer purse parties I had read about. I was urged to attend another Passion Parties event for a bride (does one register for vibrators?), then got an e-mail asking me to please come by the department office and shop through the Home and Garden Party catalog, generously placed there by an office employee. Someone else brought in their PartyLite candles catalog with the same request. I turned on late-night television, only to discover Suzanne Somers smilingly announce her new company, Mommy's Work at Home Place, where "thousands of mommies have left the daily grind of jobs to run their own businesses." It was everywhere. Except in scholarly literature.

Curious to test experiences of the college set, I informally polled my undergraduate classes. Virtually all women but none of the men related to the party plan, and I asked some of my Sociology of Women students to join ad hoc focus groups. One common wisdom that emerged from this group was that an "alcohol served" invitation gets the crowd to a product party. They specifically mentioned "Margarita Mary Kay parties," an interesting observation, given that the company discourages alcohol at product parties.[3] One young woman was actually a Mary Kay consultant and referred to the company as the Mary Kay Cult. Most invitations go out via online social groups such as Facebook and MySpace, as well as through cell phone chains; this is not surprising, given the social networking habits of this generation. Several women mentioned that they were approached in a store about their "remarkable face" or "unbelievable smile" that would make them the perfect model at a product party—a largely unethical solicitation device known as "warm chattering."[4]

This group also enlightened me to the only male party version I heard about, termed "corn and porn." Guys gather at someone's apartment, or perhaps at a frat house, eat popcorn and watch porn together. Of course, cold beverages are also involved. I suppose pornography is a type of product, but we decided this category is definitely beyond the scope of this project!

And then I thought about my own experiences. I went back to my own days as a Classique Creations jewelry consultant and later as a "beauty" consultant with Mary Kay in my small Texas hometown. The photo shows my "premiere" appearance as a Mary Kay "lady"; it was held in the bank community room because that was the largest venue I could find outside the high school gymnasium! Interestingly, at the time I never thought of these parties as *real* work (though it was actually exhausting); nor did I consider them to be particularly gendered or think of the women on both sides of the globe who are exploited through globalization, consumerism, and slave labor conditions. I do remember

Figure 1.1 Coauthor Sue Williams at her Mary Kay premier in 1982.
Note the little twin girls watching, intrigued. *(Dr. Sue's Photos)*

taking pride in what I did and being happy when my clients were pleased with the results.

After becoming aware of gender parties as a phenomenon, I searched for anything scholarly about this newfound discovery (though the party plan itself literally had been right under my nose for decades) but found nothing. I did note one critical thought–piece on the Internet that described a particular irony.[5] Mary Kay—now with huge mass production in China—sells skin lighteners to women there while marketing skin bronzers, manufactured in China, to white women in the United States. This is a vivid illustration of global exploitation as a by-product of such gender systems.

Our Gendered Eyes

Visiting with my coauthor, Michelle, we soon recognized that only a comprehensive analysis, based on a social constructionist gender perspective, would make sense of the party plan phenomenon. As gender scholars, we usually *see* gender everywhere (unlike my own blindness to the party plan phenomenon). The inevitability of recognizing gender arises because the expression of gender is embedded in action and practice. That is, people—all people—*do* gender, though the quality of such practices may vary significantly by culture.

This simple but profound concept comes from a 1987 article entitled "Doing Gender," which, among other important works in the 1970s and 1980s, marks a pivotal era in contemporary gender scholarship.[6] Candace West and Don Zimmerman, in "Doing Gender," note that although gender is learned (socialized), and gender is embedded in organizations and institutions (structure), it is individuals who *do* gender. It is individuals who, through daily practices, maintain gender. Once we consider gender as a verb, not a noun, the concept becomes crystal clear: I gender, you gender, my students at the Mary Kay party gendered, men who are disinterested (or pretend to be) are gendering, the host who invites and the women who attend and buy and book parties gender.[7] We all gender. It's a powerful, practice-based concept that helps recognize gender as embedded in relations. The challenge is to make gendering, while it hides beneath individual skirts and pants (metaphorically speaking), visible as a structure. It is equally important to recognize that it is through human initiative—referred to as agency—that resistance to power structures takes place. This book brings a structural gender analysis to the party plan economy while incorporating the role of individual motivation and contributions.

We conceive of the party plan economy as a gendered structure, identifying gender at the interactional level (individuals *do* gender) and the structural level (as an economic entity). Both are socially constructed. However, gender as a theoretical concept is more than the sum of its parts. In resisting an essentialist position, such as "we are born that way" and "that's just the way things are," gender scholars consider gender as a system of differentiation that divides people into two categories, male and female, regardless of similarities between or differences among each category.[8] That is, women and men are more alike than, say, women and oranges. And although it is true that, on average, men are taller than women, there is much greater variation *among* men and *among* women. Nevertheless, we are well conditioned to emphasize differences, not sameness, between the sexes. This practice, among others, maintains a system of power based on constructed gender that nonetheless exists under the guise of natural differences.

In considering gender as socially constructed, it is useful to think in terms of masculinities and femininities (note the plural; more than one template exists) rather than male/female.[9] Recently, I asked my students—both women and men—to write down ideal (conventional) masculine and feminine characteristics and then to rank their own gendered selves on a percentage scale.[10] I used femininity as the standard. No one ranked her/himself as 0 percent feminine, and no one ranked 100 percent feminine. We exist, as social beings, on a complex, socially constructed, and shifting continuum. Most women ranked themselves below 60 percent feminine, and most men "admitted" to incorporating at least 20 percent feminine characteristics into their identity. This brief example demonstrates that gender is not only constructed (and complex) but also a system of power. The masculine (and by association most men) is afforded greater status than the feminine. By attachment to the undervalued feminine, women are most often relegated to lower-status jobs, and much of their work is trivialized or rendered invisible. These concepts will become useful in understanding a global system of gender differentiation, one that shapes individual women's experiences as well as the entire party plan economy.

Gendering the Party Plan Economy

In many respects, the party plan economy is a financial boon. The US party plan economy alone accounts for more than $30 billion annually; Mary Kay Cosmetics, one of the direct marketing giants, declares 1.8 million independent consultants in more than thirty-five markets around the world and accounted for $2.4 billion in wholesale dollars ($4.8 billion retail) in 2007.[11] Although the study of economic forces generally characterizes markets as rational, formalized entities, sociological studies expand market research to also incorporate irrational moves such as discriminatory practices. For example, transactions in informal markets may enjoy a freer hand in more loosely defined environments such as piecework or caregiving. Many multilevel marketing companies now boost sales and recruitment through global development, where work is even less regulated. The $2.4 billion in Mary Kay sales number is from 2007. The company did not provide years for the other numbers. In 2009, Avon claimed to have "over 5 million" consultants in 100 countries.[12] During the same year, Arbonne averaged "752,052 . . . consultants worldwide and 680,449 in the United States."[13] In 2010, Pampered Chef reported 60,000 consultants in the United States, Canada, the United Kingdom, Germany, and Mexico.[14] These brief snapshots suggest a quite sizable labor market.

Yet, no one took notice, despite the seemingly obvious gendered character of the party plan economy. The language is gendered (in addition to party terms, references abound to love, romance, dreams, hearth, and other connotations associated with the feminine), and colors are almost always pink or other pastels—marks of femininity in modern society. Other imagery includes petals, hearts, patterns, florals, and demure photos of smiling women. Parties are in homes, by women and for women, and products are largely for women or for women who like to give others (usually men) pleasure.

Despite these feminine characteristics, a shadow structure with a heavily masculinist bias exists. While the party plan economy is supported almost exclusively by women's labor and women's consumer habits, the power structure looks different. For example, the home party–plan structure was the brainchild of a woman, Brownie Wise, who teamed with Mr. Tupper to boost sagging sales of his plasticware on retail store shelves, yet (as illustrated later) she was edged out early on. Even though the *portrayal* of the contemporary party plan corporations almost always includes women at the top, some claim this is a façade. For example, the president of cosmetic company Arbonne, Rita Davenport, is reported to be a figurehead who rarely if ever attends business meetings,[15] which are dominated by male executives.[16] Even the matriarch of cosmetics, Mary Kay Ash, appointed her son to manage the business. Christine Williams was the first to note a "glass escalator effect," documenting invisible forces that propel men to the top, especially in female-dominated work structures.[17] The party plan economy is dominated by men at the top and women at the bottom, a deeply hierarchical and gendered arrangement.

It's not the case that we lack scholarship to address the gendered nature of such broad-based structures. In fact, one of the earliest and most enduring gender/work concepts is the "glass ceiling," describing a transparent but impenetrable gendered barrier through which few women ascend in the work world.[18] However, it was not until around 1990 that social science developed a theory of gendered organizations. A rich set of studies emerged, led by Joan Acker. Acker convincingly argued that organizational structures are not gender neutral.[19] Assumptions about gender underlie virtually every aspect of organizations, though they are made to appear neutral by assuming a "universal" worker. On closer examination, a plethora of studies demonstrate that the image of work and workers is almost wholly masculinized (though not always in a straightforward manner).[20] For example, the ideal-type manager comes in early, stays late, works best in a highly competitive, hierarchical environment, wears a suit and tie, gives orders, appears rational and unemotional, drinks after work, plays golf with the executives, and is never expected to check on children, care for elderly parents, or pick up the dry cleaning; s/he *is* expected to have a partner at home who arranges lovely dinner parties. In other words, s/he is male or at least gendered to resemble a male.

These brief illustrations reflect a gendered party plan economy that reaches into the hundreds of billions of dollars in sales per year. Even more difficult to estimate is illegal markets. For example, knockoff purses are part of a global counterfeit trade that accounts for another $500 billion a year (though not all are sold under the party plan). Some are marketed legally, but Immigration and Customs Enforcement agents who investigate purse parties state that not only are many products smuggled into the country, but some participants are under suspicion as part of organized crime rings. Several convictions have ensued: a recent bust occurred in Omaha, Nebraska,[21] where women who sold the purses face a possible $2 million fine and several years in prison. Not so much of a party. Yet the party plan economy exists behind what some characterize as "smoke and mirrors," as one author specifically refers to the Amway organization's marketing ploys.[22] The party plan economy is big business, incorporating the glitz, glam, and sometimes questionable underbelly of a Hollywood production. Taken together, its deeply gendered character calls for a comprehensive gender analysis.

Marketplaces of Interaction

Recall that we refer to marketplaces of interaction as an organizational arrangement of relations, including both professional and personal associations that guide economic transactions. The party plan economy provides the structural arrangement for a gender analysis, but it is the interactional component that is most visible and action-based. Although it is a mischaracterization to think of the two segments—structure and interaction—as distinct, a gender analysis typically pulls the two apart. In general, the structure, here the party plan economy, gives the object of inquiry a framework within which to work, while interaction provides action and agency, or room for exploration. In particular, marketplaces of interaction accommodate a place to think about agency and resistance, whereas the party plan economy works as barriers to such movement. In reality, the two are interrelated and interdependent: as an entity, marketplaces of interaction underscore how our individual actions become embedded in structural constraints. A few personal illustrations emphasize this relationship.

Readers of this book may already be thinking about product-based parties as a part of a personal repertoire of experiences (even if actual attendance did not occur). But, if you are a woman, have you thought about your interconnectedness *as women* at these parties? If you are a man, perhaps you are curious (or not) about the absence of men in the party format. After all, one could just as easily buy tools, fishing gear, or other "manly" products while hanging out and having a barbecue in a friend's backyard. These brief wonderings elicit a decidedly gendered and local characterization of parties that includes individual and group-level features.

We've just discussed how individuals do gender, but West and Zimmerman also assert that these "doings" are situated in contexts, which lend channeling and character to the doings. Some contexts are best considered as historical and institutional, others as cultural, some as time- or geography-sensitive. All are complex, layered, multifaceted. Here, marketplaces of interaction lends itself well to thinking about situated doings. Marketplaces (the entity), like other physical places, carry history, tradition, practices, culture, institutions, trends, and conditions. The *concept* of marketplaces, however, is much broader and provides a proxy for considering ways in which social structure shapes gender and channels practices; it includes social practices and may invoke different levels of analysis.

In one sense, we can consider parties as local and markets as global. Once we envision party scenes as gendered, it becomes relatively easy to detect gendered interactions. On a global level, the connections may be further removed and more difficult to discern. How many of us stop to think about ties with workers cross-culturally? If you take a look at the products that you purchase at home-based parties, you will probably find that they were made in another country, and although the products will not explicitly state this, they are made by women whose labor is exploited. You won't readily find information that 99 percent of direct sales consultants lose money, or that Amway is being sued for antitrust violations and racketeering, or that winning on a snake-eyes roll in Vegas is about 600 times more likely than turning a profit in a multilevel marketing scheme.[23] Suddenly, the party becomes not only work but something more complex, layered and textured with a hint of the sinister or, conversely, with optimism and hope. Marketplaces of interaction provide a mechanism to assess such complexities.

The Party Plan Economy

The party plan economy sits in a peculiar position between formal and informal work: it incorporates public and private space and includes individual and collective efforts. Some follow corporate models, but others avoid bureaucratic forms. Some facets of the party plan economy defy even basic organizational conventions. This section addresses such junctures.

Worldwide, the vast majority of part-time workers are women; women represent 98 percent of this category in Sweden, 80 percent in the United Kingdom, and 68 percent in Japan and the United States. In developing countries, the informal employment comprises 50 percent to 80 percent of total nonagricultural employment.[24] Globally, women account for 30 percent to 90 percent of street vendors and about 80 percent of all home-based labor.[25]

Chances are that readers of this book have already participated in the informal labor economy. Babysitting or mowing lawns for neighbors are examples of work for which teens are often paid in cash, which may not be reported as income. There may be a benefit for the payee by not paying taxes on earnings, but the individuals who paid for the services benefited more—they escaped payroll taxes, or, saving even more, they avoided hiring a professional nanny or a landscape company. Corporations have the same desires as those neighbors—to minimize what they spend on labor—and, as a result, some build their entire enterprise around the informal marketplace. After all, why hire employees who will demand a salary, request benefits, and require a human resources department to oversee them when there are people willing to work solely on commissions?

Although the percentage of the gross domestic product (GDP) generated by informal markets is lower in the United States than in developing countries, it accounts for around 10 percent, or about $1.4 trillion dollars.[26] *Women at Work* addresses one thin slice of the informal economy—a party plan economy that seems rooted in the United States but demonstrates clear ties to other forms of women's work across the globe, which are often regarded as trivial.

Globalization movements often sit uneasily between formal and informal economies. Hernando De Soto argues that the informality of property rights in developing countries is the reason for their failure of formal capitalism to succeed beyond Westernized nations.[27] Nevertheless, the reduction of trade barriers has allowed capitalist firms to probe new markets around the world. As technology has allowed firms to become increasingly global, that same technology levels other playing fields, allowing bit players to compete with corporations many times their size. Thomas Friedman writes that "while the dynamic force in Globalization 1.0 was countries globalizing and the dynamic force in Globalization 2.0 was companies globalizing, the dynamic force in Globalization 3.0—the force that gives it its unique character—is the newfound power for *individuals* to collaborate and compete globally."[28]

But when it comes to people behind the numbers, the story is incomplete. Although some work has been done, research on gender issues within globalization is still largely uncharted terrain. As Valentine Moghadam notes, "much of the literature emphasizes globalization as an economic process; . . . the literature does not, however, consider globalization as a gendered process."[29] In particular, the field studies in this book explore ways in which optimism and hope are fostered in a system in which workers, in reality, have a very low chance of success.

Our challenge throughout this book is to theoretically frame the party plan economy as occupying a niche between "real jobs" in the corporate world and non-work-related activities and then to provide case studies as examples. As the book progresses, you will read stories that, at first glance, may not appear related to the party plan economy. In such cases, consider the field studies in terms of Table 1.1. The vertical axis represents the job's degree of structure. (Note that "real jobs" are in one corner and "attending a sales party" is in the opposite diagonal position.) Structure refers to the degree to which the system is regulated and puts requirements on members: one can simply show up to

Table 1.1 Selected units of the party plan economy, plotted along structure and formal work dimensions

					"Real job" holders
			Czech home-based workers		
		Mary Kay consultants			Counterfeit purse wholesalers
	Book club members				
Sales party attendees				Guatemalan weavers	1700s women homeworkers

Vertical axis (**Structured**): High — "It's very corporate"; Low — "I'm not told what to do"

Horizontal axis (**Formal Work**): Low — "It's occasional, a hobby"; High — "This is my job" product parties, but to get the most out of a book club meeting, members are required to have done reading beforehand. The horizontal axis denotes the degree to which the work is considered formal. In Table 1.1, the formal work designation is a combination of the degree to which the work is considered a "real" job and how readily one would identify herself as an official participant. A Guatemalan woman whose only source of income is weaving blankets would designate "participant in fair-trade textiles" as part of her identity much sooner than an American who uses the fair-trade blanket as a cover while reading.[30]

However, focusing on labor alone is limiting. We are also interested in using parties as a space for empowerment. By empowerment, we mean a bottom-up ability to exercise control over various aspects of one's social, political, economic, and personal world; the emphasis is on "power to" rather than "power over."[31] Empowerment can be approximated in different ways, and in Figure 1.2 are three types: individual economic, individual gendered, and collective. Economic empowerment requires little elaboration; financial independence invokes an overall sense of self-determination. The second dimension refers to a sense of gender empowerment when women practice autonomy, assert their right to decisionmaking, and reinforce the value of women's work.[32] In other words, they come to gain an appreciation of the historical and constructionist character of gender and how it is maintained. At the collective level, women (and others in the organization) practice empowerment when they fulfill significant commitments to social change that addresses issues especially relevant to women's lives.

Again, the usefulness of Figure 1.2 will become apparent as field studies are introduced throughout the book. However, some explanation is necessary at this point. First, understand that we subjectively judge where the various party plan "players" sit on the grid in Figure 1.2. Judgment comes from our knowledge of the positions, as conveyed by researchers who studied and wrote about them. Second, the plotted roles are neither comprehensive nor generalizable; they serve as illustrations relative to other positions in the chart. Third, the placements illustrate a vision of the party plan economy overall, as well as the unevenness among dimensions typically used to conceive of labor markets. To provide some baseline and continuity, we include the position of each unit on structure and formality as taken from Table 1.1.

Here we take evaluations of structure and formality from Table 1.1 and add assessments of gender empowerment to illustrate distinctions among several role positions. Comparing the vertical axis in Table 1.1 to the horizontal axis in Figure 1.2, observe that the position of Mary Kay consultants is scaled at six on structure and on formality. Even though one is tempted to evaluate Mary Kay as highly corporate (because it is, after all, a major corporation), the Mary Kay consultant is not. Considering that the Mary Kay consultant is specified as independent (with no corporate ties in terms of position, salary, or benefits), but is somewhat obligated to corporate principles, a six seems about right (again, relative to other roles on the grid). Moving across the horizontal axis, we see

Figure 1.2 Relative position of units in the party plan economy, by three dimensions of empowerment, individual economic (1), individual gendered (2), and collective (3)

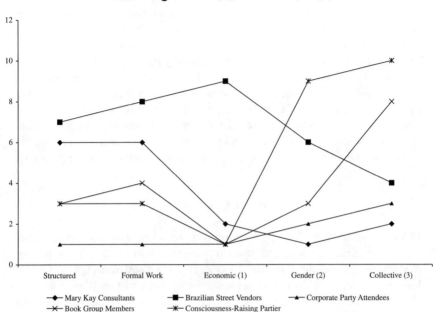

that the Mary Kay consultant scores low on individual economic empowerment (as you will learn, most make very little money on sales), even lower on individual gender empowerment (typically, they are encouraged to play a traditional feminine role), and also low on collective empowerment (even though the Mary Kay corporation professes to donate to women's causes, individual consultants are not encouraged to get involved).

Comparatively, Brazilian street vendors score higher on formality and structure measures, not because they are part of a large corporation but because they must show up to work at the same time every day, follow certain rules of the market association, and pay rent for their booth. In terms of Table 1.1 (and relative to Mary Kay consultants), they tend more toward "This is my job" and slightly more toward "It's very corporate." The street vendors score much higher on individual economic empowerment than Mary Kay consultants, higher on individual gendered empowerment (they are encouraged to be more independent-minded and autonomous), and somewhat higher on collective empowerment (they are aware of and network with other women in the same position to gain power).

Briefly, if we consider a consciousness-raising partier (including, for example, a gathering of women organized around a specific issue such as breast cancer or a political campaign), formality and structure (or corporate involvement) would be relatively low, individual economic empowerment near zero, but individual gendered empowerment and collective empowerment very high. An example we consider later in the book is women's book clubs, also plotted in Figure 1.2. The corporate party attendees (for example, guests at, say, a Pampered Chef party) are shown to emphasize their contrast to the consciousness-raising partier.

Although the methods utilized in Table 1.1 and Figure 1.2 do not allow a comprehensive analysis of the party plan economy per se, they represent a modest foundation from which to envision different entities within the party plan economy and where they lie along these dimensions relative to others. Just as the party plan economy itself is found along the hazy border between the formal and informal markets, these graphs should not be taken as absolute. Rather, use them as a tool, a conceptualization for why the party plan economy can include the work of women that certainly doesn't come to mind when one thinks of a party.

What to Expect

In *Women at Work* we look at the party plan economy within a global framework, examining connections of women around the world as they perform work that is largely invisible or seen as disconnected from structures that, nevertheless, bind together with common characteristics. We structure *Women at Work* to optimize three kinds of contributions. First, we provide seven chapters, each supplying background, context, and theoretical grit to frame issues related to gender parties and women's informal work. Second, we include case studies in Chapters 2–6, offering an exciting set of lenses that invoke curiosity and detail about how women's so-called party work functions, as well as the various configurations it takes on within different contexts and global regions. The chapters and case studies feature several photos and figures that illustrate ideas being presented. Third, we end each chapter with a short section titled "Beyond the Party," which ties the pieces together and provokes critical thought. Finally, we leave the text relatively unfettered with citations but provide ample endnotes. Below is a description of the chapters that follow.

Chapter 2: Staging the Study of Parties and Markets

Emphasizes historical, global, and local contexts and provides tools to understand the party plan economy and marketplaces of interaction.

Chapter 2 provides background to a party plan economy and introduces gender scholarship as a collective, interdisciplinary, and interdependent project established by women scholars through time and space. Exploring layered meanings of markets, parties, and gender, this chapter frames the case studies as grounded in a practice-based theory of gender. The "From the Field" section is historian Sue Zschoche's exploration of the intersections of domestic space and women's communal activities, of domesticity and commerce, intersections with deep roots in the history of women. Indeed, the idea of gendered markets—understood as spaces and products organized by and for women—brings together several essential strands in the history of women and work.

Chapter 3: How the Party Plan Economy Mutes Women's Work

Demonstrates how economic forces relegate (some) women to informal, invisible work; illustrates the party plan economy as shaping women's interactions; provides examples of how intersectionality (race, class, nationality) matters.

This chapter focuses on how the party plan economy molds many interactions among and for women. It leads off with "Now You See It, Now You Don't," illuminating a ritual of contemporary life—gender parties—through which women's production is rendered mostly invisible. The invisibility is accomplished within a context of hyper-consumerism, taking advantage of women's needs to provide for personal and family financial demands as well as their connections to one another. These gender parties, although decidedly woman-centered, work to divide women within a class-stratified culture.

Three case studies accompany this chapter. Kimber Williams, an attorney in San Diego, looks into the legal and illegal world of purse parties ("The Power of the Purse"), interviewing women in three states who report somewhat different experiences, but almost all of whom exhibit some form of status-seeking behavior. The study treads the territory between cultural trends and legal parameters. The second study, conducted by Akiko Yoshida, is entitled "A Gendered American Dream: Why Women Sell Mary Kay." Utilizing in-depth interviews, Yoshida looks at the connection between beliefs and gendered expectations, revealing gendered ideological mechanisms that contribute to the invisible nature of consultant work. Finally, in "Brazilian Women, Invisible Workers," Adryanna Siqueira observes women street vendors in her native country, researching two contemporary street markets in Goinia, Feira de Lua, and Feira Hippie and focusing on survival strategies.

Chapter 4: How Marketplaces of Interaction Modify the Party Plan Economy

Demonstrates how the structure of women's personal networks operates; illustrates how women's resistance and networks change the party plan economy; provides examples of different forms of the party plan economy.

Although Chapter 3 shows how the party plan economy shapes interactions, this chapter demonstrates how the opposite is also true. That is, women—through individual resistance and through collective networks—change the way the party plan economy works. The section "Gender Dealings: Moving Between Public and Private Spaces," focuses on ways in which the party plan economy creates "wiggle room" between public and private lives. Women are often conflicted between professional and private demands but sometimes find space for creative "knowing strategies" and common goals. In "From the Field," Michelle Bemiller examines women's participation as consumers of party plan products in "Women Helping Women on the Party Line," discussing why women participate in the party plan. The chapter ends with a collaborative event between US and Czech Republic scholars, "Womanhood and Home-Based Work in the Czech Republic." Karen Kapusta-Pofahl, Eva Kavková, Ivana Šindlerová, and Jana Smiggels-Kavková examine women's search for common ground through shared experiences as they engage in home-based work in the Czech Republic, viewing women's work as an emerging facet of globalization.

Chapter 5: When Consumption, Markets, and Movements Meet

Suggests outcomes that result from the melding of economic and interaction structures; illustrates how ideological, personal, and political forces work in concert; further promotes ideas of empowerment.

The personal is political. This famous phrase marked the second wave of the women's movement in the United States and still stands as testament to the many-faceted and overlapping character of women's lives. The section entitled "The Political Is Personal: When Personal Ideology and Markets Collide" explores the intersection of the personal and political for women. It examines how women engage in political subversion (though not always in a straightforward path) through everyday resistance. This concept is well illustrated in Leigh Fine's case study, "Sex Toy Parties, Compulsory Heterosexuality, and 'Being' in Community." Fine provides an intriguing examination of ways in which lesbians traverse sex-toy parties designed for heterosexual women. The second case study provides an apt demonstration of the politicization of everyday life when activists come together. In "Challenging the Global Economy Through Home-Based Labor," Summer Lewis focuses on groups that produce and promote fair-trade products.

Chapter 6: When the Party Reaches Beyond Products

Introduces alternative forms of "products" beyond consumerism; provides glimpses into conscious raising and idea formation; suggests groundwork for change.

The first section in this chapter, "The Promise of Parties, the Gender of Markets," turns to ways in which gender structures—defined through parties and global marketplaces—provide space for progressive change by connecting women to one another. This is not to suggest the work is easy or the outcome always favorable. But these "structural holes," which represent fissures or fault lines in a gendered system, provide promise for undermining entrenched patriarchal arrangements. The first case study, by Mangala Subramaniam, Gregory Gibson, and Beth Williford, presents an international comparative study. In "Indian Kitty Parties as Models of Women's Empowerment," the authors critically examine forms of economic empowerment for women in two countries. They compare house parties in the United States to "kitty parties" in India, a gathering in which middle-class women socialize, play games, and take turns winning a weekly money collection. The second case study, "Lasting Legacies and Sister Friends: Literacy in African American Communities," by BeEtta Stoney, conceives of African American women as "keepers of the culture," with book clubs as the venue. Following closely is Dena Wallerson's study, "The Politics and Power of African American Women's Book Groups," examining their potential for "quiet activism." The "From the Field" section concludes with Dusty Garner's "Instant Family—Just Add Eyeliner." Turning a sharp corner, Garner's contribution challenges the reader to step into a world where gender is fluid, blended, changing, daring. Exploring a community of drag queens, he finds that gender becomes muted as categories of male and female fade and as family comes first.

Chapter 7: Taking Back, Talking Back

The final chapter starts where most books end. Gathering bits of wisdom from introspection, field notes, and reflections, the authors incorporate insight from experiences gathered throughout this project to illustrate the practice and promise of gender. Integrating these revelations, this collection inspires hope toward collective practice, finding that "action is the antidote to despair."

Ultimately, the aim of this book is to bring together a multitude of diverse women's voices as they speak, in solidarity, for the recognition and celebration of women's contributions to the informal economy, the home, and our world existence. We do not presume that this little book will cause a transcendence of consumerism or capitalism, but we hope that it will prove transformative for individual women and create collective awareness for others.

Notes

1. Although some authors have written about experiences within specific companies, such as Bob Kealing's *Tupperware Unsealed* (Gainesville: University Press

of Florida, 2008), Doris Christopher's *The Pampered Chef* (New York: Doubleday Business, 2005), and Ruth Carter's *Amway Motivational Organizations* (Winter Park, FL: Backstreet Publishing, 1999), all are either journalistic or singularly based on personal accounts; none is research-based; and none covers a range of party-plan companies. Further, as far as we can determine, we are the first to use the term *party plan economy*.

2. We believe this is the first instance of using the term *marketplaces of interaction*. We sought to develop a concept that captures individual agency, networking, resistance, and determination while also advancing a term that accommodates distinct forms and patterns of interaction.

3. Apparently, the flushing of the face caused by alcohol makes it difficult to properly match products to skin tone. eHow, "How to Host a Mary Kay Party," May 2007, http://www.ehow.com (June 15, 2009).

4. Pink Lighthouse, "Warm Chatter Training," April 2008, http://www.pinklighthouse.com (June 29, 2009).

5. Sarah Wyatt, "Mary Kay Global Expansion Raises Hope, Concerns," *Women's International Perspective*, June 25, 2007, http://thewip.net (May 20, 2009).

6. Candace West and Don H. Zimmerman, "Doing Gender," *Gender & Society* 1, no. 2 (1987): 125–151.

7. Raewyn Connell, *Gender and Power: Society, the Person, and Sexual Politics* (Palo Alto, CA: Stanford University Press, 1987).

8. Beth B. Hess and Myra Marx Ferree, *Analyzing Gender: A Handbook of Social Science Research* (Newbury Park, CA: Sage, 1987).

9. Patricia Yancey Martin, "'Said and Done' Versus 'Saying and Doing': Gendering Practices, Practicing Gender at Work," *Gender & Society* 17, no. 3 (2003): 342–366.

10. The Bem Sex Role Inventory (BSRI) pioneered independent assessments of masculinity and femininity by asking a series of questions on sex-linked socially desirable personality characteristics. Hundreds of studies have been conducted using the BSRI, with mixed results. In general, feminine traits are more concentrated with female respondents, while masculine traits are more variable; see Carol J. Auster and Susan C. Ohm, "Masculinity and Femininity in Contemporary American Society: A Reevaluation Using the Bem Sex-Role Inventory," *Sex Roles* 43 (2000): 499–528. The BSRI has been critiqued on several points, including its heavy reliance on categories and stereotypes; little to no consideration of situational, interactional, and overlapping gender construction; and lack of applicability to transsexual and transgender people. For examples of this discussion, see Rose Marie Hoffman and L. DiAnne Borders, "Twenty-Five Years After the Bem Sex-Role Inventory: A Reassessment and New Issues Regarding Classification Variability," *Measurement and Evaluation in Counseling and Development* 34, no. 1 (2001): 39–55; Murray Webster Jr. and Lisa Slattery Rashotte, "Fixed Roles and Situated Actions," *Sex Roles: A Journal of Research* 61 (2009): 325–337.

11. Mary Kay, "Global Growth Quick Facts," http://www.marykay.com (June 15, 2009).

12. Avon, "Avon Around the World," http://www.avoncompany.com (June 20, 2009).

13. Arbonne, "Arbonne International," http://www.arbonne.com (June 8, 2009).

14. Pampered Chef, "Company Facts," http://www.pamperedchef.com (May 29, 2009).

15. Arbonne, "Arbonne International: Taking It to the Next Level," *Direct Selling News*, July 2006, http://www.arbonnemarketing.com (June 8, 2009).

16. Arbonne, "Global Office Executive Team," http://www.arbonne.com (June 8, 2009).

17. Christine L. Williams, "The Glass Escalator: Hidden Advantages for Men in Nontraditional Occupations," *Social Problems* 39 (1992): 253–267.

18. "Good for Business: Making Full Use of the Nation's Human Capital," A Fact-Finding Report of the Federal Glass Ceiling Commission, March 1995, http://www .dol.gov (June 30, 2010).

19. Joan Acker, "Hierarchies, Jobs, Bodies: A Theory of Gendered Organizations," *Gender & Society* 4 (1990): 139–158.

20. For example, Lorber finds that "in work organizations, position in the hierarchy does and does not override a worker's gender. The behavior of men and women doctors sometimes reflects their professional status and sometimes their gender, and it is important to look at both aspects to understand their relationships with patients." Judith Lorber, "Beyond the Binaries: Depolarizing the Categories of Sex, Sexuality, and Gender," *Sociological Inquiry* 66, no. 2 (1996): 154.

21. "Purse Parties Funding Organized Crime?" WFTV (Omaha), July 2008, http://www.wftv.com (May 7, 2009).

22. Ruth Carter, *Amway Motivational Organizations: Beyond the Smoke and Mirrors* (Winter Park, FL: Backstreet Publishing, 1999).

23. John M. Taylor, "Some Shocking Statistics: Comparing Recruiting MLM's with No-Product Pyramid Schemes, and with Gambling," Consumer Awareness Institute, http://www.mlm-thetruth.com (June 1, 2009).

24. Martha Chen, Joann Vanek, Francie Lund, and James Heintz, *Progress of the World's Women 2005* (New York: United Nations Development Fund for Women, 2005), 8.

25. Women in Informal Employment: Globalizing and Organizing, "Main Findings," http://www.wiego.org (July 2, 2010).

26. Friedrich Schneider and Dominik H. Enste, *The Shadow Economy: An International Survey* (Cambridge, UK: Cambridge University Press, 2002).

27. Hernando De Soto, *The Mystery of Capital: Why Capitalism Triumphs in the West and Fails Everywhere Else* (New York: Basic Books, 2000).

28. Thomas Friedman, *The World Is Flat 3.0: A Brief History of the Twenty-First Century* (New York: Picador, 2007), 10.

29. Valentine Moghadam, *Globalizing Women: Transnational Feminist Networks* (Baltimore, MD: Johns Hopkins University Press, 1995), 2.

30. Fair trade is a social movement as well as a market approach that helps producers in developing countries promote sustainability. The movement has been particularly helpful to women, who otherwise would be unable to find a market or fair price for their wares. Fairtrade Labelling Organizations International, "About Fair Trade," 2006, http://www.fairtrade.net (June 30, 2010).

31. Opposing empowerment is exploitation. Briefly, exploitation is characterized as hierarchical, uncooperative, and undemocratic, with practices and values centered on domination, competition, manipulation, and control. See Myra Marx Ferree, Judith Lorber, and Beth B. Hess, *Revisioning Gender* (Thousand Oaks, CA: Sage, 1999), 161–183.

32. United Nations, "Guidelines to Women's Empowerment," http://www.un.org (June 5, 2009).

2

Staging the Study of Parties and Markets

Staging the party includes plans, props, and a party persona. Preparation includes cleaning, considering design and entertainment, and arranging for food and drink. As guests arrive, the hostess (appropriately groomed and coiffed) greets them with a smile and her best party front.

Anthropologists studying roles and reciprocity recognize these actions as rituals and analyze the associated linguistic markers. These are also terms of interest to social psychologists, whereas historians are interested in how the character of each may change across time periods. To understand parties as a bundle of ideas, we call on Erving Goffman, a twentieth-century sociologist who offers a theoretical perspective and conceptual tools to analyze social settings.[1]

It is no accident that we use the term *staging the party*, for Goffman established a school of thought called "dramaturgy," using several theater terms as metaphors for understanding how people interact with one another. These metaphors make especially useful tools for understanding gender parties. For example, *frontstage* represents the party front that the host exhibits to her guests, whereas *backstage* corresponds with letting down her guard when everyone leaves. Dramaturgy is part of a larger perspective known as symbolic interactionism, and this chapter makes use of several terms in this tradition to understand gender parties.

Markets

Perhaps the easiest way to conceptualize markets is through the more concrete term *marketplace*. Chances are, the term conjures up a picture of some kind of physical space with at least a few people and some products. I (Sue) imagine lots of color—maybe sprays of red and yellow flowers and colorful, spicy food

Figure 2.1 Pike Place Market, Elliot Bay waterfront in Seattle, WA. One of the oldest farmers' markets in the United States, it is a place of business for local growers, merchants, craftspeople, and performers. It is popular with locals and tourists alike (10 million annually) and is home to the famous "flying fish" market. A public venue, it is governed by a board and offers many services, including low-income housing, child care, medical care, drug/alcohol rehabilitation, counseling services, job training, and classes. *(Dr. Sue's Photos)*

displayed in stacks and arrays, with vendors barking out the virtues of their wares. Lots of people—of all hues, shapes, and origins—mill around, some animated and fun, others curious or confused or agitated. Such places are marketplaces of business but also marketplaces of friends and family, strangers and the barely acquainted intermingling in a rich tapestry of purpose, not all of which centers on merchandise; marketplaces also tell of human stories and connections.

The term *marketplaces of interaction* captures the idea of both form and action, encapsulating related elements of gender parties. Gender parties, as a thing, include space and people and products. But gender parties, the idea, incorporates not only business but also networks of people and reciprocity; marketplaces of interaction supply a metaphor that gives this confluence of elements "legs"; it suggests activity and makes it work.

Global markets bring marketplaces of interaction to bear on what Thomas Friedman calls a "flattening of the globe."[2] The traditional reference to globalization denotes the removal of barriers for economic trade and capital ventures. A much broader interpretation includes the free flow not only of goods and international barter but also of services, technology, information, and sociopolitical exchange.

Global markets and marketplaces of interaction provide a way to include women's worldwide awareness and connections as part of this book. If we can name only one goal, it is this: that we use gender parties as a way to understand women's connections through time and space. Women have always worked in unregulated (or informal) labor, and women have always taken responsibility for relationships and social transactions. Gender parties, as a concept, provide us the ideal venue in which to explore women's local connections through informal (and most often invisible) work. But this book also goes global. That is, through case studies, we investigate other forms and functions of women's gatherings that are closely akin to the product get-togethers we call gender parties. The idea of global ground will become apparent as these field studies flatten the world of gender parties and marketplaces of interaction.

Gender Scholarship

Similar to globalization, gender scholarship belongs to a long yet shifting strand that incorporates historical and traditional ideas into modern trends—in this case, the gathering of ideas of social differences tied to sex categories, ideas that are then expanded, abandoned, or changed in tandem with changes in knowledge, sociopolitical milieux, and even technology. In its current form, gender scholarship spans a relatively wide spectrum of perspectives and takes on a somewhat different focus depending on the discipline or tradition within which it is applied. There are important commonalities, though, and this book focuses on them.

In general, we define gender scholarship as a study of the rules and patterns of social groups that organize and maintain difference between women and men.[3] In particular, we refer to contemporary gender theory—heavily influenced by feminist thought—that views gender as a social system of power, dividing feminine and masculine characteristics into two discrete categories. Note that we emphasize a *social system*, one that is based on *power*.[4] These two concepts are crucial to gender scholarship.

This chapter further elaborates on gender theory as a collective, interdisciplinary, and interdependent project established by gender scholars through time and space. It also focuses on fundamentals of gender theory that are specifically useful for understanding gender parties and global markets, especially the concept of *gender regime*, considered a "social container" of structural elements tied to gender.[5] The "From the Field" section features historian Sue Zschoche's attentive essay on the time dimension of gender parties.

Across Time and Space: Our Mothers' Parties

Remember the steam kettle; though up to its neck in hot water, it continues to sing. —*Brownie Wise*

The words of Brownie Wise, who founded home-based Tupperware parties, hint at social expectations for women throughout the history of gender parties— just keep singing (or smiling). The challenge of how to study gender parties across time and space is every bit as daunting. The problem seems insurmountable: how can we capture the essence of history, region, biographies, and economic development—as each intersects with gender? The concept of *gender regime* supplies the needed conduit.

Raewyn Connell defines gender regime as a structural inventory of gender relations.[6] Gender regime refers to a local "capsule" of gendering components— including rules, patterns, institutional arrangements, interactional events—with numerous gender regimes (thousands or even millions) embedded in a larger universe known as the gender order. The gender order is rife with structural tensions, contradictions, even crisis tendencies that may mark impending change; local gender regimes allow comparison across space and time.[7]

In this book, we consider gender parties as existing within gender regimes, some very similar, others different, but with considerable overlap because they exist within the gender order. Identifying this situatedness enables recognition of commonalities and connectedness as women work within the party plan economy in places as disparate as Boston or Kansas or Guatemala. Recalling that a full gender analysis requires both structural and interactional consideration, the gender regime again fulfills that obligation. Though there is considerable overlap, *party plan economy* generally refers to structure, and *marketplaces of interaction* captures various interactional dynamics.

The concept of gender regimes lends itself well to consideration of time and space. In fact, gender regimes represent a sort of social container, one that encapsulates gender relations in contexts as specifically identifiable as a particular place in a particular time with its host of economic, political, and social conditions. All of them are gendered. The next section provides just such an example.

The Time Tunnel

My (Sue's) grandmother's parties centered around one of two hubs—family or church. Both of them included food. When we went to her house for Sunday dinner, it was obvious that she'd been up since before dawn, preparing a host of home-cooked dishes. Having one kind of potatoes or one kind of beans was never enough. Not everyone might like the buttery mashed potatoes, so there were scalloped potatoes lathered in cheese and another dish of sweet potatoes in thick syrup. There were green beans, lima beans, and pinto beans. Fried chicken was flanked by ham on one side and roast on the other. The sideboard (a piece of furniture behind the dining table) was laden with pies and cakes and cookies. We ate two meals from my grandmother's table that day, with plenty of food left to send home with each family.

On these celebrated family Sundays, women gathered in the kitchen to taste, exchange recipes, and talk about the children, while the "menfolk" roamed around outside or sat in the living room, mulling over the weather or crops or maybe football. We knew that my grandmother also set aside time before church to starch and iron her Sunday apron and to read her Bible, while my grandfather and uncle read the Sunday paper. But the term *gender regime* or *gendered performance* never entered her consciousness or ours.

The other sort of my grandmother's parties consisted of church women gathering at one another's homes to do their Bible studies or plan missionary work or maybe do a little quilting or embroidering. Much of the narrative centered around giving to others; they were actually called Missionary Women (later to become Methodist Women). I do not know for sure, but I assume that they seldom, if ever, recognized that church was the only public space freely available to women at the time.

All these activities were decidedly gendered. Our grandmothers would never use this language, but absolutely, they were doing gender. I don't mean to say that they never valued their activities and time together; I'm sure they looked forward to and genuinely enjoyed these outings, for the most part. Certain contemporary cultural events, such as quilting, scrapbooking, or bachelorette parties, may in some ways mirror these early day get-togethers.[8] But therein lies the rub; the beat goes on because we deeply and unconsciously engage in doing gender. Our grandmothers' parties and our mothers' parties give us a tunnel to think about how gender regimes change, yet also how gender as a system endures over time.

Our Mothers' Parties

Many of us remember our mothers' parties. My own mother was a housewife of the 1950s. She lived 1 mile from the farm where she grew up, and 1 mile from where my father grew up, the three homes drawing a perfect triangle. My parents farmed in West Texas, working from daylight until well after dark, and hollowed out their own modest little piece of the American Dream. They lived among friends and neighbors, most of whom grew up together. They went to the same church as my grandparents, a little one-room structure called Carr's Chapel, named after my great-grandfather.

In addition to church activities (which were much the same as my grandmother's experiences), my mother hosted parties. As I consider it now, most of the major events were wedding anniversaries. There was my grandparents' fiftieth wedding anniversary, her best friend's twenty-fifth anniversary, and her own fortieth anniversary. Most other parties centered around the Harmony Home Demonstration (HHD) Club. (How 1950s is that?) Harmony was the name of the farming community where we lived (I'm not making that up!), and the HHD ladies focused intently on domestic arts of cooking, preserving, sewing, and, occasionally, entertaining.

The advent of Tupperware parties found favor in just such a context, and my mother and her HHD friends took turns throwing parties where they learned (over and over) how to "burp" the plasticware. These were some of the first gender parties in the United States, closely following Tupperware's predecessor, Stanley Home Products. I remember my mother hosting a product party around 1960 for "waterless" stainless steel cookware. I recently asked her about it, and she explained how innovative that was at the time. She also explained why they had the party at night—so the men could come to help make the financial decision necessary to fund such an investment (the set was around $100, which translates to about $700 in 2010 after inflation).[9] We might characterize it as a mixed-gender party since men were present. But, clearly, the men were there to control the checkbook.

Fast-forward a generation (or two or three). Gender parties today are securely embedded in a culture of consumerism and still sit primarily within the women's sphere. Home party sales now account for approximately 30 percent of the $30 billion in US direct sales, and according to AOL Small Business 13.6 million Americans bought or sold goods from home in 2004.[10] As the economy tightens, more and more people turn to entrepreneur ventures, and the party plan economy reaches out particularly to women. Though many direct sales companies introduce men's products and include a few men as sales representatives, most remain heavily dominated by women (though men executives are abundant). For example, less than 1 percent of Mary Kay consultants are men.[11]

From bras to bags to baby goods, products of the party plan economy typically bond to women and women's lives. None is more strongly representative of this trend than cosmetics and other so-called beauty products, an industry that exceeds $50 billion every year. Though L'Oreal (which sells in retail stores and includes the Maybelline label) commands the leading portion of this giant industry at almost $25 billion, direct market companies control large shares.[12] Among direct selling companies, Avon leads at $10.6 billion, followed by Mary Kay at $2.4 billion.[13] In comparison, cosmetic giant Revlon, selling in retail stores, reports only $1.3 billion in sales annually. Since World War II, cosmetics have held their own in times of war, sacrifice, and crisis.[14] Even in a rapidly declining economy, beauty products alone accounted for most new product launches in 2008.[15] Cosmetics and beauty products dominated at least five generations, from the baby boomers after World War II through Generation Y, born in the 1990s.

Though the future of gender parties seems secure, its form may adjust to a new information age. Already, marketers well understand that the world of today's young people is dominated by digital networks and virtual social worlds. MySpace, Facebook, blogs, wikis, Twitter, and other forms of new media dictate communication and interactions. The latest generations, Generation Y (the Millennials) and Generation Z, remain marked by hyper-consumerism; gender parties are already going digital, with invitations sent through electronic networks and order forms readily available online. It remains to be seen how contemporary economic crises will influence how gender parties are defined and how successfully they maintain their market share.

One thing we do know about gender change: the sudden shift to androgyny that many scholars and activists of the 1960s and 1970s envisioned did not come about; our world remains deeply gendered. It seems reasonable to say that gender parties are here to stay. Virtual parties are cropping up here and there, and the products, hosts, and consumers remain much the same—women and their purses, women and their shoes, women and scrapbooking, women and jewelry. Perhaps we will move to dressing our avatars for the next lot of gender parties!

The Party Plan Economy as Gender Regime

Gender regimes accommodate and organize various forms of structures, which in turn assist in molding gender relations. This section considers the party plan economy as a gender regime. Arguably, every component of the economy, as the institution through which goods and services are produced, distributed, and consumed, is gendered. However, in no place is this more clear than the party plan economy, where products and form depend on social ideas about and the practice of gender.

Australian gender scholar Raewyn Connell addresses three generalized structures within gender regimes: labor, power, and cathexis (or patterns of emotional attachment).[16] Though all three are applicable throughout the party plan economy, we focus on labor and power here and then refer to cathexis in the later section on marketplaces of interaction. These three structures certainly do not exhaust patterns within a gender regime, but they suffice to demonstrate how the party plan economy works.

Gender and Labor

Recalling that gender regimes exist within the larger gender order, we know that throughout modern history the division of labor has cut along gender-delineated lines. Although women may have taken primary responsibility for children and home duties for thousands of years, they also participated in the production of goods until industrialization. Once the factory-dominated mode of production dictated a clear and almost complete sexual division of labor, men became seen as primarily responsible for wage-earning labor and women for unpaid labor at home.

Work domains and home front domains became almost totally segregated by sex, or so the dominant ideology would have us believe. In fact, poor women, single women, and most women of color have always worked, but their work—whether in or out of the home—remained mostly unacknowledged. Though some women today have made great strides within the general economy, occupations and tasks remain strongly gendered. Almost a century after women first were deemed worthy of voting, women account for around 2 percent of top corporate executives in the nation,[17] comprise 17 percent of Congress,[18] and earn about 77 percent of what equally qualified men earn.[19] Most experts agree that the sexual division of labor remains responsible for much of the gender gap.

Once we acknowledge and name the party plan economy, it becomes analyzable as a gender regime. In fact, within the context of other segments of the economy—even one where women still take a 25 percent pay cut—the party plan economy can be seen as an evolutionary throwback. We would be hard pressed to find another niche of this size as clearly driven by gender relations.

Certainly, the party plan economy is dominated by commodities and services known as women's turf. But almost without exception, the merchandise could be purchased in retail stores, sometimes at a better price. Indeed, the party plan economy depends on the social expectation that women can be relied on to (1) purchase and consume gendered products that target their own personal grooming and/or home and hearth accessories; (2) maintain cultural ideals such as beauty and fragrance norms, varieties of cleaning products, and family niceties such as décor and scrapbooking; and (3) support one another's parties even when they'd rather not. The party plan economy is not simply gendered; it exists only because of gender.

Gender and Power

The party plan economy is not simply delineated by sex differences. It is characterized by gender-based power, or what Dorothy Smith calls the relations of ruling.[20] That term refers to an overarching dominance that "grasps power, organization, direction, and regulation as more pervasively structured than can be expressed in traditional concepts . . . of power." Historically, this complex formation of power has been dictated by masculinist principles—those based on hierarchy, competition, hostility, exploitation, and sometimes violence—and remains dominant by appearing to be rationally organized, impersonal, universal, and neutral.

Although power differentials exist between individual men and women, the relations of ruling—structural power—go beyond the personal. Patterns of power relations exist over time and across space; they are lasting and take on specific form and function. For example, certain physical features are emphasized to showcase masculinity in men and femininity in women. Power relations become embedded in bodily features because the masculine symbolizes power and control, whereas the feminine is seen as demure and submissive. In turn, these characterizations present dilemmas for individuals: Masculine women are seen as powerful and thus deviant and inappropriate (deserting their feminine identity), whereas feminine men are seen as weak and, in particular, incapable of violence. (It is not violence per se that is specifically valued, but the threat of violence is used consistently as a "resource for masculinity" and thus is structurally powerful.)[21] Generally speaking, a gender regime uses both universal and local strategies to sanction individuals who deviate from these social expectations.

Relations of ruling are embedded in gender regimes, which in turn are embedded in a long history of patriarchy. Although stereotypical portrayals of masculinity and femininity may seem a bit "old-fashioned," patriarchy persists, not through an overt slavery of women (though vestiges exist), but through the everyday practice of gender. Some examples: Regardless of Hillary Clinton's education, position, and power, two of the best-known remnants of her bid for the presidency were her pantsuits and the Hillary nutcracker, in which Clinton was shown holding a walnut between her knees—both aimed at discrediting not only her power but also her femininity. Though Michelle Obama is generally seen as contemporary, educated, and popular, the big news for weeks was the inappropriateness of her sleeveless dresses. While Sarah Palin was on the campaign trail, media primarily buzzed about her family values and her wardrobe. All these instances detract from women's real contributions and place them in a position one step below men.

The so-called average woman is also disadvantaged, seemingly at every turn. Students in my classes maintain that sexually active young women are still seen as "sluts" while their male counterparts are "studs" (a disturbing revelation; one would have hoped for more progress by the twenty-first century!). Girls still rarely ask guys out or to dance, and guys expect to pay (or at least maintain the appearance of paying) for meals and drinks. Many men (not all) will run someone over to open a door for a woman (especially if she's nice-looking) but are too busy to bear responsibility at home for laundry or the kids. None of these practices, taken alone, is necessarily harmful. But a universal spectrum of gender relations exists in which men and the masculine are afforded greater status, higher pay, and more allowances than women in similar positions. Taken together, women's everyday life is seen as, and made to be, problematic.

Gender, Power, and the Party Plan Economy

Although a culture of fun seems readily available within gender parties, the party plan economy harbors several gender problems. First, the party plan segment is largely unregulated, pays little (on average), and offers virtually no benefits. Despite the lack of systematic records of many of its operations, there seems to be strong evidence that most consultants' earnings fall woefully short of the much-advertised text claiming a "housewife" version of get-rich-quick.

Several alternative sites have cropped up (e.g., Pink Lighthouse, Touch of Pink, Pink Truth) that feature ex-consultants' complaints with the Mary Kay marketing plan. For example, the company claims that consultants earn 50 percent of total sales, but many layers of exceptions and expenses lie within that profit margin, including discounts, dated products, gifts, promotional materials (such as catalogs, brochures, sales slips), shipping costs, expensive training seminars, and travel. Again, very little reliable data exist; however, a 2007 press release from Mary Kay Canada reported that less than 10 percent of its consultants earned more than $200.[22] The dropout rate for Mary Kay appears to be high, from 68 percent to 85 percent.[23]

Several watchdog organizations periodically report data, claiming that multilevel marketing companies (MLMs) vastly mislead consultants, and that few of them make a profit (most experience losses). Amway, a publicly held company required to report data, has borne the brunt of several such reports, which claim that 99 percent of Amway representatives suffer significant annual losses.[24] The company has been named in criminal charges filed in India[25] and a civil suit in the United States.[26] Consistent and considerable gaps appear between the claims from many direct sales companies and the aftereffects reported by individuals and organizations disillusioned with the promises of the party plan ideology.

Virtually all consultants and most consumers are women, but the top of the pyramid is dominated by men. It's difficult to discern the power hierarchy; the true form is usually kept from prying eyes. However, we can look at anecdotal evidence. At Mary Kay, Tupperware, Passion Parties, Amway, Premier Design, and Silpada, men are listed as the top executive officers. Only at Pampered Chef, Arbonne, and Avon is a woman's name listed at the top. Even so, some claim that women serve only as figureheads at those companies.[27] These facts are even more significant because of the heavy representation of women in the lower ranks; in fact, it is almost exclusively in the top ranks that men can be found at all. As with Mary Kay, it might have begun with "one woman's dream," but there's usually a man holding the purse strings.

A second dimension of gender power within the party plan economy, even more difficult to ascertain, is marked by global stratification. The loosening of regulations for multinational companies, which began in earnest during the 1980s, coincides with heavy growth among the largest direct sales companies, such as Avon and Mary Kay. Lesser-developed countries provide cheaper and more plentiful labor, as well as tax shelters and little to no regulation. Within a context of the universal gender order, shored up by patriarchy, women outside fully industrialized nations are especially at risk. With lower levels of control over sexuality, fertility, partner choice, and work options, women fall prey to the most exploitive conditions.

Although it certainly is not true that all companies within the party plan economy exploit their salespeople, many do. Women most often participate without full knowledge of the market forces that take advantage of gendered conditions. Not only are unregulated markets subject to sweatshop conditions, but other inequalities abound. According to the Women's International Perspective (WIP), women in poor countries (as well as poor women in the United States) may be especially vulnerable to the ideals of the American Dream, borrowing money and bypassing education and other opportunities in order to join a workforce that is a long shot at best.

Third, as surely as humans need oxygen, gender inequality feeds on gender ideology. One WIP article quotes a former consultant who compares the chances of success in the party plan economy (at least in some segments) to winning the lottery: "You could win $27 million."[28] As the contributor goes on to explain, the verbiage is only slightly different from the golden lottery language, typically couched in terms of "earning" or "producing" or, even more devious, "becoming"—as if one's entire being may be transformed. Ideology can be defined in several ways, ranging from heavy-handed, even oppressive, conditions that dictate thought to a set of cultural ideals that convey positive self-persuasion and motivation. Playing on women's drive for independence and sometimes the very survival of their families, the veiled promises of the party plan economy can become quite provocative and exploitive.

Marketplaces of Interaction and Partying Down

We've just seen how one type of structure, the party plan economy, gives form to gender regimes, and how particular contours of the structure vary over time and across places. We've acknowledged that the gender order sustains a generalized gender power but also accommodates considerable variation among gender regimes. The variation doubtless occurs because of many social, economic, and political factors. But some of the variation, and (arguably) all the maintenance of such a system, occur due to interaction among people and between people and institutions. Social structures take on scope and permanence, but it is through human interaction that such paths are forged and preserved—in a word, it depends on how we *party*.

Marketplaces of interaction, as a concept, refers to both individuals and situations. In a wide-angle view, it certainly takes on structural features. A marketplace, as an arrangement of relations, displays configurations that organize associations and dealings; it offers models for contact and communication; and it provides a blueprint for actions that will work toward a particular goal. All these structures have breadth and enduring features; structures put up boundaries to action. In our study of gender parties, we leave much of the structural job to the party plan economy. Marketplaces of interaction, as an idea, helps make visible the millions of encounters that take place within structures.

The Everyday

Marketplaces of interaction capture everyday happenings. Commonly, the everyday takes on a somewhat trivial sense. We think of everyday clothes or routine activities or day-by-day tasks that quickly become humdrum. Even something that we absolutely loved the first time—say, watching a polar bear yawn at the zoo or tasting strawberry ice cream—could quickly become mundane if we replicated that same experience many times a day, every day. In fact, we would soon forget the wonder of the gigantic white creature and fail to appreciate the taste and feel of cold, pink, sugary ice cream. Smith warns of the same taken-for-granted assumption of the everyday when she says that the

> pieces of a world—"power elites," "formal organization," "stratification," "social class," the "state"—are thus littered all over a sociological landscape. Locating the knower in the everyday world and constituting our inquiry in terms of the problematic arising from how it is actually organized in a social process enable us to see the "micro" and the "macro" sociological levels in a determinate relation—though it is one that scarcely makes sense any more in these terms. . . . Making the everyday world our problematic instructs us to look for the "inner" organization generating its ordinary features.[29]

Smith encourages gender scholars to see the everyday as problematic. The sense of a party plan economy takes us out of the everyday familiarity of gender parties, setting it in the larger framework that we seldom think about, much less glimpse. Party preparation becomes a long, necessary, and arduous task. Décor, food, and dress take on extraordinary qualities; interactions range from slightly showy to ostentatious. Women host and attend, food is often petite and elegant, and the color pink typically crops up in various ways. Talk usually centers around shopping or clothes or children. The products may be jewelry or housewares or makeup, or even that certain cream made to titillate erogenous zones. Gender parties are not simply an exercise in the everyday; they are firmly entrenched in women's worlds. They are at once unusual and tantalizing, but with their ideology and power relations held from everyday sight.

Gender parties separate the everyday and the extraordinary and in some ways help make gendering more discernible, underscoring the assertion of Beth Hess and Myra Ferree that gender is most visible at boundaries and points of change.[30] As they argue, gender is not an innate characteristic that develops as a naturally occurring phenomenon. Because gender is *not* natural, it is marked with struggle, conflict, and contradictions; gender requires considerable work in order to maintain its appearance and performance. Thinking back to the characteristics that identify the apparatus of gender parties—preparation, putting on a show, keeping up appearances—all these take considerable work. So does sitting, talking, walking just so, dressing, applying makeup, deferring, acting demure, and the thousand other markers that identify the female sex. It is just as much work (though with a very different relationship to power) for men to pose, work out, stride, jockey for position, act chivalrous, and in general take charge.

Gendering is hard work, and we all participate. Because gender is a struggle, it is often more visible at boundaries and points of change, and gender parties mark one of those boundaries—between the exceptional and the everyday.

Paradoxically, gender parties also represent deception and disguise. Visibility isn't always without ruse. Despite the time and toil that parties entail, the perception is that once the party begins, work disappears; only fun and frivolity remain. To the contrary, it is at this point that gender work begins in earnest. Interactions keep a system of power in place and may even gather speed and intensity. What appears to be leisure is actually invisible work; what seems pleasurable may be uninspiring or even painful; what looks like a casual visit can be strategic manipulation.

Important distinctions lie between these stealth business endeavors and an environment that overtly invites commercial negotiations. First, there is a sense of pretense that veils the seriousness of business transactions; some partygoers may be more or less aware of these transactions, setting them at an advantage or making them more vulnerable. Second, stakes appear considerably lower than in the corporate world. The trophy may seem to be no more than a trophy (or perhaps some free plasticware). Third, and most important, partiers participate in a system that, on average, ultimately disadvantages them personally (by detracting them from more viable options) and women everywhere (by entrenching a system of power that affords men and masculinity the upper hand).

Cathexis, Relationships, and Resistance

Recall that Connell refers to "structural models" within gender regimes—labor, power, and cathexis.[31] Cathexis—defined as patterns of emotional attachment—provides an opportunity to reach beyond individual relationships that take place within gender parties. Certainly, relationships are personal, private, and expressive; women's relationships, in particular, mark critical and lasting life guideposts. The idea of cathexis allows comparison across time and space of the patterns in those emotional attachments, which in turn reveals much about the gender system. Gender parties as gender regimes accommodate particular arrangements of emotional attachments, some of which are described above as embedded in work and strategic power plays. When women craft power plays, the moves are generally perceived as negative, unlike the same behaviors initiated by men.

Gender parties, though, are not singularly negative. At least for women, relationships remain at the heart of the gender system, and women generally manage relationships very well. From childhood, families and teachers and society in general condition girls to value connections to others; indeed, girls and women are rewarded through relationships. Consider Girl Scouts who fund their local and national organizations by selling cookies to community citizens; high school girls who suddenly find that popularity depends on whom they date; and the up-and-coming corporate woman who discovers she must attach herself to a male mentor to have a chance at climbing the ladder. Such situations do not represent casual, anecdotal observations; they are supported by research.[32]

Gender parties are not *simply* fun; they also provide ample opportunity for networking, forging new associations, and deepening existing friendships. Such relationships are a source of strength and empowerment for women. Studies demonstrate that when girls and women are able to come together, without male interference, they often thrive.[33] Throughout history, women have leaned on one another. Recalling my grandmother's Methodist Missionary Women and my mother's Harmony Home Demonstration ladies, I now understand why they dressed and fussed and laughed and cried together. Their parties were about much more than products—they fashioned advice and empathy, services and savvy, and sometimes endorsements or vetoes about the most important parts of their lives. In such intimate groups, women find degrees of control over their environment.

When structures of gender regimes are revealed (that is, when we gain awareness), the first step toward resistance becomes actualized. Resistance—a clearly intentional act of critical and political opposition—occurs when two related events happen.[34] First, it becomes possible when people see that what is defined as normal is actually "a definition of what the holders of social power wish to have accepted."[35] Further, exceptions to what is defined as "normal" must be seen as part of a larger pattern, not simply as individual eccentricity or deviance. Second, resistance follows when a collective sense of possible change is perceived and activated. Certainly, individuals can become dissatisfied with current (gender) arrangements, but when individual comfort is achieved no further action follows. Resistance, as conceived in gender theory, refers to group consciousness and group engagement. Gender parties offer a milieu in which resistance fomentation is viable.

Real Women, Real Stories, and Intersectionality

The abstract concepts just described (e.g., gender regimes, power, labor, cathexis, resistance) demand concrete models that we can use to visualize bona fide life events. For that, we turn to real women and real stories. In fact, gender theory grounds its ideas in just such factual, anecdotal narratives and instances. A major tenet of a woman-centered methodology is that women fully participate as subjects, not simply objects of research. Certainly, this does not mean that individual stories are always seen as science or that science is not the bedrock of gender theory inquiry. Indeed, we argue that gender theory and concomitant methodologies include both quantitative and qualitative schemes; each should be held to standards of social science research. But for too long women's experiences were totally absent from research. Contemporary gender theory places women at the center of inquiry but fully incorporates stories, coaching, training, and awareness for all gendered beings.

The term *real women* invokes different images for different people. Another tenet of contemporary gender theory is the inclusion of women from various times and places. A basic theoretical premise is that all women do not experience gender in the same way; again, comparative research illuminates patterns otherwise obscured. Gendering processes, as socially constructed, vary according to other constructed points of difference; intersectionality is the associated term that captures this matrix of differences. Examples include race, ethnicity, social class, sexual orientation, ableness, and age. Patricia Hill Collins is attributed with bringing intersectionality to theoretical prominence with the pivotal work *Black Feminist Thought*.[36]

Hill Collins underscored Smith's premise of standpoint knowledge—that all knowledge is constructed from a particular set of traditions and perspectives. Emphasizing that African American women's contributions had been "thrown away" and thus were absent from feminist knowledge, Hill Collins argued, "Black women intellectuals have laid a vital analytical foundation for a distinctive standpoint on self, community, and society and, in doing so, created a Black women's intellectual tradition."[37] Concurrently, other gender scholars, such as Judith Lorber, began building a body of theoretically rich ideas and research to underscore the concept of intersectionality. Lorber wrote, "As researchers, as theorists, and as activists, sociologists have to go beyond paying lip service to the diversity of bodies, sexualities, genders, and racial-ethnic and class positions. We have to think not only about how these characteristics variously intermingle in individuals and therefore in groups but what the extent of variation is within these categories."[38]

Building on this idea, intersectionality as a concept quickly rose to eminence in gender theory. Again, borrowing from Lorber: "The goal of sociological research should similarly be multiple levels of analysis that include the heterogeneity of people's lives, the varied dimensions of status categories, and the power relations between and among them."[39] We owe a great deal to these pioneers in gender theory. These two ideas—intersectionality and recognition of gendered power—remain the cornerstone of gender theory work. As a result, women and girls from many life experiences are included as "knowers" (and thus teachers) within the folds of gender theory.

In my own work, intersectionality brings a richness that otherwise would be lost. For example, in "Trying on Gender," I included teenage girls as "knowers" in the study; they came from two communities with very different characteristics.[40] One community was primarily working class (blue-collar industries) and the other predominantly middle class (with a large university). What we discovered is that the way in which girls "try on gender" (that is, experiment, engage in) was significantly different in each community. Further, the social class of the community (as an environment) exerted stronger influence on the girls than the social class of their respective families. I could not have seen these class-based dynamics without full input and sharing by the girls in this research.

Similarly, in another study, young Latina teens who had recently immigrated to the United States gave me deep insight into their lives.[41] The girls were basically warehoused in an understaffed English as a second language (ESL) class, making little to no progress, and isolated from the rest of the school. They also had different experiences from their brothers (who were able to get outside jobs) and from other Chicanos/as (who could speak English). As a measure of resistance, they refused to accept Americanized standards of beauty, retaining their hairstyles, Mexican jewelry, and ways of dress. (They especially denounced the peculiar American way of singling out particular high-priced name brands.) The young immigrants were seen as different from mainstream kids yet indistinct from others in their own group. In response to this sort of pigeonholing, one of the Latinas explained that others called her "María" (as in a generic designation), leading her to proclaim, "My name is not María!"

These brief examples clearly demonstrate intersectionality. The trying-on-gender girls and the Latina immigrants experienced gendering very differently from others in their surroundings. Studying gender parties offers exciting opportunities to apply gender theory, including intersectionality, in ways heretofore not apparent to us. It is vital that we understand how gendering processes sometimes control and other times empower women and men, girls and boys. Therein lies the potential of greater control over one's own life. We turn now to a brief foray into selected gender party environments, experimenting briefly with the concepts we've introduced in this chapter.

Ding-Dong Ladies: A Gender Analysis

Recall that a gender regime holds an inventory of structural arrangements, including unwritten rules, that sustain a gender system of differentiation. Two broad categories (structures and interactions) will help classify different kinds of mechanisms. For the purposes of this analysis, the party plan economy is treated as structure and marketplaces of interaction as, well, interaction. Within the party plan economy, two structures are defined—labor and power; within marketplaces of interaction, cathexis (a pattern of emotional attachment) is embedded. To complicate things just a bit more, we've identified doing gender, intersectionality, resistance, and Smith's term "the everyday as problematic" as concepts that inform an analysis of gender parties.

We start at the top. Avon is the number one direct marketing company in the world, with five million representatives in almost 150 countries. One of only eight Fortune 500 companies with a woman at the stern, Avon is headed by Andrea Jung, who is now chief executive officer (CEO) and chair of the board. Of its seventeen-member senior management team, six are women, and 75 percent of the company's district sales managers are women. Jung has brought in top women executives from Revlon, Prada, Ford Motor Company, and Kraft Foods.[42] What could a gender analysis possibly offer this bright scenario?

First, a critique asks probing questions, examines all sides of the issue, and looks for what is not apparent. What we do see is a company with a sales force and customer base that is 99.9 percent female, yet for 113 years it had only men at the top of its hierarchy. Even now, by its own count, 65 percent of Avon senior management is male. The company that adopted the slogan, "a woman's company," admittedly depends on its representatives—those almost two million women who are the on-the-ground sales force—to generate the company's hefty profits and hearty dividends (Avon is a publicly held company). However, the turnover rate for the sales force is "almost one hundred percent." Though we can't find an average income for Avon sales representatives, we assume that with this kind of turnover rate, nobody is achieving the "fame and fortune" that Avon (and virtually every other direct marketing company) promotes.[43] A gendered division of labor always maintains a steep hierarchy, and almost always keeps men in positions of power. One CEO and other powerful women represent a great start but do not mean that gender power of men has been dismantled.

In particular, a conscientious gender analysis will ask, at whose expense? Who are the women on whose backs Avon's sales are won? What we do know is that Avon laid off 3,500 workers (8 percent of its workforce) in 2002, closing an entire jewelry plant in Puerto Rico.[44] Further, workers who print Avon's brochures describe a "campaign of threats, harassment, and intimidation, claiming that Avon fails to live up to its ethical code and slate of workers' rights."[45] As of 2008, Avon began outsourcing its call center and transaction processing, reducing direct connections to the "Avon lady."[46] By considering these brief scenarios, we can figure out how significant power can be maintained through positions traditionally held by men. An even greater power dynamic runs through the exercise of ideology—a sense of how we should think.

Ideologies incorporate ways to maintain the status quo. Gendered ideologies, then, support a hierarchy that privileges males and masculinity, including a gendered division of labor. In a book about Avon endorsed by Jung, she boasts about "empowering women," "core values," and "improving women's lives."[47] She speaks to the representatives of this $7.7 billion mega-company, calling them the "heart and soul" of Avon, saying that they are her role models and that "everything we do is about helping to make their job easier."[48] However, in a situation in which the turnover is almost 100 percent, it's difficult to believe that their jobs are ideal.[49]

The book's author, journalist Laura Klepacki, refers to Avon's company mission of "making women around the world both more beautiful and more financially independent."[50] She refers to a promotion in which the company ran a banner of the Statue of Liberty with the following message: "A Monumental Makeover: Avon Helping to Make the Face of America Beautiful." The book packs in many, many such ideological messages, which constantly conflate beauty with independence, patriotism with cosmetics, and the American Dream with the Good Housekeeping Seal of Approval.[51] Yet, the real billion-dollar power structure of the company, headed exclusively by men for 113 years, seems far removed from the women (often, working single mothers) who are promised fame and fortune within Avon's "culture of caring."[52]

None of this takes away from the tremendous strides Avon made to advance women within its ranks. Nor does the brief analysis outlined here suggest that Jung or any of the other top executives in Avon are insincere. In fact, because ideological power runs in the background, clandestine and mysterious to its strongest advocates, it becomes even more insidious. Because gender is a master status for individuals and a ubiquitous force throughout the world, the ideologies that uphold it are especially authoritative.

I have no doubt that Klepacki, author of *Avon: Building the World's Premier Company for Women*, is unaware that she bracketed women, literally and figuratively, when she entitled a chapter "Hire the Best Man (or Woman) for the Job."[53] This misstep dramatically illustrates what Smith meant when she referred to the everyday as problematic, because the everyday uses the male as the default standard. To paraphrase Smith, gender parties are a strongly gendered regime, one that should be dismantled.[54]

From the Field

Plotting a historical map of the party plan model by way of women's stories, in the case study below, Sue Zschoche tells a tale of Tupperware and its growth from local production to mass-produced plastic, both of which found their way into homes. Although other scholarship documents the progression of labor and goods from private to public realms in the United States, Zschoche's study is unique in that she clearly situates the underpinnings of the contemporary party plan economy at the intersection of production, sociability, and everyday happenings in women's lives. This historian, like all historians worth their salt, skillfully lays open a social landscape we should have seen all along. That she also gently demonstrates the urgency and politics of a gender consciousness is an added bonus.

Case Study 2.1
The Party Plan Economy and the History of American Women
Sue Zschoche

Like any phenomenon worthy of the name, direct sales "home parties" have their very own creation story: in the beginning, there was a very special plastic bowl. The creator in question was Earl Tupper, an inventor with a visionary faith in modern plastics. In the 1940s, his experiments with polyethylene led him, finally, to his holy grail: a cone-shaped bowl for which he designed and patented a lid with a cleverly operated airtight seal. He had created—what else could he call it?—Tupperware.

And then came a surprising plot twist: unlike most creation stories, the Tupperware story became a distinctively feminine tale.[55] Despite positive reviews, including one in *House Beautiful* that celebrated the "art" of Tupperware, the company's attempts to sell the "poly-t" goods in retail outlets were largely unsuccessful. The one sales arena that demonstrated growth potential were orders from "home demonstration" sales companies: dealers for other, more familiar, household items like brushes and cleaning supplies discovered that including Tupperware in their sales presentations had jazzed up both their presentations and their sales. More to the point, their experience revealed that potential customers needed to be shown what was so wondrous about Earl Tupper's "Wonder bowl"; plastic bowls sitting on shelves, clever burping lids or not, could not sell themselves.

In 1951, Tupper took the surprising step of hiring Brownie Wise, a divorced mother with no corporate experience but an impressive record in direct sales. In Detroit, Wise, her mother, and a growing crew of female dealers had been selling and distributing Tupperware products along with a line of silverware and various personal products. Earl Tupper made her the vice president in charge of Tupperware Home Parties (THP); her charge was to construct a national sales and distribution plan, all to be centered upon hostess party direct sales.

Brownie Wise fulfilled her charge with a vengeance. Though the company did direct some appeals to racial and ethnic minorities, the THP's bread and butter lay in the burgeoning white suburbs of the postwar era, the epicenter of the explosion of consumer buying in the 1950s. Targeting suburban housewives, Tupperware mixed appeals to traditional frugality with promises of chic but affordable living. Just as one container with its airtight seal could save the housewife's crackers from staleness, a set of Tupperware glasses (with matching stirrers and coasters) were perfect for that evening party on the patio when, presumably, those crackers would be dressed up with cheese spread. More significantly, in the new suburban neighborhoods Tupperware found the population most likely to be willing to spend an afternoon with friends and neighbors, playing games, sipping punch, and learning how to burp plastic bowls.

Wise was not, of course, actually selling plastic. Her job was to sell the *idea* of selling plastic to women looking for work that could dovetail with home responsibilities. By 1954, she had signed up 20,000 dealers in a national network, almost all of them women, and many of them women like herself.

Brownie Wise had gone into direct sales to supplement the secretarial salary that supported her and her young son. Using a relentless gospel of positive thinking and the enticement of both personal empowerment and material gain, her charismatic recruitment and cultivation of Tupperware dealers and distributors built what she called "A Woman's World." Once a year, two thousand dealers made the pilgrimage to THP's sprawling Orlando campus for the "Homecoming Jubilee," five days of evangelical-style exhortation, corporate recognition, and a fantasyland of prizes that, for the most successful dealers, might include a mink coat or a convertible. *Business Week* put her on their cover in 1954, the first woman so honored. As she put it to the magazine: "If we build the people, they'll build the business."[56]

In 1958, however, Brownie Wise discovered that it was not necessarily a woman's world after all. Depending upon who was telling the story, Wise either resigned or was fired, but either way, Earl Tupper got rid of her. Wise was the victim, not precisely of her own success, but rather her flamboyant flaunting of it. The reclusive Tupper (he had never appeared at a THP sales meeting) had become increasingly disenchanted with Wise's extravagant rewards system for her dealers, her very public promotion of the Tupperware sales gospel of self-fulfillment, and what had become something of a Wise personality cult within the company. Her tactics and high profile, he believed, had overshadowed his product, the one unforgivable transgression.

Tellingly, however, Tupper dismissed Wise, *not* her sales plan. In that respect, she had left an indelible mark. In seven years, Brownie Wise had successfully charted the multibillion-dollar future of direct sales: a nearly all-female sales force motivated by the power of positive thinking, selling in homes, to other women, in a setting invariably described as a "party."

The legacy of the Tupperware plan is contemporary business enterprises in which seeming opposites are aligned. Here we find a mixture of commerce and domesticity, profit and sociability, work and leisure, public and private, even two distinct groups of women—the sellers and the buyers—and in each pairing the potential for both exploitation and empowerment. Oddly enough, what throws these contradictions into bold relief is not that they exist but where they occur. Whatever else may be said about the party plan business model, the plan at its point of actualization—a party held in someone's home—mixes one gendered domain, the "male" world of business, with another gendered domain, the "female" world of sociability. The jarring feature is not that the two are mixed but that the latter is bartered for the sake of the former—by women whose businesses remain largely invisible, at times, even from themselves.

How is this explained? Or, for the purposes of this chapter, what historical antecedents can guide our understanding? Perhaps the simplest place to begin is with the observation that, despite the modern insistence on the home as private and set apart from the world, the norm throughout human history has been for the household to be a central site of both production and commerce. The uniting of the "social" and the "economic" is the hallmark of the modern gender party, but to understand the significance of the pairing, we must see it as a "reunion" of what had once been commonplace.

The Gendered World of the Household: The Venue
Consider, for example, the events that transpired in the home of Ephraim and Martha Ballard in the early autumn of 1788. The Ballards lived in the Maine community of Hollowell, and in 1788, they were on the upper edge of middle age, their children mostly grown. Martha Ballard was the community's most respected midwife, and the diary she kept for almost three decades provides an extraordinary glimpse into the ways of an American household of the late eighteenth and early nineteenth centuries.[57] We know, for example, that Martha's daughter Dolly completed forty-four yards of checked linen cloth on September 15, 1788, and that Mrs. Savage, a hired helper, spun forty double skeins of linen thread that same week in exchange for, among other things, seven yards of newly woven diaper material.

These processes involved a number of women—Martha's daughter, her nieces, hired help, and neighbors, in and out of each other's households, trading skills and goods, and, we may assume, indulging in the daily sociability that such proximity to each other offered. At times, the site of primary weaving activity shifted to another household; at times work was halted so that needed equipment could be borrowed. Men wandered through occasionally, but cloth production was women's work, and men were only called upon to perform distinctively masculine tasks such as fixing a bit of hardware on a loom. In a traditional agrarian society, the household was the seat of economic production, and though tasks were clearly demarcated by gender, women, no less than men, were part of that economic activity.

Is this, then, the prototype of the gender party economy? Certainly it juxtaposes domesticity, commerce, and female sociability. Ultimately, however, such a comparison breaks down on one ironclad reality. Women's work produced articles for human consumption, but it was a consumption based on the hard fact that what was to be consumed had first to be produced. A linen shirt required that a female someone grow and harvest the flax, spin it into thread, weave it into cloth, cut out the cloth, fit it, and sew it. The poultices for a winter's respiratory disease required the cultivation and harvesting of herbs and then the preparation and preservation of the carefully mixed recipe. There was the tending to livestock, the milking of cows, the production of cheese and butter. Women made ale as well as soap, killed chickens and baked bread, and all the while, they also toiled at providing the most basic of human needs: they cooked, kept the hearth fires lit, laundered, cleaned, and watched over children.

What is clear is that in most places, they did this in the frequent company of other women: in and out of each other's houses, they traded with each other, special skill for special skill. Martha Ballard's diary records myriad forms of payment for her considerable midwifery skills: cheeses, ham, butter, lard, bushels of ash, seed potatoes, a skein of wool yarn, the sewing for a special dress—all of them the product of another woman's skill. In the late eighteenth century and throughout most of the new nation, households operated just as did the Ballard household, its members producing most of what was consumed and trading their surplus or bartering their particular skills with their neighbors for what they did not produce.

Along the way, they no doubt exchanged a good deal of neighborhood gossip and offered woman-to-woman advice, but it is difficult to believe that any of them would have called these activities a "party." To the contrary, they lived within a web of relationships in which it was impossible to mark the social as discrete from the economic.

Woman as Consumer: Party Plan Participants
Martha Ballard and her female contemporaries performed labor fundamentally indistinguishable from women's labor a century, or two centuries, before. But whether or not Ballard and her acquaintances knew it, they were living on a historical cusp in which the social and the economic were in the process of severing: in the young nation's larger cities, commercial manufacturing had begun to remove economic production from the household. And though what was ultimately left to the household was immediate and essential, it was also increasingly deemed as unworthy of respect.

In 1791, the nation's first secretary of the treasury, Alexander Hamilton, noted that production for use directly by families or bartered for other goods was still prevalent. But he pointed to the superiority of the third type of production—the manufacturing that fueled cash-based commerce—as the engine of American growth. Indeed, he announced that labor performed for cash was the most "productive."[58]

As the pace of manufacturing quickened in the nineteenth century and more and more economic production moved out of the household, women were left behind in a domestic world that looked very much like the traditional world of their grandmothers. There was one difference: their labors were no longer recognized as economically valuable. "Work" was now defined as the human activity that created profit or earned cash: it was public, and though poor women labored in the bowels of factories, "work" was gendered as male. The capitalist economy simply took for granted the domestic labors of women, the work that tended to the most basic of human needs: child care, decent food, clean clothing, warm blankets, and a hundred other basic human needs that required unremitting labor. Separated from the cash nexus, women's work formed the underpinnings of the economy, but it was invisible, confined to the realm of the private and the social. A new and eternally annoying question presented itself: "Do you work, or are you just a housewife?"[59]

By the end of the nineteenth century, American housewives—at least the ones of middle-class status—had earned a new title: it was now said that women were the nation's "consumers." They provisioned their households, less by making goods themselves and more by thoughtfully purchasing the myriad household items for sale. One might even say that such women began to possess something that Martha Ballard never had—a lifestyle. I insert the term *lifestyle* quite deliberately because this very modern word forces us to look more closely at the meaning of women's work in a traditional context, the better perhaps to illuminate our own time.

"Lifestyle" may be defined in several different ways. One of the more neutral definitions is simply that a lifestyle is "a manner of living that reflects the person's values and attitudes."[60] Martha Ballard's life certainly did that, but to say it was a "lifestyle" is somehow discordant. What was missing from her environment is the subtext of the term's modern meaning: lifestyles are known to us by their accoutrements—the *products* that demonstrate values and attitudes. In short, we tend to use "lifestyle" to denote differential consumption patterns.

In the years after the Civil War, mass-produced items had lightened some aspects of women's work—ready-made clothing, for example, had become prevalent. But in addition, mass production also included decorative and personal items, items that might be used for expressive rather than utilitarian purposes. Victorian homes were filled with such items—antimacassars, figurines, fine linen, volumes of Shakespeare, heirloom silverware, pianos—displayed to show the respectability of the family who lived there. In the words of one historian, a woman's "ability to create a satisfying domestic environment through the manipulation and placement of domestic objects was an essential part of the late Victorian woman's sense of herself, as well as her awareness of what it meant to be 'civilized.'" So powerful was this ideal that the same historian has probed the reality behind the legend of the prairie schooners filled with china and spinet pianos. The legend is true: women were intent on bringing the artifacts of culture with them into the rawer circumstances of the West. In dugouts and sod houses, no less than in eastern homes, one could find gilded birdcages, bric-a-brac, and wallpaper.[61]

The new culture of consumption promised something akin to personal transformation as well. The herald of what one historian calls this new "imaginative culture" was the department store, an institution that, beginning in the 1870s, brought together a nearly unfathomable array of goods and offered them in an atmosphere that used glass, color, and light to display a phantasmagorical world, all of which was, of course, for sale.[62]

Designed to appeal particularly to women, the department store invited them into a realm of possibility far beyond the familiar and mundane. The managers of department stores acted as curators for a modern consumer culture, creating displays that emphasized the exotic potential of personal items. That those "possibilities" were often artificial—fake fur, synthetic silk, and cosmetics, for example—mattered less than the fact that one was invited to play, to try on new identities. One measure of the attraction was the rise of the disorder "kleptomania." Respectable women could scarcely be accused of base thievery; they were only guilty of irresistible impulses, impulses the department store was designed to induce.

By the 1950s, the democratization of the consumer culture hit its zenith in the United States; mass production flooded an increasingly affluent society with "unique" goods for every budget. And modern advertising accentuated the dream worlds now attainable by presumably everyone, conjuring worlds of multiple and highly individualized meanings out of the products of mass production. A number of scholars have struggled with the larger significance of American society's dedication to consumerism. But at the very least, the most thoughtful among them recognize, in the words of one commentator, that consumer goods "are for modern societies central elements in the establishment and circulation of meaning."[63]

It was in this context that Tupperware introduced its iconic products in the reimagined selling venue of the home. Earl Tupper's utilitarian zealotry for his plastic notwithstanding, the company sold multilayered meanings to the housewives who were its target market. The plastic's airtight seals allowed the housewife to imagine her connection with her mother's Depression-era motto of "waste not, want not." But simultaneously, one could buy the product line that imagined the affordable sophistication of a patio party. The housewife could even connect with her imagined colonial foremothers with Tupperware's provocatively odd heirloom piece, a polyethylene tea service. THP sold not so much plastic products, but the idea of what those plastic products could mean if woven properly into the fabric of everyday life. They sold, in short, a lifestyle, or more accurately, multiple expressions of a lifestyle that one could alter by mood or occasion or even time of day.

No one in the party plan business has improved upon Tupperware's essential insight into selling. To an extraordinary degree, the gender parties of contemporary society operate on identical premises, promising an array of goods that will either mark one's home as a place of refinement or, more commonly, remake one's individual style along more sophisticated lines. The success of the party plan economy rests to a large degree on the cultural centrality of consumer goods as "a defining feature of personal identity."[64]

Consumerism at least partially explains the seemingly mysterious question of why a private venue is effective as a point of sale. In the 1950s, less than 40 percent of American women between the ages of twenty-five

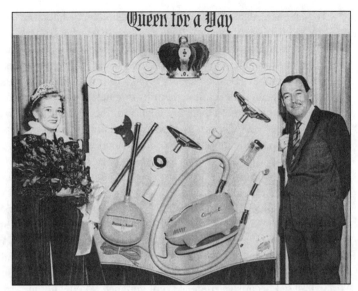

Figure 2.2 *Queen for a Day,* pop culture TV show of the 1950s.
(Charles Richard Lester © 1995–2009)

and fifty-four worked outside the home; the party plan took products to where women were. But in today's society, where more than three-quarters of the women in that age range are employed, the party plan makes less apparent sense.[65] As far as can be determined from a quick perusal of the Internet sites for current home sales companies, none of these companies sell particularly distinctive products. Some version of the jewelry, candles, home decorating items, luxury bath products, makeup, decorative baskets, gourmet cooking utensils, and children's toys—to name only a few—can be readily found in department stores or specialty shops; indeed, a good many of the wares are indistinguishable from what can be found at Wal-Mart. Even sex toys require no broker: "adult" shops may be uncomfortable terrain for most women, but owing to the wonders of the Internet, no one has to leave the privacy of her own home to buy them.

In this regard, Tupperware once again provides the model. In an age of mass production, the apparent exclusivity of a product sold only in homes offers additional sheen. Initially no one would buy the Tupperware displayed in the company's coordinated store displays. Later, no one *could* buy Tupperware in a store, lending the product the aura of uniqueness, and suddenly, Earl Tupper had difficulty in keeping his production high enough to meet demand. To some degree, the same premise is at work in contemporary parties: they offer products rendered more valuable because they presumably cannot be had at the local department store.

To leave it at that, however, is to diminish the considerable sway exerted by women's relationships to each other. In Martha Ballard's age, women were constantly in each other's presence because the sexual division of labor threw them together in similar tasks. As the consumer age opened, women became the primary targets for merchandisers because gender discrimination had excluded them from much of the public world and consigned them instead to the maintenance of the household, a job redesignated as "consumer." Consumerism offers a distinctly personal type of fulfillment, but ironically, mass-produced consumerism implicitly accentuates the importance of one's group as a guide. In creating their sense of themselves, be it how to behave or what to buy, women's reference points were most often each other.

The party plan economy tugs on those long historical threads. Women buy at such parties at least partially because they encourage each other to do so: to buy in such a private and personal venue invests a mass-produced commodity with the rituals of friendship and "sisterly" advice. And, of course, even their presence at such parties is part of a "gift" exchange. Women attend because a friend or acquaintance asked, and one suspects that their willingness to attend involves more than a little bit of implicit bartering (some cynics prefer the word "extortion"), one social obligation paid or another incurred.

Invisible Women: Dealers of the Home Party Plan
Perhaps the most extraordinary aspect of Brownie Wise's rise in the corporate world of the 1950s was that she was that most suspect of women: a divorced mother raising her child on her own. Throughout the history of American women, but particularly since the economic transformations of the late eighteenth century, women who lived without male economic support were particularly vulnerable to both financial disaster and social censure.

The economic vulnerabilities are the most obvious. Well into the twentieth century, women who needed to support themselves or their children found a job market that routinely hired women and minorities at a fraction of the amount paid to white men; job mobility was virtually nonexistent. Should a poor woman find work, her situation was (and still is) further complicated by the problems of child care, or rather, the scandalous lack of it. To cite just one example, a perusal of the records of early twentieth century social welfare agencies reveals one heartbreaking story after another. Single mothers without work faced losing their children for "lack of support"; single mothers with jobs faced losing their children because their absence made them guilty of "neglect."

The economic catch-22 was matched with social attitudes that labeled self-supporting mothers as somehow defective. (For the staying power of such attitudes, see any debate over welfare reform.) Such attitudes were born in the same economic revolution that had removed economic production from the household. The utter *interdependence* of male and female work within the traditional household economy of Martha Ballard's world had, at least to some extent, mitigated the profound legal and political disadvantages under which women lived. But the new invisibility of women's domestic work beginning in the eighteenth century—its "uselessness" in a world that increasingly required cash—underscored women's economic dependence upon men.

Women's economic vulnerability was further obscured by the ascendancy of an ideology regarding the "separate spheres" that men and women were to occupy in life. The ideology cast men and women as virtual opposites and naturalized women's exclusion from political and civil rights. Men would create the American economic empire; women, using gentle persuasion and refined sensibility, would provide a private moral ballast for the competitive public world. The ideology reified domestic space as "woman's place" and though it granted women's work within the home a political and cultural significance, such "influence" came at a steep price. The moment a woman asserted her need for independent economic security (or political rights or equal education), her claim on respectability was nullified.

By the end of the nineteenth century, the double bind that crippled the lives of self-supporting women had become a recurring theme in campaigns for economic opportunity for women, even in some unlikely quarters. Consider, for example, Bertha Palmer, the socialite wife of the Chicago merchant Potter Palmer and the chair of the Board of Lady Managers, which directed the construction of the Women's Building (designed by a woman architect) and all its exhibits for the 1893 Columbian Exposition. Palmer could scarcely be considered a rabid women's rights advocate, but she chose the opening of the Women's Building as an occasion to chastise those who used separate-spheres ideology to alternately ignore and castigate working women.

The Women's Building featured exhibits promoting the talents of women, including their capacity for work that was thought of as exclusively male. Palmer had been asked whether it was proper for her board "to promote a sentiment which may tend to destroy the home by encouraging occupations for women which take them out of it." Palmer bowed to the ideology by conceding that "presiding over a happy home" was woman's highest calling but called out those who refused to see the "stern facts." Living up to the ideology required that a woman be married to a reliable male, or as Palmer put it, "a manly and loving arm to shield her from rough contact with life." But many women had "no manly arm": they were widows supporting children or mothers who found themselves married to drunkards and criminals who casually ignored their family's needs. Perhaps, she noted archly, those who criticized women who worked outside the home might excuse women the "offense" of attempting "to earn for themselves daily bread," given the reality that such women "must work or they must starve."[66]

Brownie Wise was born two decades after Bertha Palmer gave her speech, but with only minor updating, she might have been one of the women whom Palmer was describing. Abandoned by her husband three years after the birth of their son (though not before Mr. Wise's drunken driving had put her in the hospital for an extended period), Wise had been employed as a secretary after the divorce. The burgeoning "pink-collar" sector represented an improvement in the job market for women, particularly women with a high school education, during the first half of the twentieth century. Most certainly, secretarial jobs were considered more respectable (for one thing, the worker had to dress better than factory workers), but for a mother supporting a child, the difficulties remained daunting. Salaries were meager and job advancement and reliable child care still virtually nonexistent.

Wise had launched her "outside of work hours" direct sales business in response to her limited opportunities for economic advancement. In recruiting new dealers for her own company and later for Tupperware, Wise recruited women very much like herself: women who lived on the edges of economic solvency, with or without a man in their lives; women for whom the middle-class "American Dream" was seemingly out of reach.

Tupperware recruitment promised the realization of that dream, a promise for which Wise's glamorous lifestyle served as touchstone. During her glory days at THP, Wise and her son lived in a luxurious lakeside home, appointed lavishly with all the accoutrements of an upscale consumer lifestyle: modern appliances, beautiful furnishings, lush gardens, a pony, even a cabin cruiser.

In-house publications, written or edited by Wise, made extensive use of her lifestyle as a reference point for what could happen to those who followed her relentlessly enthusiastic creed of self-actualization through positive thinking, or in the language Wise preferred, "hitching your wagon to a star."[67] Moreover, Wise's approach allowed women to frame their work as an indelibly feminine activity. She invited women into "work" that drew upon ancient feminine tropes of sharing and giving. Dealers, Wise insisted, were using their initiative to share their knowledge with other women while advancing their own "self-determination." Tellingly, selling Tupperware was not framed as "working at your job," but rather sharing one's "know-how" in demonstration techniques and accounting. "Your knowledge," she said to her dealers, "becomes a reality only when you *give it away*."[68] And, one could add, the proof it was a reality could be found in the consumer goods that would rain down upon the successful.

Wise's model of women's advancement became and remains the dominant trope among gender party direct sales companies. As such, it is important to underscore how profoundly Wise subverted the earlier message of women like Bertha Palmer. Palmer had called upon her audience to see the ways in which the ideology of separate spheres penalized women who lived outside the comfortable economic circumstances that made adherence to the ideology of separate spheres remotely plausible. There was nothing wrong with such women, Palmer insisted, but there was a great deal wrong with an ideology that failed to recognize the hideous choices confronting women who lived without reliable male support. She argued for a new "public sentiment" that would recognize the "rights and duties" of women, including "the propriety of their becoming not only self-supporting but able to assist in maintaining their families when necessary."[69]

Palmer in effect called for public sympathy and support for women forced to live outside the respectable confines of middle-class domesticity. Wise had been one such woman, but perhaps because of it, she recognized that the "job opportunities" Palmer championed were usually dead-end desks in patriarchal structures. When the glass ceilings were so low that women were constantly bumping their heads, the "stern fact" was that they were still excluded from the wonders of the "consumer's republic." Whether it was realistic or not, Wise subversively offered precisely the middle-class respectability from which so many single mothers like her were barred. With or without a man, you too could fulfill the ideology that claimed that "feminine" women were the underpinnings of the American Dream, this one measured by a full inclusion in the consumer paradise that advertising portrayed.

In our own time, the various recruiting pitches made by direct sales companies in their online ads are directed not toward consumers but to potential dealers, and to an uncanny degree they replicate Wise's approach. What is revelatory about such pitches is that the product in question takes a distinct second place to advertisement copy hailing what the company can do for "you." Directed, frequently by name, to work-at-home moms (WAHMs) and featuring an inordinate number of exclamation points, the companies promise income but, more than that, "empowerment" so that the "you" in question can "live your dream." A firm recruiting dealers for a "body fat wrap" opens with an appeal typical of many companies: "when you choose [name of company] you are making a statement that you've finally arrived and are ready to *create a new life for yourself* and your loved ones that will be bigger, better, and more satisfying than ever before."[70] Equally typical is that this product, like all of the products, is allegedly easy to sell (several are said to "sell themselves!"). Moreover, all the companies promise the "best support in the business!" and allow "you" to take care of your families. One clearinghouse site geared specifically toward stay-at-home mothers prominently displays a photograph of two small children and asks, "*What is Most Important in Life?*"

One can presumably fulfill all the expectations of conventional domesticity and still achieve the dream. Certainly, the company ads suggest one of the reasons that this multibillion-dollar industry is a nearly invisible part of the economy: whatever else it is, becoming a dealer is never defined as work in the conventional sense. The companies ask prospective dealers to think of what is, in fact, actual work not as a job at all, but rather—dare we say it?—a lifestyle enhancement.

Gendered Domains, Gender Consciousness
Finally, I would be remiss if I did not address the 400-pound pink gorilla in the living room: what is the relationship between the gender party economy and contemporary feminism? The knee-jerk answer is simple: "not much." Though this book takes as its central premise that the party plan economy is a profoundly gendered domain, it is for the most part a domain that seems to exclude a consciousness of that fact. As a necessary—though not sufficient—first step, feminism requires women's recognition of their membership in the category named "women." From that recognition can emerge not only the sensibility that women as a group face common obstacles but, more importantly, the conviction that they can confront these obstacles as a group. Feminist scholars may recognize the actual and potential exploitation of the women involved in the party plan economy, but there is little sign that the actual participants do.

Certainly, there is nothing in the structure of the party plan economy that would preclude that recognition. The history of American women is replete with accounts of reform movements born over the low murmur of conversation as women worked together in domestic space, either at home or in the newly feminized public space of nineteenth- and twentieth-century churches. From these spaces and through the stories that women shared in those places came campaigns dedicated to temperance, health care reform, the eradication of prostitution, abolition, educational rights, child labor laws, municipal reform, and hovering over them all, women's rights defined in a dozen different ways.

Though it would be false to claim that such campaigns ever engaged the majority of American women at any given point, it is undeniable that in the last decade of the suffrage campaign, the insistence that women be granted the most basic right of citizenship had become a mainstream movement, gathering—though not necessarily uniting—women across class, racial, and geographic lines. Indeed, it is not stretching the point to claim that the advancement of women in the United States is owing to that feminine sharing of hopes and dreams. In myriad groups across time and space, women gave each other the one inestimable gift: the belief that they could, as one historian put it, "accomplish for themselves what the Revolution had failed to do."[71]

It is, I believe, noteworthy that several of the chapters in this volume tell the stories of groups in "gender parties" in which women's sharing with each other contains the promise of the kind of consciousness that allows women to act together as a group. It is, however, also noteworthy that none of those examples is drawn from the experience of white women in the United States. In the accounts of white women in the United States, the dominant trope appears to be one drawn explicitly from consumerism. The problem is that, as Michael Schudson has written, in "a consumer society 'lifestyle' surpasses a person's work life as the defining feature of existence."[72] And because a lifestyle, by definition, centers on personal fulfillment rather than common dreams, one has to wonder about whether a feminist consciousness is even possible in such circumstances.

Again, perhaps history is instructive. In the decade following the achievement of suffrage in 1920, the broad-based coalition that had won the vote fell apart. The coalition dissolved for a number of reasons, the profound ideological differences among its leadership being one of them. But it was also clear that a generational shift had occurred as a younger generation of women, mostly privileged, declared their "emancipation" from tiresome prescriptions for feminine personal behavior.

In an often quoted essay written in 1927, the journalist Dorothy Dunbar Bromley came as close as anyone to explaining the resistance of her contemporaries to the movement of their mothers and grandmothers. Declaring herself a "Feminist–New Style," Bromley acknowledged her allegiance to the importance of meaningful work and her conviction that a woman's life could not be wrapped up completely in home and family. She also recognized the continuing arenas of discrimination against women. But the most telling aspect of her analysis was her attack on her predecessors, "the old school of fighting feminists who wore flat heels and had very little feminine charm." The "old-style" feminists were, she proclaimed, too often "strident creatures," and besides, she added, the "Feminist–New Style professes no loyalty to women *en masse*, although she staunchly believes in individual women." Most of all, she proclaimed herself as "intensely self-conscious whereas the feminists were intensely sex-conscious."[73]

One way to read Bromley's manifesto is as an early seductive callout, as yet incompletely formed, from and to the consumer society that would shortly declare that all individual wishes could come true through hard work and pluck, so long, of course, as one had the money to buy them. Why bother to emulate one's foremothers when they so clearly lacked "style"? More to the point, why bother to consider their demands for a more just society when, just on the horizon, there had appeared a brave new world in which any woman of talent and initiative could, if she just "reached for the stars," fulfill her wildest dreams? It is perhaps churlish to pick on Bromley for an inadequate reading of the future. But it is encouraging to be reminded that forty years later a new feminist movement arose to address a good deal of unfinished business. At a time that cannot be accurately predicted, one supposes that personal fulfillment will once more be found lacking as the be-all and end-all of existence. As Mark Twain allegedly put it, "History doesn't repeat itself, but it rhymes."

Beyond the Party

This chapter shows that many features of gender construction remain a constant through time and space. The parties of our grandmothers and mothers foreshadowed the events that we participate in today. Predating even our grandmothers' parties, Zschoche weaves a picture of women's work that emulated the party plan during the late 1700s—what she refers to as a "prototype" of the gender party economy.

Such historical accounts are important because they demonstrate that participation in a larger gender order is cyclical. In many ways, we keep coming back to where we started. Brownie Wise, wittingly or not, designed the great escape from the doldrums of one brand of domesticity to the celebration of another. After all, domesticity is not a thing; it is an idea. And Wise transformed the idea of domesticity into a marketplace where women could have their domesticity and eat it too—that is, they could take what they knew best and turn it into good cash, with the potential, at least, of much higher earnings than a file clerk. That Wise herself was ousted by the greed and power of one man now seems, with the glory of hindsight, ironically prophetic. Having said that, let's not get caught up in what we have missed or have not done; instead, this project urges us to move ahead and see possibilities for raising gender consciousness.

By using the past to look forward, we see a significant potential to raise awareness within the party plan economy. It is certainly true that there are examples of consciousness-raising activities throughout history; arguably, two of the most significant were the gatherings that marked the suffrage movement in the United States during the nineteenth and twentieth centuries, and the second-wave feminist consciousness-raising parties during the 1960s and 1970s. Further, contemporary feminists have begun to raise a global consciousness through significant empirical and theoretical works (e.g., Ferree and Tripp's *Global Feminism*;[74] Mohanty, Russo, and Torres's *Third World Women and the Politics of Feminism*;[75] Naples and Desai's *Women's Activism and Globalization*;[76] and Purkayastha and Subramaniam's *The Power of Women's Informal Networks*[77]). The goal now is to produce a sustained effort that brings women together worldwide.[78] The party plan economy provides seeds for just such action.

Notes

1. Erving Goffman, *The Presentation of Self in Everyday Life* (New York: Doubleday, 1959).

2. Thomas L. Friedman, *The World Is Flat: A Brief History of the Twenty-First Century* (Boston: Farrar, Straus and Giroux, 2005), 49.

3. Myra Marx Ferree and Beth B. Hess, "Introduction," in Beth B. Hess and Myra Marx Ferree, *Analyzing Gender: A Handbook of Social Science Research* (Newbury Park, CA: Sage, 1987).

4. Raewyn Connell, *Gender and Power: Society, the Person, and Sexual Politics* (Palo Alto, CA: Stanford University Press, 1987).

5. Connell, *Gender and Power.*

6. Ibid.

7. Ibid., 158–163.

8. See Beth Montemurro, *Something Old, Something Bold: Bridal Showers and Bachelorette Parties* (New Brunswick, NJ: Rutgers University Press, 2006); Marybeth C. Stalp, *Quilting: The Fabric of Everyday Life* (New York: Berg, 2007).

9. Dollar Times, "Inflation Calculator," http://www.dollartimes.com (May 19, 2009).

10. AOL Small Business, "Home Party Sales," March 1, 2007, http://smallbusiness.aol.com (June 11, 2009).

11. Dena Harris, *Lee Kirkman: Breaking In to a Woman's World,* Common Boundaries, 2004, http://www.commonboundaries.com (June 6, 2009).

12. Nick Antonovics, "UPDATE 2: L'Oreal 2007 Sales Rise 8.1 Pct, Confident for 2008," Reuters, January 24, 2008, http://www.reuters.com (June 6, 2009).

13. Even so, these figures are underestimated. Most direct sales companies such as Avon and Mary Kay report wholesale figures, whereas companies whose products are sold in department stores and similar venues report retail figures. For example, if Mary Kay reported retail numbers, its rank might be higher. AOL Small Business, "Home Party Sales."

14. A partial list of other home-based party plan companies includes Adora; Anna William; Azante Jewelry; BabyCrazy; BeautiControl; Fuller Brush Company; Goldshield Elite; Hat Creek Candle Co.; Jewels by ParkLane; Lady Emily; Matol Botanical International; Nest Family; Omnitrition International; Pampered Chef; Petlane; ProMaSystems/Grace Cosmetics; Self Indulgence; Shade Clothing; Shure Pets; SimplyFun LLC; Tarrah Cosmetics; Tastefully Simple; Two Sisters Gourmet; Wachters Organic Sea Products Corp.; WineShop at Home.

15. NielsenWire, "New Products Generate $21 Billion in Sales in 2008," January 30, 2009, http://blog.nielsen.com (April 28, 2009).

16. Connell (*Gender and Power*, 111–112) defines cathexis as a structure that organizes the emotional attachment of one person to another (including objects or even ideas). The concept is commonly used to refer to patterned dimensions of sexuality (like heterosexuality or homosexuality) and/or sexual practices (such as using fetishes or creating fantasies). Connell seems to say that cathexis, as a structure, constrains people's social practices with regard to sexuality but also in terms of overall emotional attachments, which allows us to talk about women's relationships with one another, and their relationship to femininity or to power dynamics. These practices can be both positive and negative for any one individual but should be examined with a critical eye, questioning how such emotional attachments can feel good in the short run while also undergirding a power structure that disadvantages women as a group. As a matter of fact, Connell points out that cathexis can be affectionate or hostile, or both at once (i.e., ambiguous),

which further expands how the term may help analyze relationships within marketplaces of interaction.

17. Del Jones, "Women CEOs Slowly Gain on Corporate America," *USA Today*, January 2, 2009, http://www.usatoday.com (May 23, 2009).

18. Gloria Penner, "The Pitiful Progress of Women in Politics," KPBS, February 27, 2009, http://www.kpbs.org (June 16, 2009).

19. Institute for Women's Policy Research, "The Gender Wage Gap: 2008," April 2009, http://www.iwpr.org (June 14, 2009).

20. Dorothy Smith, *The Everyday World as Problematic: A Feminist Sociology* (Boston: Northeastern University Press, 1987).

21. James W. Messerschmidt, *Masculinities and Crime: Critique and Reconceptualization of Theory* (Lanham, MD: Rowman and Littlefield, 1993).

22. Mary Kay Canada, "Earnings Representation," 2000, http://web.archive.org (May 3, 2009).

23. Nathan P. Moore, "Re: Comments of Mary Kay Inc. to the Proposed Business Opportunity Rule, R511993," Federal Trade Commission, July 17, 2006, http://www.ftc.gov (May 3, 2009).

24. Several organizations report this same finding. Examples include the Women's International Perspective (WIP), Pyramid Scheme Alert, Pinktruth, False Profits, Pyramid Schemes, and Common Cause. Eric Scheibeler, *Merchants of Deception* (Charleston, SC: Booksurge, 2009).

25. Freedom of Mind Center, "Criminal Charges Filed Against Amway in India," 2008, http://www.freedomofmind.com (April 18, 2009).

26. "Amway Sister Company, Quixtar Inc., Sued by Distributor Group Represented by Shughart, Thomson and Kilroy," Business Wire, 2007, http://www.businesswire.com (June 17, 2009).

27. Robert L. Fitzpatrick, "The Myth of 'Income Opportunity' in Multi-Level Marketing," Pyramid Scheme Alert, 2004, http://www.pyramidschemealert.org (June 20, 2009).

28. Sarah Wyatt, "Mary Kay Global Expansion Raises Hope, Concerns," Women's International Perspective, June 25, 2007, http://thewip.net (June 25, 2007).

29. Smith, *The Everyday World*, 99.

30. Beth B. Hess and Myra Marx Ferree, *Analyzing Gender: A Handbook of Social Science Research* (Newbury Park, CA: Sage, 1987).

31. Connell, *Gender and Power,* 112.

32. Rosabeth Moss Kanter, *Men and Women of the Corporation* (New York: Basic Books, 1977).

33. American Association of University Women, "Shortchanging Girls, Shortchanging America," Executive Report, 1991–1992, http://www.aauw.org (January 15, 2010).

34. Henry A. Giroux, *Theory and Resistance in Education: Towards a Pedagogy for the Opposition* (Santa Barbara, CA: Greenwood Publishing, 2001), 110.

35. Connell, *Gender and Power*, 52.

36. Patricia Hill Collins, *Black Feminist Thought: Knowledge, Consciousness, and the Politics of Empowerment* (New York: Routledge, 2000).

37. Ibid., 3.

38. Judith Lorber, "Beyond the Binaries: Depolarizing the Categories of Sex, Sexuality, and Gender," *Sociological Inquiry,* no. 2 (1996): 143–159.

39. Ibid., 154.

40. L. Susan Williams, "Trying on Gender, Gender Regimes, and the Process of Becoming Women," *Gender & Society* 16, no. 1 (February 2002): 29–52.

41. L. Susan Williams, Sandra D. Alvarez, and Kevin S. Andrade Hauck, "My Name Is Not María: Young Latinas Seeking Home in the Heartland," *Social Problems* 49, no. 4 (2002): 563–584.

42. Laura Klepacki, *Avon: Building the World's Premier Company for Women* (Hoboken, NJ: John Wiley and Sons, 2005), 41–59.

43. Ibid., 45–46.

44. "Company News: Avon to Lay Off 3,500 Workers, 8% of Work Force," *New York Times*, March 19, 2002, http://www.nytimes.com (June 8, 2009).

45. Voice Network, "Tell Avon to Support Workers Rights," 2004, http://www.union voice.org (June 5, 2009).

46. Serena Penn, "Avon Calling for Layoffs," TheStreet.com, January 8, 2008, http://www.thestreet.com (June 5, 2009).

47. Klepacki, *Avon*, vii.

48. Ibid., viii.

49. Ibid., 45.

50. Ibid., 2.

51. Ibid., 17.

52. Ibid., 31.

53. Ibid., 41.

54. Smith, *The Everyday World*.

55. This account of Tupperware is drawn from Alison J. Clarke, *Tupperware: The Promise of Plastic in 1950s America* (Washington, DC: Smithsonian Institute Press, 1999).

56. Ibid., 130.

57. Laurel Thatcher Ulrich, *A Midwife's Tale: The Life of Martha Ballard, Based on Her Diary, 1785–1812* (New York: Vintage, 1991).

58. Hamilton's "Report on Manufactures" was delivered to Congress on December 5, 1791. "Alexander Hamilton Report on Manufactures to Congress 1791," December 13, 2008, http://open.salon.com (July 7, 2010).

59. A number of historical works deal with the economic and political transformations of the late eighteenth century as they pertained to women, but an excellent place to begin is with Nancy Cott, *The Bonds of Womanhood: "Woman's Sphere" in New England, 1780–1835* (New Haven, CT: Yale University Press, 1977).

60. "Lifestyle" (WordNet Search 3.0), http://wordnetweb.princeton.edu (June 18, 2009).

61. Angel Kwolek-Folland, "The Elegant Dugout: Domesticity and Moveable Culture in the United States, 1870–1900," *American Studies* 24 (1984): 21–37.

62. William Leach, "Transformations in a Culture of Consumption: Women and Department Stores, 1890–1925," *Journal of American History* 71 (September 1984): 319–342.

63. Michael Schudson, "Delectable Materialism: Second Thoughts on Consumer Culture," in *Consumer Society in American History: A Reader*, ed. Lawrence B. Glickman (Ithaca, NY: Cornell University Press, 1999), 341–358.

64. Ibid., 349.

65. US Department of Labor, Bureau of Labor Statistics, TED: The Editor's Desk, "Changes in Women's Labor Force Participation in the Twentieth Century," February 16, 2000, http://www.bls.gov (June 12, 2009).

66. Bertha Palmer's 1893 address is reprinted in Susan Ware, *Modern American Women: A Documentary History* (Chicago: Dorsey Press, 1989), 6–11.

67. Clarke, *Tupperware*.

68. Ibid., 136. Emphasis is mine.

69. Palmer, quoted in Ware, *Modern American Women*, 8–9.

70. Home Party Millionaires, "The Ultimate Body Wrap by It Works!" 2008, http://www.wrapnlosefat.com (July 1, 2010).

71. Linda Kerber, *Women of the Republic: Intellect and Ideology in Revolutionary America* (New York: Norton paperback edition, 1986), 12.

72. Schudson, "Delectable Materialism," 349.

73. Dorothy Dunbar Bromley, "Feminist–New Style," *Harper's Magazine* (October 1927): 552–560.

74. Myra Marx Ferree and Aili Mari Tripp, eds., *Global Feminism: Transnational Women's Activism, Organizing, and Human Rights* (New York: New York University Press, 2006).

75. Chandra Talpade Mohanty, Ann Russo, and Lourdes Torres, *Third World Women and the Politics of Feminism* (Bloomington: Indiana University Press, 1991).

76. Nancy Naples and Manisha Desai, *Women's Activism and Globalization: Linking Local Struggles and Transnational Politics* (New York: Routledge, 2002).

77. Bandana Purkayastha and Mangala Subramaniam, *The Power of Women's Informal Networks: Lessons in Social Change from South Asia and West Africa* (Lanham, MD: Lexington Books, 2004).

78. Notable is the Fourth World Conference on Women, held in Beijing, China, in 1995, sponsored by the United Nations (the first was in 1975). Approximately fifty thousand women and men attended the conference, representing more than two hundred countries. United Nations Department of Public Information, "Fourth World Conference on Women 1995," http://www.un.org (June 9, 2009).

3

How the Party Plan Economy
Mutes Women's Work

What does it mean when we say that work is invisible or muted? Why does it matter? Much work that people perform is visible. We see what people are doing within a structured work environment, and we acknowledge it as work. Work can, however, be invisible to the naked eye. Such work may be done in invisible places (think of the work of costume designers or set operators in movies) or by invisible people (such as domestic workers).[1] Or, work may be invisible because it involves informal processes that do not coincide with one's formal job description (e.g., unplanned office meetings, gendered aspects of secretarial work).

Invisible work has real consequences. If work (or workers) is perceived as unnecessary (i.e., expendable), the elimination of such work is not questioned.[2] In this chapter, we attempt to make visible the invisible work of the party plan economy. Acknowledging the labor performed by women in this economy, as well as why it is invisible to most people, is one step toward changing women's workplace experiences.

Whether in the United States or other countries, a gendered party plan ideology serves to mute work that women do at, or for, home-based gatherings. The invisibility of women's work in the party plan economy falls between women's labor in the formal, paid labor market and their informal paid and unpaid labor. Because of this structural location, we refer to work within the party plan as *wedge-work*. The unique structural position of the party plan economy aids in keeping women's work invisible, perpetuating a gendered culture that devalues women's work.

In addition to its structural location, party plan labor does not occur in a formal work environment (e.g., corporation, industry) but instead often centers on activities that happen in the home. That this work is performed mostly by women does not help to make it noticeable.

Making party work invisible occurs on both a micro- and a macrolevel—

the two are, in fact, interconnected. Party plan work is devalued within the broader society for the reasons cited earlier. It is not seen as real work, but instead as a hobby or a way to earn a little extra cash for the family or for personal use. US-based party companies use the enticement of a little side money as a way to lure women into the business. Once there, women are convinced of opportunities available to them in this line of work. It is fun, exciting, and flexible. As a result, women may not see the job as work until after they have been in the business for a while. In some cases, women may never see party work the same as work in the corporate world. This is all part of the smoke and mirrors behind which the party plan economy operates.

This chapter and the field studies that follow describes the types of work performed by women within the party plan economy, as well as the ideology that silences them. In addition, the field studies illustrate the role of social class in influencing women's decisions and experiences. The journey through this section will consist of a guided tour of consultants' experiences from within a legitimate American company, Mary Kay, to the underside of the party plan economy—illegal purse parties. Moving beyond the United States to the streets of Brazil, readers learn about female street vendors in marketplaces of interaction.

Now You See It, Now You Don't: The Invisibility of Women's Work

> Freedom. Fulfillment. Financial security. Fun! That's what life is like for thousands of people just like you. —*Partylite promotional material*

Does the above quote sound like the perfect job? Sounds like fun, right? What a great career opportunity. At least, that is what corporations within the party plan economy encourage women to believe. A cursory examination of home-based party websites demonstrates a commitment to "making women's dreams come true,"[3] providing women the opportunity to spend time with friends and family,[4] and earning the income they want.[5] Tupperware specifically tells potential consultants to "imagine life on your terms—complete with more time for family, friends and fun, more flexibility, and more financial freedom." Such words of encouragement are targeted at women—many of whom are stay-at-home mothers, women who want to work part-time, or women who are working the party circuit as a second job.[6]

These tag lines distract from the work that goes into direct sales, making the job sound fun, exciting, and rewarding. Some women certainly may agree that the work is fun and exciting, but many will also tell you that it is *work*.

A standard definition of work is "activity involving mental or physical effort done in order to achieve a result."[7] The image that this definition probably brings to mind is someone laboring in a formal work environment such as a corporation. This is not unusual. Our perceptions of work connect with a particular workplace ideology and structure.

A formal ideology of work encourages some level of visible action on the part of the worker and receives monetary payment. Formal images of work tend to be organized around a white working- to middle-class man who is completely dedicated to his work and has no day-to-day responsibilities for raising children or household chores. His job is to earn a living.[8]

In terms of structure, workplaces are outside the home and operate within a bureaucratic system such as a corporation, industry, or factory.[9] Notions of work are so formalized that we even have designated times that we go to work. Again, these understandings are based on the white male's work experience.[10]

The structural details of work are not apparent to us when we are young, but we are certainly aware of what work is or should be. As a child I (Michelle) remember hearing that Mom and Dad had to go to work, and I automatically formed an image of my parents getting into the car, driving to our family restaurant, and serving other people food. Now, thirty years later, my three-year-old daughter, Riley, talks about Mommy and Daddy working, too—she even role-plays, pretending to type on her play computer much like I do at work. Even at the age of three, Riley understands the concept of work, and why Mom and Dad both must have jobs. At least twice a week she will tilt her head to the side and say, "Mommy, you have to work to pay bills, right? If you didn't have a job, we wouldn't have a house, right?" Her response is, admittedly, very cute, but it also illustrates how central work is to our lives.

Yet as a child, I (and I assume my daughter, and perhaps even you) never thought about work that fell outside the boundaries of paid, formalized work. I never thought about workers who worked within the home or who were not tied to some formal organization. My life was centered on patriarchal processes (though I did not recognize them as such until much later in life) that dictated a male-centered model of work.

In addition to this narrow view of work within my own family, my small-town mentality never allowed for the opportunity to explore women's and men's work on a global scale. I had no idea about working conditions in other countries or the gendered division of labor. Had I been able to step outside my world, I would have learned that 60 percent of women in the developing world participate in some form of informal labor. In fact, although the rates of women's participation in paid labor are much lower than men's in these countries, data indicate that women's participation in home-based work as well as street vending is of great importance to these countries' economies. I also would have learned that, worldwide, millions of workers do not have benefits (e.g., retirement, maternity leave) and will never have a job that provides for such benefits.[11]

Obviously, I led a sheltered, privileged life that lacked a sense of consciousness of the world around me. But I was not alone. This formal work ideology and structure took hold of me, and the rest of us, at a very early age. The result is the invisibility of women's paid and unpaid work in both the formal and informal marketplaces.[12]

Scholars who study work recognize this tendency to lean toward these formal notions of work and push us to question traditional conceptions, encouraging definitions that include all women's and men's productive activities as work. When these activities are considered, the result is a more encompassing understanding of work that incorporates all forms of labor—paid and unpaid—into definitions of work.

The party plan economy provides a unique opportunity to better understand women's work that is wedged between formal and informal, paid and unpaid work—these concepts have been discussed in Chapter 1 of this book and will be elaborated upon later in this chapter. In addition to its unique structural location, party work reinforces a gendered culture. Such reinforcement occurs on an individual level as party participants (i.e., workers, attendees) purchase products, forge relationships, and embrace the idea of domesticity.

On a structural level, cultural production occurs as women work within a female-dominated organization that encourages a gendered division of labor with gendered rewards (i.e., lower pay, few benefits). This gendered cultural production may be viewed as positive, seeing women embracing being women, having fun together, and exacting some level of agency over their workplace options.[13] But it would be disingenuous to ignore the fact that participation in such cultural production also upholds a system that exploits women's labor.[14] The problem is that women often do not see such exploitation because it is masked as "fun with friends" and "what women do." This sense of false consciousness contributes to the invisible nature of women's labor within the party plan economy.

Before turning to the field studies in this section, it is important to establish a foundational understanding of work that goes into the party plan economy on a local and global scale. As Zschoche illustrated in Chapter 2, women's historical participation in paid and unpaid labor constitutes the roots from which work in the party plan economy has grown. Throughout all points in time, women's labor has been invisible and, subsequently, devalued.

Party Work

As I (Michelle) write, I am also preparing for a Pampered Chef party at my house. I can speak firsthand to the labor that goes into throwing a home-based party. I have thrown such parties in the past. Each time I do, I always say "never again." Yet here I am having another party.

The ideology of the party plan economy—fun and friendship—mutes the work that is performed by women as consultants, hosts, and guests. Structurally, party plan work falls into the private realm of the household. Because parties are supposed to be fun and because they are what many women do, the work that goes into such gatherings is either trivialized or remains completely invisible. Yet it is work from beginning to end.

First, invitations must be sent. Determining whom to invite and not to invite is a challenge. Options include family (though I have none here in Kansas), friends, and coworkers. As I think about these different groups of people I wonder: Who should I invite from work? Should I invite everyone? Maybe I should just invite the people whom I speak with regularly. But wait—then people who are not invited might feel left out. Suddenly, this doesn't sound like as much fun as I had originally thought.

Once I finalize my guest list, the menu needs to be planned and ingredients for the meal purchased—as a party host I must purchase the grocery items so the consultant can prepare a meal for the party guests. Between now and the day of the event (in exactly two weeks), I will wonder who will attend the party and whether they will have a good time. This brief illustration of what will happen before and after my party provides insight into the physical, mental, and emotional labor it requires.[15] And I'm not even being paid to do this! Of course, I am hoping for some free items, though I won't need them since I don't cook (the irony is not lost on me).

My labor as a host coincides with the work of the consultant. Perhaps the work that *she* (of course the consultant is a woman!) will perform seems obvious to most of us. After all, these are the individuals being paid (though not much) by parent companies to sell products to consumers at home-based gatherings. We can imagine what her labor looks like (i.e., what types of tasks she participates in, how she is compensated) and, in some cases, why she is performing this labor. In the case of my consultant, she is "just a mom trying to make living."

Pampered Chef consultants' physical labor consists of helping to arrange the party, keeping the host on target with the invitations and menu, driving to the party (my consultant lives two hours from my house), doing a cooking demonstration at the party, and processing the product orders from start to finish.[16] Yet the consultants are trained to make this work seem effortless, seamless in fact. Their enthusiasm is contagious, meant to keep the party atmosphere light and entertaining. It is amazing how good these women are at creating a party atmosphere while coring an apple. Much of their preparation work is invisible. Even the work performed in front of the guests appears to be fun and easy, contributing more to the invisible nature of the work.

Beyond this physical labor, consultants participate in mental labor (e.g., remembering what ingredients go into the pie first and last, how long it needs to be baked) and emotional labor—hiding the fact that they are having a bad day or that they are disappointed with the number of party guests in attendance.

Even less obvious than the work performed by hosts and consultants is the work performed by party guests. Parties are supposed to be fun, yet not all invited individuals are excited about the prospect of attending a product party, resulting in guests' participation in emotional work similar to that of the consultant and host. Guests' apprehension centers on pressures to attend, pressures to purchase, and uncertainty about whom they may or may not know at the gathering. Again, these concerns become invisible as the women put on their party faces.

The invisibility of party plan work is compounded by the fact that many of these organizations operate under the auspices of empowering women, which is true in some cases but not in others. Based on this ideology of empowerment, some party plan organizations may be viewed as feminist organizations.

Twenty years ago, Patricia Yancey Martin shed light on what constitutes a feminist organization. In her research, she acknowledged that there is variability but outlined some key characteristics: (1) it endorses feminist ideology or beliefs; (2) it supports feminist goals of political change that improve women's lives; (3) it encourages feminist guiding values that support care, cooperation, and personal growth; (4) it produces feminist outcomes; and (5) it was founded during the women's movement.[17]

Based on these criteria, some organizations within the party plan economy may be construed as feminist in nature. Other organizations may be perceived as empowering, but in reality they exploit women's labor. For example, some US-based organizations espouse a commitment to empowering women through economic growth even though they use women's labor for their own profit. Outside the United States, some global counterparts to the party plan economy may exploit women's labor (e.g., sweatshops), but others may help women feel empowered (e.g., fair-trade markets). Thus, empowerment and exploitation exist in degrees and can contribute to the invisibility of women's labor.

Parte Plan Mundial

As you continue to read *Women at Work,* you will see that the global party plan mirrors (at least to a degree) the US model (e.g., Indian kitty parties; home-based workers in the Czech Republic), but at times the similarities are not as obvious (e.g., female street vendors in Brazil). What all these examples have in common is the invisibility of labor that is connected in some way to the private sphere. Perhaps women are not having product parties in their homes or working as party plan consultants, but what they are doing is producing and distributing products and services that are often used within the home. Such work consists of weaving, basket making, embroidery, and personal services, just to name a few.[18]

Women's experiences within the party plan economy provide similar talking points. Whether a woman works as a US party consultant, a street vendor, an artisan, or a textile producer, her work is often unregulated and almost always devalued. As one illustration, textile workers in the United States earn $15.78 per hour, whereas the same workers earn $2.19 per hour in Mexico. Roughly 90 percent of such factory workers are young women.[19]

Performance of global party plan work involves the same forms of labor found in the US party plan. Women physically produce and sell products (e.g., clothing, jewelry, food) to consumers. Such production and distribution involves mental labor as well as emotional labor. All the while, the work is made invisible partly because of its location between an informal and formal economy, and partly because of our inability to see the connections between our experiences and those of women in other countries.

This inability to see our connections as women became clear while I was doing research for *Women at Work*. I was teaching two courses while also collecting data for the case study "Women Helping Women on the Party Line," which appears in Chapter 4. Some of the women from one of my courses agreed to talk to me about their party participation. When I asked them whether they thought about how we are connected to women around the globe, they looked at me blankly. One young woman said, "I don't think that we think about that right away. Maybe after we look at the tag in our shirt and see that it was made in Bangladesh. Then we think . . . oh crap." This "oh crap" moment points to a sudden awareness that they are participating in a system that exploits women's labor. Yet in most cases, this sudden awareness is brief and does not result in any activism on the part of participants.

Another young woman remembered a Passion Party that she attended. At this party the consultant told the young women not to be alarmed if they saw the face of a Chinese man on their dildo. Apparently, the faces are put on the dildos so that they can be sent through customs as novelty items (not as aids for sexual pleasure) to the United States.[20] This, of course, led to lots of laughter at the party and also in the interview. After their laughter subsided, the women acknowledged that they simply do not think about global connections unless they are very apparent—as clear as the face on the dildo.

Similarly, when I interviewed a group of older women at a meeting of a national service organization about party attendance, none of them thought about our global connections.[21] While they did not have any examples as colorful as the dildo story, their lack of acknowledgment was the same. We do not see our connections to other women. As a result, we indirectly (and subconsciously) help to keep their labor invisible.

My guess is that readers of this book are not much different from the women I interviewed. We simply do not think about our connections with women around the globe. These global connections, however, are everywhere. Look around you. Flip your shoe over. Where was it made? What about your purse or your pants? In many cases, you will find that the products were mass-produced in other countries (often by women), imported to the United States, and sold through some form of direct sales marketing plan or in local stores.[22]

If products are not made in other countries, they are certainly sold in other countries. Pampered Chef, for example, sells its products in the United States, Canada, the United Kingdom, Germany, and Mexico.[23] Mary Kay sells its products in thirty-five markets worldwide, with a global independent sales force exceeding 1.8 million.[24] Tupperware is sold in almost 100 countries.[25] These few examples are not meant to be exhaustive (there are many other direct sales companies who do business around the world) but to further illustrate the global connections that exist between women within the party plan economy.

Whether local or global, the party plan economy overlaps the formal and informal economies. The party plan is, in fact, wedged between these two markets, making women's work within this sector less and less visible. To further illuminate the implications of this structural location, I use the term *wedge-work* to refer to local and global work performed in the party plan economy.

Wedge-Work

The structural location of the party plan economy—between formal and informal work—lends itself to further discussion and clarification. As noted earlier, the formal economy follows a bureaucratic, rational structure. It is regulated by the government, which results in the creation and implementation of rules, policies, and procedures.[26] The informal economy, however, is unregulated and does not follow a rational model. The result is that workers are underpaid, work long hours (often in poor working conditions), and have little to no autonomy.

The US party plan and its global counterparts are subject to exploitation by capitalists. Owners within the formal economy look to the informal economy for a cheap, reserve labor force. The result is work that is subject to ambiguous employee-employer relationships, which creates uncertainty about worker rights and employer obligations.[27] A lawsuit (*Woolf v. Mary Kay Inc.*) filed against Mary Kay Cosmetics for wrongful termination serves as one example of this ambiguity.[28]

Other companies are not without problems similar to those of Mary Kay. Tupperware, as one article notes, presents a "salad bowl full of problems." As in the Mary Kay lawsuit, one consultant spoke out about questionable practices in the Tupperware company (e.g., hidden costs to consultants, difficulty quitting the company).[29]

Problems surrounding worker rights and employer obligations also appear within the party plan economy in countries outside the United States. Examples include poor working conditions for women in developing countries who make clothing, textiles, and other products used in the private sphere.[30]

Women's party plan work exists on a continuum of visibility. Secretarial work is one example. Most people understand what kind of work secretaries perform. These tasks are visible, but less obvious are the gendered tasks secretaries perform, such as running errands for the boss, doing housekeeping duties in the office, and participating in the emotional labor of maintaining good client relations.[31] Despite these invisible components, people recognize the formal tasks associated with secretarial work. The location of secretarial work in a formal, structured work environment helps to further solidify its membership in the category of *real* work.

The party plan economy does not provide as much clarity. Earning a living takes a backseat to perceptions of pleasure and enjoyment. In the United States, consultants work within the home, not a structured work environment. Their work, as well as the work of hosts and guests, is less visible to the general public. This is also true for women globally. Women working for free-trade marketplaces, for example, may not be in a formal work environment. Instead, they may be working in open-air markets or making their wares in their homes. As a result, these activities are perceived as not being real work.

Comparing a party consultant to a housewife, however, results in a completely different analysis. The housewife—an undervalued, unpaid worker—is even more invisible than the party consultant. Consultants' work, done in front of other women at women's homes, is definitely more visible than the tasks performed by housewives day in and day out. The consultant, therefore, falls in between the housewife (unpaid, informal laborer) and the secretary (formal, paid laborer) in terms of invisibility of work.

This continuum of invisibility is important to understand because it highlights the distinct nature of the party plan. Other scholars note that visibility varies depending on the structure of organizations and that awareness of such inequalities may be intentional or unintentional. These analyses, however, focus mostly on the invisibility that exists within formal organizations.[32] Missing is an assessment of wedge-work. As such, the party plan economy provides an opportunity to further understand the mechanisms that assist in contributing to (and disguising) women's low pay, lack of benefits, and long hours within the party plan.

Giving Back, Gender, and Invisibility

In addition to other issues that contribute to invisibility of the party plan, the exploitation of women's work within the US party plan economy is mitigated by product companies through charitable giving programs. When consumers go to a product website or when they attend a product party, they are quickly told about the wonderful work the company is doing to support children's schools or to cure juvenile diabetes—just two examples of a multitude of causes supported by party plan organizations.

A quick Internet search of party plan companies provides an overview of other causes supported by product companies, almost all focusing on helping women and children. Pampered Chef, for example, is battling hunger in the United States, raising funds to help combat breast cancer, and enriching family well-being in communities by supporting education and community development efforts in impoverished communities. Tupperware supports sustainability and gives tips on its website for living a sustainable life. Silpada wants to help "polish off juvenile diabetes."[33]

In mentioning these companies' charitable works, I am not trying to minimize their humanitarian efforts. Recall, in fact, that we mention women's collective efforts to help one another in the party plan economy. Yet another outcome (possibly unintentional) is that charitable giving aids in minimizing the work done on the ground by company consultants, hosts, and guests. Consultants encourage party guests to buy special recipe cards, towels, or cooking pads. All proceeds will go to the breast cancer foundation. By drawing attention to these important causes, women's work within the party plan is further relegated to the margins.

Consultants feel as if they are working for a company that really cares about its workers and society, shifting attention away from their poor profits, long work hours, and lack of job security.[34] Guests overlook the fact that they are buying products that help to sustain a capitalist organization that cares more about industry profits than people. Hosts feel a bit less guilty about asking friends, family, and coworkers to buy products. The proceeds from these purchases are going toward a good cause, after all.[35] The end result is a contribution to the invisibility of women's work. By focusing attention on charitable activities, people forget about problems inherent in party plan organizations— problems that devalue women as workers and consumers.

In the case studies that follow, invisibility and the power of social class serve as common threads that influence women's choices and experiences within a local and global party plan economy.

From the Field

In the following case study, Kimber Williams provides a unique opportunity to peek into an illegal realm. Women's participation in illegal purse parties is particularly well-hidden, contributing to the greater invisibility of consultants', hosts', and guests' labor at these gatherings. Williams discusses the illegal aspects of selling these goods while assuring us that our purchase of such products can be legitimate. The motivations for purchasing illegal purses, however, are deeply embedded in issues of gender, status, and class. Belonging to the upper class is desirable, adding to the allure of accoutrements that prove you belong.

Case Study 3.1
The Power of the Purse
Kimber R. Williams

Can a purse save a friendship? Can it ruin one? Will it make you look rich, or will it send you to prison? With "designer-inspired" purse parties supplied by black market sources, purses have played a role in all of the above. For one purse partier, it salvaged a friendship between two coworkers. For others involved in this recent phenomenon, participating in a purse party can mean anything from an excuse to have a girls' night out to a criminal conviction with serious jail time.

Purse parties follow the party plan marketing scheme in which women gather to select from an assortment of items at a host's house. Typically, the host is not the organizer of the party but instead acts as just that—the host. The organizer recruits other hosts, provides merchandise, and sets up and displays the purses. Although purses are typically the main attraction, parties will also offer hats, scarves, belts, and other accessories.

Two characteristics set purse parties apart from the other parties and informal markets discussed in this book: (1) the merchandise often includes illegally counterfeit (or "knockoff") purses, and (2) the purchasing drive associated with buying knockoff purses is almost exclusively the quest for status and plays specifically to perceived vulnerabilities of women. The illegality of the merchandise at purse parties and the subconscious—or overt—desire to acquire a status piece is the focus of this case study.

Invisible, Informal, or Illegal Work?
Although it is a crime to *sell* counterfeited trademarked goods such as knockoff purses, it is not a crime to *purchase* them. The fashion police might go after a woman for her recent purchase of an atrocious purse, but the real police will not. However, people who organize and supply purse parties (or sell out of their minivan on a street corner) cannot rest so easily.

Selling knockoff purses certainly is no longer a party for a father-son duo in Virginia. The two supplied fake designer purses for purse parties until a tip from a partygoer led federal agents to seize over 30,000 fake purses from their warehouse. Of those confiscated, over 6,000 were deemed to infringe on trademarks, with a retail value of $198,000. In one of the nation's largest counterfeiting prosecutions, the duo now faces up to five years in prison. Before the two men pled guilty to conspiracy to traffic in counterfeit goods, the prosecution geared up for a designer trial—representatives from Kate Spade, Gucci, and other luxury designers were set to take the stand; key pieces of incriminating evidence were the bags themselves.[36] At trial, the US attorney's office intended to parade hundreds of the counterfeit purses in front of the jury.

As a threat to public safety, purse counterfeiting is generally perceived as nonexistent, spinning the issue into more of a consumer game than a real crime.[37] But high-end retailers do feel the effects of knockoffs, and bags are the most widely infringed product (followed by clothing, watches, wallets, and cell phone covers).[38] In fact, just one unit within the US Customs and Border Protection Office of San Francisco conducted over 150 busts in one year and confiscated approximately $17 million worth of fake purses.[39] Because fake purses are so easily attained, the general public perceives them to be legal.

So why are knockoff purses illegal? Simple: intellectual property and trademarks. While most purse connoisseurs never delve into the complex legal issues of intellectual property and trademarks, they do know the unmistakable LV from Louis Vuitton, the interlocking double C from Chanel, the big G from Gucci, and the upside-down Prada triangle. These are powerful symbols and are fiercely protected.

The problem is that purse imitation isn't flattery; it's counterfeiting. A counterfeit item is anything that is "forged, copied, or imitated without the perpetrator having the right to do it and with the purpose of deceiving or defrauding."[40] Intellectual property laws are designed to protect against counterfeiters, but high-end designers are finding that the line between trademark infringement and acceptable knockoffs is increasingly blurred.[41] Imitation, which was once a desirable benchmark of success in the fashion industry, is now a hotly contested legal issue for high-end designers. Because knockoffs and counterfeit items have become a multibillion-dollar business, designers and manufacturers are starting to view imitation as a mortal threat.[42]

Yet is it fair to call wealthy designers the victims? Coach representatives think so: "The counterfeiters illegally profit at the expense of Coach and affect the entire economy through lost revenues and taxes."[43] Although designer sales may be dented, what is more important to the fashion giants is that the prestige of their brand is degraded by fakes. More ethically problematic, many contend, is that several counterfeit manufacturers use sweatshops and child labor to produce the designer lookalikes. Coach is quick to point out that counterfeiters often do not honor safety and environmental regulations, particularly child labor and anti-sweatshop laws.[44] Even though knockoff purses have been widely popular and can be a huge business, the purse party also presents a major challenge for law enforcement. Consumers continue the illegal trade despite a wave of stings and arrests because citizens rarely turn anyone in, and most would not know whom to report. This is where invisibility and the informal market structure of purse parties play a role in their continued success. Most parties are hosted by a suburban housewife and are organized by a behind-the-scenes supplier whom no one knows or sees. As one supplier indicated to Gina, a hostess interviewed for this case study, she "flew under the radar" because of the illegal nature of dealing in fakes.[45] Parties can turn a big profit for organizers, as lower prices make the wares affordable to all attendees. Knockoff purses at the parties are priced at $40 to $50 each, whereas the prices of genuine designer purses range from $200 to $3,000.[46]

So why are women willing to go to such lengths for a purse? What kind of power do purses actually wield? In a society fixated on status, the purse has become an accessible and acceptable form of status attainment for women. What better outward status symbol for a woman than a Coach bag or a Gucci clutch? It's so easy—just throw it on your shoulder or tuck it under your arm when you leave the house and you have an instant status upgrade.

Purses and Prestige

Using a snowball sampling technique—a process where respondents are located through personal referrals—I conducted unstructured interviews with eighteen women who had attended and/or hosted purse parties. Interviews lasted from thirty minutes to two hours and were conducted in California, Nevada, and Arizona.

Exactly what draws thousands of women to the purse party phenomenon? According to those contacted for this study, there's one driving force: affordability. Aside from price, a few other themes arose, including showing support for the hostess and socializing with the girls. But what seems to represent the underlying motivation? Status.

Status symbols vary from culture to culture but share a uniform purpose of making social standing clear. A particular designer brand may represent the upper class in Western civilization, but a totally different brand or style may rule in another part of the world. What is important within a certain culture or society may also depend on its level of economic or techno-

Figure 3.1 An enthusiastic partier at a (legal) purse party. *(Becky Keller)*

logical development. For example, before books were mass-produced (and thus affordable), having a large library was a status symbol.

Additionally, status symbols reflect the cultural values of the time. With the ever-expanding commercialization of our society, the ability to purchase material goods is a sign of status, and the goods themselves become status symbols. Luxury cars, houses, clothing, and accessories are modern examples of status symbols in Western civilization and most industrialized countries.

It is also important to note that status symbols and their popularity can change dramatically over time. On the one hand, even though "Hammer pants" were all the rage in some places in the late 1980s, a teen today wouldn't be caught dead in a pair and would rather be wearing True Religion or a pair of skinny jeans. On the other hand, luxury designers like Chanel, Versace, Louis Vuitton, Gucci, and Fendi have experienced staying power for decades.

In the purse party world, women are able to fulfill their desire for the status one gets from carrying a Louis Vuitton purse, even though they can't afford the real thing. In short, women who buy knockoff purses want the status without having to pay for it. For those on the cusp of upward mobility, why pay $2,000 for the real thing when no one will likely know the difference?

Some argue that a good knockoff can fool most people, but as one partygoer commented, "They're just trying to look like the real thing, but they're not gonna fool anyone." Others believe that although a purse connoisseur will be able to distinguish between the good fake and the designer, the average woman probably won't. Perhaps the beauty (and the status) lies in the eye of the beholder.

It can be a sore subject, though, for women who *do* know the difference or do own the real thing. One Internet purse blogger commented on the war between the "fake haters" and the "fake lovers," noting that both sides are quickly offended by the other.[47] For example, one interviewee reported that she reacted emotionally to a fleeting compliment about her designer bag, stating that yes, hers was real and expensive, but many of her friends owned knockoffs and had paid a fraction of what she had paid. As she rolled her eyes, the contempt she held for knockoffs was clear. There is resentment and a sense of entitlement from those who own the real thing— they can afford a genuine bag and resent those who buy the knockoffs that diminish the good image of the designer and women who pay for authentic items.

But there is more to the haters than that. When approached about the subject of this case study, one young woman proudly stated she was "not into little kids in Third World countries being mistreated for profit." So while the fake-haters may often appear to be only worried about protecting their own status, there are some who cite a higher moral calling.

Owners of genuine purses may deride fakes, but there are plenty of women who love their knockoffs. In fact, when Michelle found out that her good friend Mia's Chanel purse was a fake, she was shocked and commented that it looked so real. In response, Mia said with an attitude, "Honey, I know! Pshhh." Mia was obviously proud of her lookalike, and why not? It had ultimately fooled even her closest friend, and she hadn't broken the bank to pay for it.

It seems there is something magical about owning the real thing. Several women talked lovingly and nostalgically about their "first Coach"—almost as if it were a milestone in their lives as young adult women. And perhaps it was. Maybe it was a sign that they had made it or that they had reached womanhood. Whitney reminisced about buying that first Coach purse, recalling proudly that she got a big discount because of a pen mark on it, which she was later able to remove. More interesting, however, is that Whitney specifically recalls buying a knockoff designer bag when she started a new job—she remembered feeling like she needed to have the bag, the symbol, the status in order to fit in as a newcomer in the corporate world. Another purse partier, Emma, recognized that owning a designer bag (or a good lookalike) was all about prestige: "Why pay for the real thing when you can fool most people for pennies on the dollar?"

Fendi and Friendship
Although getting a bargain on status is often on the minds of female shoppers, there's more to purse parties than just the good buy and the label: there's the interaction between and among groups of women. Purse parties are often held by an experienced host and accompanied by drinks, snacks, and even entertainment. Selling parties turn into just that—a party. Most of the women interviewed for this case study commented that they went to the purse party because it was hosted by a good friend. Several women even stated that they went because the host "just really knew how to throw a party."

Although the draw of both a good purse and a good deal was strong, what seemed to be even stronger was the female bond. The purse parties had a social feel to them. And the atmosphere, centered on partying rather than selling, became the ultimate marketplace of interaction. In this informal marketplace, women exchange more than just products—they share ideas, experiences, and jokes that bind them together as women, friends, and purse fiends alike. Although no one reported feeling pressured to buy, most did feel an obligation to the hostess because they were friends. In fact, Katie, a one-time partygoer, didn't count herself as a huge purse buyer but still ended up buying two purses at the party she attended. So, is it really the power of the purse, or is it the power of the party?

For one interviewee, it didn't matter—the purse party Tanya attended healed a failing friendship. Tanya had had a falling out with a coworker but had still been invited to a purse party hosted by her. She didn't particularly want to go but went anyway to make a friendly gesture and possibly mend fences. By the end of the party, Tanya had bought two purses and felt that her presence helped bring them back together. Tanya commented, "Had it not been for me going to that purse party, I'm not sure we'd still be friends, and I certainly wouldn't have the purse collection I have today!" The friendship between Tanya and her coworker was successfully repaired, and they continue to be friends today. Ah, the power of the purse party! Saving friendships, saving money.

Wallets and the Worldwide Web

So what does the future hold for purse partiers? The knockoff purse industry has been hit hard by sting operations and arrests, but it certainly hasn't disappeared. Rita described a dealer who has her own MySpace page. After viewing the site, it was clear to me that business is booming. The peddler advertises fake purses, wallets, Ed Hardy bikinis, and Tiffany jewelry on her page, claiming that hosting a party will get you free merchandise. Indeed, Rita had hosted a party and received a free wallet and purse. The My-Space page contains pictures of the items that are for sale (you can purchase direct if you don't want to host or attend a party) and states that they specialize in "designer-inspired" merchandise.

In a "culture of constant sampling and remixing," knockoffs will be around as long as there is demand.[48] With the fashion industry and our culture being so fixated on image, the demand won't fade anytime soon. Counterfeiting is a $600-billion-a-year problem that has grown over 10,000 percent in the past twenty years, growth attributed in large part to consumer demand.[49] Indeed, consumer demand has risen, but big business, artists, and public figures plastering brands on just about everything imaginable has only fueled the fire.

Totes to Tasers: Gender Appeal

Women are often attracted to designer purses and thus succumb to the purse party because of society's particular pressure on women to fit in according to class and the latest fashion trend. But even though it may seem that the purse party is the perfect modern manifestation of gender consumption, there is another emerging trend that may better capture the essence of the gender party: the Taser party. A Taser party doesn't *sound* particularly gendered—after all, Tasers are the ultimate nonlethal weapon and are carried by thousands of police agencies.[50] However, the Taser party specifically targets women because the female gender is often perceived as weak and in need of protection. More important, it plays on the contemporary woman's need for autonomy and personal safety. One saleswoman who has been trying to push for Taser parties for years comments, "It's a girl power kind of thing."[51]

Seeing an untapped market, Taser developed a new line that is small, lightweight, and comes in a variety of colors, including, of course, pink. The party plan scheme has now taken a twenty-first-century turn. But it hasn't veered too far from the original plan—that is, to bring women together in a social setting, allow the host to make some extra money, and sell a product to which women might not otherwise have access. What is most interesting about the Taser and purse parties is that they specifically illustrate how the party plan manipulates the idea of an appropriate modern-day woman, just as the original Tupperware parties and Stanley Home Products did in the 1950s. Perhaps the ultimate compliance is to enhance one's status with a pink Prada and claim the right to safe public space by tucking a pink Taser inside.

Beyond Purses: Excessive Branding
Bullets, guns, and even an electric chair have been branded with the Louis Vuitton label, aiming to make compelling political statements. Although artists and activists seek to resist consumerism through such acts, they may actually expand excessive branding.

Obviously, purses are among the more reasonable products to be designer branded. But what does it say about a society that is so fixated on brands, status, and labels that a famous designer logo is placed on a gun or an execution device? To what lengths will we go for the label?[52]

Akiko Yoshida reveals several mechanisms that contribute to the invisible nature of consultant work within Mary Kay. Central to this study is the interrelatedness of structural (social class), ideological (guided beliefs), and gendered expectations. All these devices constitute strong gendered channeling that affect women's beliefs and choices. Seeing their own work situated under the guise of parties, most consultants fail to recognize the pitfalls and consequences associated with invisible work, believing that success is just around the corner. Yoshida illustrates several aspects of cosmetic work as couched in a "gendered American Dream," explicating a system that would be inapplicable if not for a gender order that segregates work (and idealized lifestyles) by sex. Among other strategies, women are sold a story that privileges femininity at the expense of individual independence and collective empowerment. Using qualitative interviews with ten independent sales consultants, Yoshida exposes the power of a gendered, classed ideology in shaping women's views of themselves and their work.

A Gendered American Dream: Why Women Sell Mary Kay
Akiko Yoshida

> The women who have made it big in Mary Kay tell how they started on
> the doorsteps of poverty. And they've gone all the way to the top. So, we
> know that people can do it, because countless numbers have done it.
> —*Linda, Mary Kay team leader*

Mary Kay, a cosmetic giant and one of the most prominent direct sales
companies in the United States, was founded in 1963 by Mary Kay Ash and
her son Richard Rogers.[53] According to the company, Mary Kay has over
1.8 million distributors ("consultants") in more than thirty countries and
had more than $2.4 billion in wholesale revenue in 2007.[54] The company
uses multilevel marketing in which consultants are highly encouraged to recruit other Mary Kay distributors. According to informal estimates, wholesale volume per consultant averaged $1,818.18 per year,[55] and the
consultant turnover rate was 68.6 percent in the United States in 2005.[56]
Even so, the business continues to attract large numbers of consultants.

To understand the wide appeal of Mary Kay, I conducted in-depth interviews with ten current and former Mary Kay consultants, finding that
most earn little income (and/or are in debt) but anticipate high future earnings. I call this belief a gendered American Dream: the idea, as promised by
Mary Kay, that all women can become rich entrepreneurs without sacrificing womanhood. This ideology is accomplished through methods of persuasion including "fuzzy math," religious attachment, and individual
recognition, which seem to divert women from focusing on actual earnings
or losses and sustains their belief in the gendered American Dream.

Understanding Mary Kay
Mary Kay provides consultants two ways to earn income: by selling products and by earning commissions on the wholesale purchases made by consultants they recruited.[57] To sell products and recruit future sellers, Mary
Kay consultants are instructed to offer a free facial (skincare class) to potential customers, often using personal networks for sales and recruitment.[58] In addition to earnings from sales and commission, reaching certain
sales goals enables consultants to earn various prizes as well as recognition
awards at Mary Kay's annual sales meetings, or "Seminars."[59]

Becoming a Mary Kay consultant requires no particular skills or cre-
dentials. According to "Mary Kay Is the Perfect Opportunity,"[60] for the
price of a $100 starter kit, any woman can start her own business.[61] Her
title is independent sales consultant, and she receives a 50 percent discount
on all products. She can then attain higher ranks by recruiting team mem-

bers (consultants beneath herself). Recruiting one or two active team members makes her a senior consultant, followed by star recruiter with three or four, and so on (see Figure 3.2).[62] A consultant earns 4–13 percent commission from wholesale purchases made by her "offspring." That is, Mary Kay commissions are based on a declining scale where independent sales consultants earn a percentage of sales by everyone they recruit, and from all those in the pyramid-like structure under the direct recruit. When a consultant earns a new title, she wins prizes such as pins, jackets, bonuses, and car use eligibility. Mary Kay reveals minimal financial information, so few reliable sources exist for consultants' earnings,[63] yet based on reports from Canada, over 90 percent of consultants had no earnings from commissions.[64]

Methods

To understand the reasons for, perceptions of, and meanings attached to women's Mary Kay participation, I interviewed eight current and two former consultants who have engaged in the Mary Kay business. I contacted

Figure 3.2 Mary Kay Pyramid

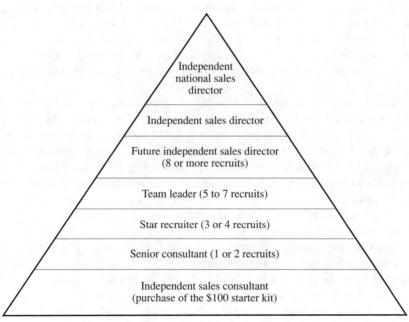

Independent
national sales
director

Independent sales director

Future independent sales director
(8 or more recruits)

Team leader (5 to 7 recruits)

Star recruiter (3 or 4 recruits)

Senior consultant (1 or 2 recruits)

Independent sales consultant
(purchase of the $100 starter kit)

This visual representation of a pyramid-like scheme characterizes
Mary Kay and similar corporate party structures.

an independent sales director (ISD), Caroline, in a small town in the southern United States.[65] She agreed to be interviewed, invited me to her weekly Mary Kay meetings, and allowed me to recruit other consultants for interviews. Four women (Elaine, Joan, Evelyn, and Monica) immediately agreed to be interviewed. Caroline also introduced me to Meghan, another ISD, who then introduced me to her mother (Linda), who was Meghan's team member. Some of my acquaintances gave me a few names and, among them, Jennifer (a current consultant) and Maxine (who left Mary Kay fifteen years ago) agreed to be interviewed. I met another former consultant (Lisa) who left Mary Kay a year ago and was eager to share her experiences with me.

The interviewees' levels of education varied from high school diploma to master's degrees.[66] All the women were very sociable, welcoming, and willing to talk about the Mary Kay business (see Table 3.1).[67]

Why They Sell
Even though the number of interviewees was small, the women's views and practices were remarkably similar. It was as if I was listening to members of a tight-knit family who shared common beliefs and a common lifestyle.[68] Four major findings are as follows: (1) All the women believed strongly in the Mary Kay story, which I call a gendered American Dream; (2) these women are highly encouraged to continue investing in Mary Kay despite financial losses and are rewarded for their dedication; (3) some associate their Mary Kay participation with religious (Christian) faith; and (4) although stable finances and flexible schedules are deemed questionable, most interviewees reported that they valued their Mary Kay participation.

Belief in a gendered American Dream. All interviewees believed that earning substantial sums of money via Mary Kay was absolutely achievable. This was the case for former consultants as well: Lisa, an outgoing woman in her thirties, said that while she was in Mary Kay, she thought she would become rich. Maxine, a widow and former consultant, still believed such wealth was possible and wished she had continued her business.[69] All current consultants cited other Mary Kay women who supposedly had already achieved such high income. For instance, Caroline, an ISD in her forties, told me that her national sales director's highest check was over $50,000 for one month, and that other directors were making "sixty-, seventy-, eighty-thousand, or millions." Elaine, who earned $22,000 a year from her full-time job outside of Mary Kay, showed me the Mary Kay magazine *Applause,* which listed monthly incomes ranging from $3,974 to $111,654 in the October 2007 issue. Elaine exclaimed, "This is what they're making! I can double my salary in just one month! See, this is why I want to go full time!"[70]

Such wealth is presented as attainable by anyone, including those who

Table 3.1 Demographics, Yoshida field study sample

Name[a]	Age[b]	Race/Ethnicity	Marital Status[b]	Mary Kay Title	Years in Mary Kay[b]	Other Occupation
Caroline	49	White	Remarried	Independent sales director	16	No
Meghan	29	White	Married	Independent sales director	9	No
Linda	60	White	Married	Team leader	9	No
Jennifer	22	White	Married	Team leader	2	No
Elaine	49	White	Remarried	Senior consultant	20	Yes
Joan	56	White	Remarried	Senior consultant	3	No
Monica	27	White	Married	Senior consultant	2	Yes
Evelyn	56	Asian	Cohabiting	Independent beauty consultant	6	Yes
Lisa	38	White	Remarried	Left when star recruiter	3[c]	Yes
Maxine	66	White	Widowed	Left when independent beauty consultant	2[c]	No

Notes: a. All names are pseudonyms.
b. Age, marital status, and years in Mary Kay are at the time of the interviews.
c. Lisa and Maxine left Mary Kay after three and two years, respectively.

have no capital. "Anybody can do it" and "Everyone should try" were phrases repeated by all current consultants. Linda, a housewife in her early sixties, told me about Mary Kay women she saw at a Seminar: "The women who have made it big in Mary Kay tell how they started on the doorsteps of poverty. And they've gone all the way to the top. So we know that people can do it, because countless numbers have done it." In the face of such living proof, achievement of wealth became real for consultants despite the fact they hadn't actually achieved it.

Mary Kay promotes independence. Consultants all identified themselves as independent business owners and referred to their work as "my business." Jennifer, a college student, talks about the main reason she liked the Mary Kay business:

> JENNIFER: The fact that it's up to me. It's not up to anybody else. It's my work. Whenever I want to do, I can do, however much or however less I wanna do with the company, and nobody could say anything.
>
> AKIKO: So, you mean freedom?
>
> JENNIFER: Freedom, yes! Not that boss breathing over your shoulder, making sure you met your quotas.

In addition to gaining wealth and independence, women believe these goals can be achieved without sacrificing womanhood, that the business accommodates itself to the needs of women, allowing them to care for their families. When recommending the business to others, flexibility was one of the most commonly named advantages: consultants cited a philosophy of "God first, family second, career third." Caroline had been in Mary Kay for sixteen years and said her now-grown children were ages seven and ten when she started. She told me, with confidence:

> They would both tell you today that they never missed out having their mom. I was there at their school functions, every class party, every band concert. Anything that went wrong. If they got sick at school, I was the one who picked them up. If they forgot their lunch, I took it too. You know? I was their mama! So they never really knew I worked. Sara [one of her daughters] has been so sick, . . . I missed seventy-five days of work, and guess what? In that seventy-five days, Mary Kay still brought me a free vehicle to drive, I was still getting paid, every month. I didn't get fired!

Some interviewees reported that relationships they had with customers were also personal and genuine. Consultants personalized such relationships by giving roses at parties (Jennifer) or placing a small chocolate bar in each customer's order (Caroline); they reported that customers loved these special touches. As Elaine explained, Mary Kay is about relationships: "You develop relationships with your customers. And you're helping them get the skincare quality, and it's not just skincare, it's body care and everything. . . . You're offering them a way to make themselves look prettier. . . . It offers them a chance to let them feel prettier by using the product and stuff. And also spending time with them. It develops relationships."

Consultants could depend on customers. Joan, a retired teacher in her late fifties, said: "Customers! If I call ten of my customers and say, 'I did thirty facials already and I need ten more. Could you give me a hand? Can I come by sometime this week and facial you?' They'll do it for you! It's just that relationship and they'd come on board and help you do anything."

Some consultants compared Mary Kay to other jobs, or what they referred to as "corporate America." Caroline elaborated:

> I have a friend who worked here in a bank, had been there for thirty years. About eighteen months ago, she had a medical leave for cancer treatments. Just a few months ago, she got a letter in the mail, terminating her from her position. She had a medical leave, worked there for thirty years. They terminated her. I thought, "How sad. How sad!" And I thought how fortunate I am! Because, I know that's not gonna happen to me. . . . In most jobs, they don't care about your family. It's job, job, job. You're supposed to be here. You're supposed to clock in and clock out. We'll pay you for the time you're here. You can't be sick, your kids can't be sick. That's Corporate America!

Caroline and others projected that most other jobs were impersonal, merciless, and unaccommodating to women's needs, whereas Mary Kay women could expect warm, personal, and cooperative relationships, as well as an accommodating job.

Further, consultants believed that women could gain (or retain) beautiful, feminine looks by participating in Mary Kay. Maxine admired the "gorgeous" appearance her acquaintance acquired after she started selling Mary Kay products, which influenced Maxine to join. All the current consultants were proud of their younger-looking skin. They were also encouraged to dress in a feminine manner, as Elaine explained: "Mary Kay wants you to wear a suit or skirt or dress, and nylons. Mary Kay just stresses 'You are a woman.' It teaches you to feel proud about who you are, as a woman. [These days,] women wear men's clothing, you know, men's T-shirts and stuff like that. And you know, you don't have a pride in yourself."

Indeed, all the Mary Kay consultants I interviewed were dressed in ways that accentuated femininity. Slacks were discouraged. Many told me that they represented Mary Kay and enjoyed this aspect. For example, Meghan, another ISD and mother of two young children, said: "Just for my delivery, for my errand, I'm always dressed [in] a skirt, a dress, or something. I always wear some sort of dress on. And people notice. . . . My customer'd say, 'Why are you all dressed up? You know, it's just Wal-Mart!' . . . It's fun to do that every once in a while. You'd feel feminine, kinda dressed up and feel good."

Elaine commented on photos of directors in the magazine: "Aren't they just gorgeous? These women are just beautiful!" Top directors serve as role models, as women who achieve wealth while retaining a young, beautiful, feminine look.

The insidious emphasis on feminine beauty seems to encourage Mary Kay women to differentiate themselves from women who work for corporate America, who are stressed and fatigued, have no time for themselves, and act/dress like men. In contrast, Mary Kay women presumably maintain or even gain glamorous feminine beauty as they attain economic success.

These women believe in a gendered American Dream, in the idea that in the United States opportunities are open and anyone can achieve material prosperity through hard work and perseverance. Women, however, often expect (or are socially expected) to take the primary role in child care and household chores. Nineteenth-century gender ideology (emphasizing piety, purity, submissiveness, and domesticity) assigned women to the domestic sphere, an ideology still alive today.[71] Many women are employed outside the home, yet most feel (or are expected to feel) they should be the primary caregivers for their children, conflicting with economic achievement.[72] Mary Kay promises that women need not sacrifice womanhood to realize economic success—a gendered version of the American Dream.

Because these consultants strongly believe in Mary Kay's gendered American Dream, recruitment is seen as giving opportunities to other women, not as exploitation of personal networks. As Elaine put it, recruitment is "to get them the opportunities to have a career where they can stay home. It's not just to get women under me. It's to help them, to let them see the opportunities and money they can make; it's just sharing." Every interviewee (except Lisa, a former consultant) confidently said they would recommend this business to other women, in line with Caroline's claim that "sharing the opportunity is part of my job description."

Earnings and fuzzy math. "How much do they actually earn?" is a question people may ask regarding direct sales. Curiously, *none* of my interviewees could give a definite answer to my question, "What is your income from Mary Kay?" Because such incomes are not set, it is understandable that figuring earnings is not a straightforward task. However, it seems that Mary Kay offers no solid financial advice or training to its consultants. Most business owners keep meticulous records of costs (e.g., inventory, losses, other overhead costs) and amounts of retail sales so that profits can be calculated, yet I observed no such practices among my interviewees. Most of them simply moved money in and out of their Mary Kay accounts and gave a rough estimate of their profits from each retail sale. Caroline and Jennifer told me how much they thought they made in the past year ($50,000 to $55,000 and $8,000, respectively). These figures appear to be unreliable for many reasons.

First, words such as *profit* and *sales* were not used in a conventional sense. For instance, Joan first told me, "I made $1,400 from one party." That figure turned out to be the total retail value ordered, and since she gave 20–30 percent discounts on some of the products sold at the party, profits must have been even smaller than the standard profit margin. The use of the term *sales* was even more unconventional, referring to the retail value of purchases *consultants* made from the company. So when Joan said she received the Queen of the Sales award (for selling $15,000) and Linda said she made $10,000 in retail sales per year, it meant they bought products worth those retail amounts (paying wholesale prices of $7,500 and $5,000, respectively) from the company. Lisa confirmed what Mary Kay does:

> You're taught to look at the retail number. I was once Princess Quarter of the Sale one year. That's not selling. That's based on how much products you ordered from the company. . . . Nobody at the corporate ever told me that "Okay, we need to know how much you sold." That never happened. My Director never cared that much. She just wanted me to order. You know, we got prizes for ordering, not for selling.

Second, Mary Kay consultants were advised (via their directors) to consider only 40 percent of their retail sales as profits. In Jennifer's words, "I do a 40/60 split. Whatever Mary Kay products you sell, like, a foundation is $14. You make $7 off each. You make 50 percent. Well, instead of doing 50 percent, you do 60 percent: 60 percent back in my business and keep 40 percent for myself." Under the 40/60 split, Jennifer would consider only $5.60 of her $7 markup as profit.

When Caroline said she thought she made "roughly about $50,000 to $55,000," she was gazing at the certificates on her wall, which she received for her unit achieving a certain "sales" figure. To maintain the ISD position, her unit must order a minimum of $72,000 per year.

Going back to Jennifer's illustration, I assume that Caroline used the 40 percent rule to calculate her profit based on her unit's "sales." But the 40/60 rule does not apply to "sales" made by her unit: she earns just 4–13 percent commissions from these. I attempted a rough estimate of the retail sales required for her to earn $50,000 in profits. Putting aside inventory costs and other expenses, she would need either $125,000 in personal retail sales ($50,000 being 40 percent of $125,000) or $385,000 in retail sales made by her unit members ($50,000 being 13 percent of $385,000), or a unit total between the two.[73] If she had such large sales figures, would she not have moved up in rank?

Another common business practice among consultants is to purchase inventory packages at fixed levels (retailed at $600, $1,200, $1,800, $2,400, etc.), instead of purchasing from actual orders. Consultants are given prizes as incentives (from a small wallet to jewelry and fur coats) to buy such packages. Linda said the prize for a $2,400 wholesale order was "a beautiful pearl and rhinestone ring, and I really wanted that ring," so she purchased the package.

Do consultants typically sell off all purchased inventory? The interviewees answered "No," but some were not concerned about it. For instance, Evelyn, who worked full-time for $9 an hour, spent $3,000 on inventory but thought she was not losing because she got a 50 percent discount on products she loved (i.e., she would use them if not sold). But products eventually expire, and, according to Lisa, consultants are not allowed to sell expired products. In addition, some products become discontinued or are sold as seasonal products (e.g., Christmas edition).[74]

Still, the two ISDs (Caroline and Meghan) probably earned some income, though much less than they claimed. As for low-ranked consultants, I

Figure 3.3 Mary Kay consultants who buy enough products may get prizes like a pink blender, pink toaster, or a pink phone in the shape of a classic Cadillac. *(Akiko Yoshida)*

doubt they made any; more likely, they were in debt. I asked Lisa why consultants do not realize this fact:

> You're just kind of oblivious to it. You think you're successful. You know, one of the mottos you hear all the time is "You fake it 'til you make it." And you just kinda teach yourself to believe that, well, I'm gonna fake it 'til I make it, because I only sold $50 this week but next week I'm gonna sell $250. . . . Once you make a Director, they'd begin giving you the Director check and you can pay off any debt you built up. So you kinda have this mindset going, well, I'm gonna get the big check, so I'm gonna be able to pay off all the debts later.

God is behind my business. Mary Kay consultants I interviewed often mentioned the role that religious belief played in their business; God is cited as an important part of their Mary Kay participation. Caroline stated, "I know God is my business partner." Elaine elaborated:

> Mary Kay speaks, you know, about putting God first in your life . . . and I said [to God], "I give this over to you." And ever since then, every single job I applied for, I've been turned down. It just closed the door. I haven't gotten interviews or anything, but my Mary Kay business is growing. And so that's, you know, God is just saying, "Hey, we're gonna go with this!" . . . Because, you know, the Lord is closing doors in every other area, and income for me, and he's opening up the path to Mary Kay.

Though consultants made little to no money, they reported believing it was the right thing to do because God was behind it. I observed Bible scripture on consultants' Mary Kay binders. The former consultant, Lisa, complained that Mary Kay was "abusing God" and said that people always prayed and used scripture at Mary Kay conferences. Elaine reported liking Mary Kay women because they were all "good Christians." From these accounts, a claim to Christian faith is part of company culture and perhaps is another motivation for selling the cosmetics.

Gains. If not money, what do consultants gain from doing Mary Kay? One might expect that they enjoy flexible work schedules. However, despite claims of accommodating schedules, some consultants perceived the business as an obstacle to caring for families. Joan had to look after four grandchildren (ages three to eleven) when her son moved back after his divorce, and at that time she "had to figure out how to make [my Mary Kay business] work." Linda did not think she would continue with Mary Kay once her (or her husband's) aging parents required care. Monica stopped going to Mary Kay meetings or even making contact with the other women after becoming pregnant with her first child.

Earlier, Caroline emphasized that she could accommodate her then-young children's needs. However, Caroline's typical work schedule did not appear mother-friendly: "Usually, my afternoons are spent at making deliveries. . . . I spend most of my mornings [in my home office]. Most nights are spent delivering. Wednesday night we have a conference with the National Sales Director, and Monday mornings, we have a meeting just for Sales Directors with our National Sales Director [in a city 150 miles away]." I asked Caroline where her daughters were when she worked, and she said that her mother watched them or they went to after-school programs, explaining it "was a treat for them."

Lisa's story also contradicts the Mary Kay philosophy that women can prioritize their families over work. She said that the Mary Kay job was in general "labor-intensive," and that consultants were expected to attend meetings even at the expense of their families. Lisa told a story of being forced to attend a Mary Kay meeting even though the Department of Human Services had planned a visitation to check on children who had been placed in her house. "Looking back, I go, 'Oh, my gosh! What was I thinking?' . . . They say 'God first, family second, Mary Kay third,' but they don't mean it. I think they lie. It was 'Mary Kay first, Mary Kay second, Mary Kay third!'"

Social connectedness, identity, and self-worth. Though flexibility did not seem to be a gain for most interviewees, the women appeared to enjoy other aspects of Mary Kay. Warm, caring, social relationships were emphasized as things they could enjoy, and they claimed that relationships with other team members were genuine and personal.

> CAROLINE: I can call any one of my Mary Kay friends right now, and if I needed anything, they'd rush to my side to help me.

> JENNIFER: It's not really us fighting against each other for customers. It's really us becoming, you know, sisters, and taking care of each other, and making sure everybody is doing good and cheering each other on. I really like that.

"Positive," "uplifting," "caring," "true friends," and "like real sisters/sisterhood" were words often used when describing other consultants. Meghan emphasized this aspect more than that of staying home with her children.

> [Mary Kay people] know what the big picture is. Something more than just a day-to-day, eight to five. They're positive; they're happy about what they do. I think of the people I used to work with [other beauticians

at a hair salon] . . . I don't want to be in contact with them. I think the
Mary Kay people, they have higher morals. . . . When you're not present,
they'll not talk about you. . . . [Mary Kay women are] true friends. . . .
People I used to work with wouldn't lift you up. Whereas Mary Kay people, they can!

For Evelyn, other women were the main reason she stayed in the business. She described weekly meetings as "girls' night out" and looked forward to them. Elaine thought Mary Kay women were friends connected
through a common goal. Lisa met her best friend through Mary Kay.

The consultants also seemed to receive a boost of self-esteem from
Mary Kay involvement. Caroline said, "It brought me out of my shyness. It
taught me how to be more of a people person. . . . Mary Kay really gave me
back my self-esteem that I had lost in thirteen years of marriage to an abu-
sive husband."

Motivation and recognition were important: "I love to have something
to focus on" (Meghan). "I love those awards" (Evelyn). "I just loved all that
recognition" (Lisa). Caroline and Jennifer were proud of their fast ascent.
For Monica, "Glamour!" was her biggest reason to be in this business.
Maxine "wanted to be gorgeous and confident" just like her acquaintance
who transformed after starting Mary Kay. Many enjoyed feeling pretty and
young from dressing up and maintaining young-looking skin. Still others
(Caroline, Elaine, Jennifer, and Meghan) enjoyed helping other women
transform physically and/or psychologically. In sum, Mary Kay consultants
seem to gain a sense of connectedness, identity, and self-worth.

Conclusion

This study suggests that women participate in the Mary Kay business because of the strong belief in a gendered American Dream. The social exchange perspective informs us that individuals participate in an exchange
when they perceive or anticipate rewards from it.[75] These women anticipate
rewards (being rich and feminine), so they continue with the company despite the fact that they are far from accomplishing such goals. The remarkable level of consistency in the interviewees' accounts suggests that a
gendered American Dream ideology is embedded in the Mary Kay culture.
This ideology becomes an instrument, consciously or not, that convinces
consultants to join the Mary Kay ranks.

My findings may also reflect other pathologies in our society. Some social critiques have pointed out that individuals are increasingly self-focused
and communities are in decline in the United States.[76] Thus, for my interviewees, the sense of connectedness, self-worth, and the dream itself may
be priceless. In our capitalist society, we pay for countless commodities and
services that supposedly provide pleasure. For some, spending money on

Mary Kay inventory may be a justifiable expenditure, well worth a price-less sisterhood.

As I commented to Meghan, "It sounds like Mary Kay is giving you a dream." She immediately and excitedly responded, "Yes, yes, yes! So many people don't dream any more. You have nothing to work for. Why? You don't have anything to look forward to or try to achieve. Yes! She [Mary Kay] wants you to do this."

But the difference between spending money on services that provide such psychic rewards and the Mary Kay business is that, in the former, individuals are aware that they are the customers. This is not the case for Mary Kay consultants, who believe that they are business owners on their way to becoming rich entrepreneurs. Would these women still consider the dream and sisterhood priceless with the clear understanding that they are paying in cash? I know that for Lisa and many other women the answer is a resounding "no."

In Chapter 2, Sue Zschoche provided a historical examination of the invisibility of women's labor in the United States. In "Brazilian Women, Invisible Workers," Adryanna Siqueira explores the invisibility of women's work globally. Using fourteen one-on-one interviews with Brazilian street vendors, Siqueira's findings demonstrate the invisibility that stems from the hidden production of goods that occurs in the home and the devaluation of work that occurs in the street markets. Through analysis of women's home-based production and street-based entrepreneurship, Siqueira uncovers a combination of tough, pragmatic tactics needed to survive on the street and internal strength that she terms *luta,* or "fighting spirit."

Case Study 3.3
Brazilian Women, Invisible Workers
Adryanna Siqueira

A self-made entrepreneur starts an ordinary day of work, proud of the successful business developed months before. Sales are good, customers are coming back, and the company is already making a profit. It's two in the afternoon, and the wire stalls are already set up in the city square where sales happen. The stalls are covered in colorful plastic with products hanging on all sides. Even though customers are not going to arrive until four or five p.m., the products are already on display, ready for one more day of sales. Maria—the business owner or *feirante,* as the workers in the street markets are called—wears Bermuda shorts, a T-shirt, and tennis shoes and generally has a "fanny pack" where she stores her money and change. It is hot, an av-

Figure 3.4 This marketplace in Goiania, Brazil, buzzes with customers shopping from Feira da Tarde street vendors. *(Adryanna Siqueira)*

erage of 90 degrees Fahrenheit. The marketplace gets louder as feirantes communicate with each other in a very informal way, and traffic gets more intense with the arrival of more feirantes and customers. In the air is a strong smell of oil from the food being deep-fried in the "food court" area.

Maria is only one of the thousands of feirantes who make a living in the informal street markets of Brazil. Street markets, one of the many shapes the informal economy may take, are a creative way of accommodating individuals outside the formal labor market. Hernando De Soto, on his search to find the sources of the development of an extralegal economy, found that this sector of the economy flourishes in developing countries due to the impediments that the local governments impose on aspiring entrepreneurs.[77] What he found was that taxation and bureaucracy discouraged or even hindered citizens from following legality.

Participants in this alternative form of market economy have specific characteristics. Studies show that greater percentages of women than men work in informal economies worldwide. Of the nonagricultural workers in sub-Saharan Africa, 84 percent of women are informally employed, compared to 63 percent of men. Overall, 60 percent or more of women workers in the developing world are informally employed.[78] Women in this context are generally home-based workers and street vendors, as are the women who are part of this study.

The higher incidence of women participating in the informal economy does not happen by chance but is influenced by an ideology that professes that being a man or a woman is relevant in the generation of expectations and rewards. Even though bodies can differ physiologically in many ways, they are "transformed by social practices to fit into the salient categories of society, the most pervasive of which are 'female' and 'male.'"[79] Based on these social constructs, work opportunities, social power, patterns of emotional attachment, and desire are unequally distributed between men and women. These elements, although still disguised by arguments of essentialism (such as men being "naturally tough" or women as "naturally emotional"), function as constraints on further practice, in which individuals are under constant scrutiny as to whether or not they fit the expectations created for their gender.[80]

In this study, it is possible to have a personal account of how these ideologies come into practice in the realities of women street vendors in Brazil. Through the development of an unconventional entrepreneurship, the vendors challenge traditional expectations dictated by self-feeding cultural, religious, and gender ideologies.

Methodology

This case study aims to reveal the perceptions women street vendors in Brazil have of work in the marketplace, specifically how individual and contextual factors influence these women's participation in the informal sphere. Two main subjects are the starting point for this discussion: the opportunity structure that is available to women in that context and the cultural milieu in which they are immersed.[81] Although informal markets have been the subject of various studies worldwide, the work of women in Brazilian street markets remains largely unexplored.

This study took place in Goiania, the twelfth-largest city in Brazil. The city's economy is based on agriculture, cattle production, and a large industrial sector. Informal street markets became another characteristic of the city; in 2007, there were 144 known markets operating.[82]

Data were collected in the summer of 2007 (June, July, and part of August) in five markets, called here *Feira da Tarde, Feira do Artesanato, Feira do Dia, Mercado dos Trabalhadores,* and *Feira Central.* I completed face-to-face interviews with fourteen feirantes (thirteen women and one man). The age of the participants ranged from twenty-six to sixty-three. All participants were informal business owners in street markets in Goiania. All but one of the participants was white.

Conversations with participants were guided by a semistructured interview schedule that inquired about the lives of participants before and after the markets. Some of the questions asked during the interviews involved previous work activities, the beginning of their work in the market, daily market routines, and plans for the future. Besides interviews, participant observation was another method used for data collection, in which subtle details of work in the markets could be observed, offering a closer understanding of the markets from an insider perspective.

The data were hand-coded, with themes emerging after extensive scrutiny. Themes were included when they were present at a frequency of 50 percent or more of the cases.

Findings

I divided my findings into four main categories: "opportunity structure," "cultural milieu," "*luta*," and "beyond the decision."

Opportunity structure. Participants discussed the limitations they faced in the formal labor market prior to their initiation into the markets. They shared stories about how discouraging their prior activities were for many reasons, but above all financially. The formal labor market is described as age- and gender-selective, and financially uninviting. The women made clear that their informal business generates more income than any other job they ever had. Clara said, "[The market stall] pays a lot more than any job I have had. I was a secretary and . . . could pay for college and a couple of bills, and the money was gone before the middle of the month." Clara's gains in the informal economy are double what she had in the formal economy, where only low-level positions were available to her. Even women holding college degrees attest to the difficulty in finding jobs.

Another issue that women in Goiania face is that the job market is age-restrictive. Clarice pointed out, "Ninety percent of the feirantes are women. There is not available work for women in the formal economy, especially for women older than forty. There are no jobs available for us and we are all coming to the markets, because there is no age limitation to work here."

With a career as a teacher and a housewife for most of her life, Clarice felt that the venue of the informal markets would be more inviting to women like her, struggling to meet their personal and financial needs. This reality is true for women of all skill levels. These characteristics illustrate the pervasive gender ideology that is present in their experiences, producing limited opportunities for these women because of gender, class, and race. Due to the unequal distribution of opportunities—and therefore power—they are kept from reaching their potential in totality and are restricted to certain occupations. The informal markets offer them the choice of playing a new role in a new context.

Cultural milieu. Women's participation in the street markets happens not only in the context of a job market restrictive to them but also in the context of a cultural milieu that is embedded in their identities. Religiosity is marked in their discourse, not surprisingly, as Brazil is the largest Catholic country in the world.

Kathleen Young describes virgin martyrs, used as the depiction of most Catholic female saints, as reinforcing patriarchal mandates of behavior.[83] In this context, "cultural paradigms of virginity and martyrdom have implications for the construction of sexuality, codes of reproduction, gender identity, and life experience for Catholic women." By emphasizing suffering as a means of redemption and femininity as a synonym for motherhood and submission, Catholic values shape women's lives by making their behavior accountable not only in the eyes of the community, family, and themselves, but also in the eyes of God.

God was a repeated theme in the interviews with women street vendors. There was a constant need to show appreciation and thankfulness, but in a manner different from mechanically saying "Thank God" without meaning it. This omnipresent figure was identified not as an enforcer of restrictions but as the one who made vendors' dreams possible. The faith these women express in their appreciation of God, regardless of which religious denomination they follow, has profound influence on the way they see their achievements, but their beliefs vary. At times they adopt a passive attitude, by transferring to God all the achievements and successes they have had and the strength they use to keep going. Sara explained, "I stretch my arm and feel that I am sore, because of all the heavy lifting and I always say, 'Thank you, Lord.'" Ana was even more direct: "I don't know what I will do in the future; whatever God tells me to do, I will do; wherever He guides me to go, I will go."

God is perceived as offering constant companionship, guidance, and confidence through difficulties or disappointments. The women street vendors seem to be aware of the gender rules they have to play by and the constant scrutiny of their gender role by society and even themselves. Because the vendors have been socialized within these rules, they are part of the knowledge repertoire the women use to evaluate themselves. By attributing their work and success to God, they continue the status of compliance mandated by their religious beliefs but still maintain their business. It is a negotiation strategy in an attempt to break with old beliefs that are so embedded in their identities.

Luta. When recalling the moment they decided to invest in the formal markets, women vendors point not only to growing family needs but also a need to change their personal lives: fulfilling the role of a housewife and mother or working at a low-paying job was not enough any more. The vendors expressed their search for a better life, unwilling to simply accept a role expected of them, a role that would be insufficient to reach their goals.

Sara explained, "I was staying home and taking care of my child, but realized that I needed to do something with my life. I did not want to follow that pattern of being just a wife and a mother. I thought I should also work to increase our income and give our daughter a better future. That desire gave me the strength to try. I knew I could succeed with a lot of *luta*."

The overarching theme described by vendors is called here *luta*, or fighting energy, indicating a strong element of agency that is clear in their discourse.

Beyond the decision. Once their business was established, the street vendors had to choose between two different entrepreneurial outcomes. One path remains stuck in the present, whereas the other reaches beyond their current position.

Some street vendors saw the enterprise as a temporary solution to a financial problem, never intending to work at it very long, and others decided to permanently keep their shop but had no goals to improve or expand it. These individuals are called here *feirantes*, and they are characterized by the fact that they made the entrepreneurial decision to start a business but ran it in a stagnant or temporary manner, avoiding further risk taking after the business was established. Joana said, "I don't have plans for working in other markets, or starting a store, because the taxes are too high to have a formal business. I just want to stay here." To Joana, who has maintained her business without change for the past ten years, the markets have become a source of frustration. She is tired of the routine and feels that her health has deteriorated from the market experience.

The other part of the sample group was composed of women who see their business as the beginning of an entrepreneurial career. They have plans to expand, diversify, formalize, and export. These individuals are seen as having a true entrepreneurial vision and are called *empreendedoras informais*, or informal entrepreneurs.

The combination of all these factors in the opportunity structure and the cultural milieu shows that these women have developed an entrepreneurial vision that will guide them through the creation of a business, even though most of them have no experience in or preparation for starting a business. "We were talking about taking a course to learn to plan the business better, and learn to make our work more efficiently. We are planning to fly high. This is such an innovative product, and we intend to market it abroad, because we understand that handcrafts are more valued out of Brazil," said Karina.

The plans and aspirations of these women are far beyond those of a stagnant *feirante*. Their attitudes and goals are indicative of the qualities of a true entrepreneur. Even though that term is commonly used to describe individuals in formal markets, the same characteristics can be seen here in the informal economy. The limitations of the gender regime have restricted these women from engaging in formal businesses. However, in the informal markets they have found an opportunity, regardless of their gender, age, or class, to learn about business. The informal markets are to the *empreendedoras informais* a stage in which they play a new role, the role of an entrepreneur. This preparation will strengthen their confidence, increase their capital, and provide them with the tools necessary to enter the formal economy in a globalized way.

Beyond the Party

Economist Adam Smith spoke of the presence of an invisible hand in free-market capitalism.[84] According to Smith, the invisible hand encourages participants to maximize self-interest by exchanging goods and services. The result is a stable marketplace where all participants appear to benefit. Similarly, this chapter of *Women at Work* reveals institutions working as an invisible hand, shaping women's experiences within the party plan economy and reinforcing cultural ideas of the "good woman." It is not to be denied that many women find their roles in the party plan economy to be positive. However, our job as gender scholars is to bring a critical eye to the analysis, pointing to outcomes that may be harmful. When traditional gender arrangements, already demonstrated as based on masculinist power, are uncontested, they remain stable within the party plan economy.

Often, women are not conscious of how institutions influence party plan participation. The women in the field studies in this section, for example, do not fully recognize the role that religion, family, and consumption play in their experiences as producers, distributors, and consumers of products. We all participate, making the performance seem natural. The field studies bring concrete examples of how the party plan economy is supported.

Women aspire to have products that display, or simulate, their high-status position within the gender order (e.g., pink Cadillacs, "designer" purses). In the case of women who buy knockoff purses, owning a designer-inspired handbag gives the illusion of status and style for half the price. As a result, they continue to work and throw gender parties. Consumption brings women together. We may not know fellow guests at product parties, but we assume that we attend for the same reason; we instantly feel an affinity with other women. Family obligations serve to further encourage participation in the party plan. The party plan economy promises that women will be financially successful and have flexible work hours. The result—women may stay in party plan work for several years before realizing that they are not making money and that their work hours are not flexible.

Religion may further persuade women to work hard because it is God's will. Mary Kay, for example, encourages women to put God first, family second, and Mary Kay third. The belief that one's work is supported and encouraged by God's mission is a powerful conviction for many women. Emphasis on religion is not solely part of Mary Kay, Inc., but was also evidenced in Siquiera's study of Brazilian street vendors. In both cases, the women believed that faith in God's plan ensured their financial success.

To ignore women's agency within the party plan economy is problematic. Women certainly may make choices to participate in work that is construed as fun and rewarding, but often such choices are mired in structural conditions that result in the limiting of "choice." As such, we participate (often unconsciously) in institutions that maintain poor working conditions and limited life chances. One outcome of the invisible hand of institutions is the maintenance of party plan work that is hidden or trivialized.

The structural position of party plan work, wedged between formal and informal markets, adds to the invisibility of individual workers and the companies themselves. We do not automatically see Mary Kay or Silpada as part of the formal economy. Instead, we think of Wal-Mart as a capitalist company with a capitalist agenda. Party plan organizations fly under the radar. This is due in part to the feminized nature of these companies' products and in part to the invisible hand of institutions that encourage women's participation in this economy.

Notes

1. To learn more about this form of invisible labor, see Pierrette Hondagneu-Sotelo, *Domestica* (Berkeley: University of California Press, 2001). This book discusses immigrant workers' experiences with domestic labor and child care.

2. Bonnie A. Nardi and Yrjö Engeström, "A Web on the Wind: The Structure of Invisible Work," a special issue of *Computer-Supported Cooperative Work*, May 17, 1998, http://www.darrouzet-nardi.net (June 4, 2009).

3. Longaberger, "Become a Home Consultant," http://www.longaberger.com (May 15, 2009).

4. Silpada Designs, "The Silpada Story," http://www.silpada.com (May 15, 2009); Tupperware, "Opportunity," 2009, http://order.tupperware.com (May 15, 2009).

5. Pampered Chef, "Come Join Us," http://www.pamperedchef.com (May 15, 2009).

6. Statistics from the Direct Sales Association (DSA) in 2007 indicate that direct sales employ 15 million salespeople, 87.9 percent of whom are women. Direct Sales Association, "Estimated 2007 US Salespeople," http://www.dsa.org (June 5, 2009).

7. "Work," *Compact Oxford English Dictionary Online*, http://www.askoxford.com (June 8, 2009).

8. Joan Acker, "Inequality Regimes," *Gender & Society* 20 (2006): 441–464.

9. Bureaucratic structures have a hierarchical arrangement, with an owner or manager at the top of the hierarchy and workers organized in rank order according to earnings, benefits, and so on.

10. Acker, "Inequality Regimes."

11. Women in Informal Employment: Globalizing and Organizing, "Programme

Areas: Social Protection," http://www.wiego.org (May 20, 2009); and "Street Vendors," http://www.wiego.org (May 20, 2009).

12. Valentine Moghadam, *Globalizing Women: Transnational Feminist Networks* (Baltimore, MD: Johns Hopkins University Press, 1995).

13. Marybeth C. Stalp, "We Do It Cuz It's Fun," *Sociological Perspectives* 51, no. 2 (2008): 325–348.

14. Liz Gordon and Paul Willis note that cultural production occurs as a result of particular social conditions. In this case, women's participation in party work ties to a patriarchal system that devalues and subordinates women. Gordon and Willis, "Education, Cultural Production, and Social Reproduction," *British Journal of Sociology of Education* 5 (1984): 105–115.

15. Arlie Russell Hochschild defines emotional labor as management of one's outward expression of emotions. Such labor is performed in occupations that require contact with the general public (e.g., service work). Performing emotional labor involves creating a particular public and bodily display that is considered appropriate for the situation. It often results in worker stress and feelings of inauthenticity. See Hochschild, *The Managed Heart: Commercialization of Human Feeling* (Berkeley: University of California Press, 1983).

16. The labor performed by party consultants will vary depending on the type of product party. Regardless of the type of party, consultants participate in some form of physical, mental, and emotional labor.

17. Patricia Yancey Martin, "Rethinking Feminist Organizations," *Gender & Society* 4, no. 2 (1990): 182–206.

18. Women in Informal Employment: Globalizing and Organizing, "Sub-Group Case Studies: Home-Based Work," http://www.wiego.org (June 5, 2009), for an extensive discussion of the home-based work performed by women in other countries.

19. Werner International Management Consultants, "International Comparison of the Hourly Labor Cost in the Primary Textile Industry, Winter 2004/2005," *New Twist*, March 8, 2006, http://www.werner-newtwist.com (June 5, 2009). See also www.wiego .org for statistics and readings on home-based labor.

20. The face detracts from the purpose of the product. Thus, it is an adult toy but not necessarily a sexual toy.

21. This national organization, referred to as a "sorority" by its members, was developed around a service orientation and consisted of women between the ages of 40 and 80.

22. Moghadam, *Globalizing Women.*

23. Pampered Chef, "Company Facts," http://www.pamperedchef.com (June 2, 2009).

24. Mary Kay, "Mary Kay Around the World," http://www.marykay.com (June 2, 2009).

25. Tupperware, "World Wide Presence," http://www.tupperwarebrands.com (June 2, 2009).

26. Acker, "Inequality Regimes."

27. Martha Alter Chen, "Rethinking the Informal Economy: Linkages with the Formal Economy and the Formal Regulatory Environment," DESA Working Paper no. 46 (New York: United Nations, Department of Economic and Social Affairs, July 2007), http://www.un.org (May 15, 2009).

28. *Woolf v. Mary Kay Inc.* was a lawsuit filed by Claudine Woolf in 2002 for wrongful termination as a Mary Kay director. Woolf was fired from her post due to her unit's lack of productivity. Woolf claimed that she was wrongfully terminated due to medical circumstances (she had cancer). She won this case, but it was later overturned on appeal

in 2005. Peter Page, "Fired Mary Kay Worker Wins Job Suit," Law.com, December 12, 2002, http://www.law.com (June 2, 2009).

29. "Selling Tupperware Results in a Salad Bowl of Problems," Advocate, *Times Union*, Albany, NY, October 12, 2008, http://www.timesunion.com (June 2, 2009).

30. The informal economy is very prominent in developing countries. Eighty-three percent of new jobs in Latin America and the Caribbean are located in the informal sector. The International Confederation of Free Trade Unions estimates that 84 percent of female workers in sub-Saharan Africa work in the informal economy. International Confederation of Free Trade Unions, "The Informal Economy: Women on the Frontline," *Trade Union World: Briefing* 2 (2004): 1–16, http://www.icftu.org (June 8, 2009).

31. Michael Wichroski's research on secretaries illustrates the invisibility of labor experienced by female secretaries. For female secretaries, secretarial work consists of actual secretarial duties as well as emotional labor (manipulating one's own emotions as well as the emotions of others), political labor (e.g., making sure the office runs smoothly by working with clients and vendors), and peripheral labor (e.g., housekeeping tasks in the office, doing personal favors for the boss). Much of the work that female secretaries do is not part of their formal job description and thus remains invisible. The gendered nature of this invisibility is apparent. Wichroski, "The Secretary: Invisible Labor in the Workworld of Women," *Human Organization* 53 (1994): 33–41.

32. Acker, "Inequality Regimes."

33. Silpada Designs, "Polishing Off Juvenile Diabetes," http://www.silpada.com (June 2, 2009).

34. Consultants' poor profits and earnings are related: women feel that they are making a good living because they have money coming in, but they do not take note of the cost of investing in the products or other start-up and maintenance expenses.

35. In North America, women participate in volunteer activities more than men, demonstrating the gendering of such unpaid work. It is presumed to be in women's nature to participate in such caregiving. John Wilson and Mark Musick, "Who Cares? Toward an Integrated Theory of Volunteer Work," *American Sociological Review* 62, no. 5 (1997): 694–713.

36. Jerry Markon, "Va. Men Plead Guilty in Fake Purse Scam: Designer Knockoffs Were Sold at Parties," *Washington Post,* February 3, 2007, http://www.washington post.com (June 1, 2009).

37. Lauren D. Amendolara, "Knocking Out Knock-Offs: Effectuating the Criminalization of Trafficking in Counterfeit Goods," *Fordham Intellectual Property Media and Entertainment Law Journal* 15, no. 3 (2005): 789, 819.

38. Kara Platoni, "What a Steal! Counterfeiters Apply Tupperware Business Model to an Illicit New Enterprise: Purse Parties," *East Bay Express*, November 3, 2004, http://www.eastbayexpress.com (May 25, 2009).

39. Platoni, "What a Steal!"

40. Sarah J. Kaufman, "Note: Trend Forecast: Imitation Is a Legal Form of Flattery—Louis Vuiton Malletier V. Dooney & Bourke, Inc.," *Cardoza Arts and Entertainment* 23 (2005): 531, 533.

41. Ibid., 537–538.

42. Ibid., 533.

43. Platoni, "What a Steal!"

44. Ibid.

45. The names of those interviewed in this study have been changed to protect their privacy.

46. Markon, "Va. Men."

47. Platoni, "What a Steal!"

48. Amanda Mull, "Can Counterfeit Bags Make You a Bad Person?" The Purse Blog, April 9, 2009, http://www.purseblog.com (May 10, 2009).

49. International AntiCounterfeiting Coalition, "Get Real—The Truth About Counterfeiting," http://iacc.org (May 15, 2009).

50. Ross D. Franklin, "Forget Tupperware; It's Taser Party Time," Associated Press, MSNBC.com, http://www.msnbc.msn.com (January 4, 2008).

51. Ibid.

52. FashionPhile blog, "Done to Death," September 8, 2008, http://www.fashion phile.com (May 15, 2009).

53. Catherine Egley Waggoner, "The Emancipatory Potential of Feminine Masquerade in Mary Kay Cosmetics," *Text and Performance Quarterly* 17 (1997): 258.

54. Steven Oberbeck, "Utah Woman a Star in Pink," *Salt Lake Tribune*, May 15, 2008, reproduced on Sequence, Inc.: Forensic Accounting Answers, http://www.sequenceinc.com (June 15, 2009).

55. Unfortunately, I could find only "informal" sources for consultants' salaries, as Mary Kay does not publicly divulge this information. The citation given here is an informal, not scholarly source; however, it is the best estimate found. "Mary Kay Earnings," Wikipedia, 2008, http://en.wikipedia.org (June 15, 2009).

56. Nathan P. Moore, "Re: Comments of Mary Kay Inc. to the Proposed Business Opportunity Rule, R511993," Federal Trade Commission, July 17, 2006, http://www.ftc.gov.

57. Richard E. Hattwick, "Mary Kay Ash," *Journal of Behavioral Economics* 16 (1987): 64.

58. Nicole Woolsey Biggart, *Charismatic Capitalism: Direct-Selling Organizations in America* (Chicago: University of Chicago Press, 1989), 76.

59. During the "Seminar," consultants attend workshops, celebrity shows, and so on. The climax is "Award Night," which is described as a combination of the Academy Awards and a beauty pageant by these authors: Maureen Connelly and Patricia Rhonton, "Women in Direct Sales: A Comparison of Mary Kay and Amway Sales Workers," in *The Worth of Women's Work: A Qualitative Synthesis,* ed. Anne Statham, Eleanor M. Miller, and Hans O. Mauksch (Albany: State University of New York Press, 1988), 247–250; Jane Banks and Patricia R. Zimmerman, "The Mary Kay Way: The Feminization of a Corporate Discourse," *Journal of Communication Inquiry* 11 (1987): 92–93; and Waggoner, "The Emancipatory Potential," 260–267.

60. Mary Kay, "Mary Kay Is the Perfect Opportunity," http://gillianortegansd.com (June 15, 2009).

61. I use female pronouns to refer to Mary Kay consultants because the company overtly targets women for recruitment, most consultants are women, and the present section of this chapter concerns women who sell or sold Mary Kay products.

62. Team members are *active* if they made at least $600 in wholesale purchases from the company, according to my interviewees.

63. "Mary Kay Earnings," Wikipedia, 2008; Michael J. Webster, "How Much Can You Earn in Mary Kay?" Bizop News (blog), June 6, 2007, http://bizop.ca (June 16, 2009).

64. Moore, "Re: Comments of Mary Kay Inc."

65. My interviewees, who were ISDs, informed me that they have their own "unit" that consists of their recruits as well as recruits of the recruits (what they call "offspring"). ISDs are responsible for organizing weekly meetings with distributors and must meet quarterly quotas (minimum $18,000 wholesale by the unit) to stay in this position. ISDs are under their national sales director. All the names given to my interviewees and their family members are pseudonyms.

66. These facts confirm past research findings. John C. Crawford and Barbara C. Garland (1988) and Harriet Presser and Elizabeth Bamberger (1993) found no association between education and direct sales involvement or other home-based jobs, but the latter found that those who work wholly at home are likely to be married. Among my interviewees, Maxine was widowed at the time of the interview but was married when she was involved in Mary Kay. Caroline was divorced for a short while in the early stage of her Mary Kay business but was married for fourteen years at the time of the interview. Evelyn was engaged to her cohabiting partner with whom she had lived for eleven years. See Presser and Bamberger, "American Women Who Work at Home for Pay: Distinctions and Determinants," *Social Science Quarterly* 74 (1993): 815–837; Crawford and Garland, "A Profile of a Party Plan Sales Force," *Akron Business and Economic Review* 19 (1988): 28–37.

67. Interview length averaged an hour and twenty minutes. Interviews were tape-recorded, transcribed, and coded for analysis, with the exception of Evelyn's and Monica's interviews. They refused to have their interviews recorded or to be directly cited.

68. A simple Internet search exposes a large number of opinion pieces referring to Mary Kay as a cult or cult-like, not necessarily due to its ties to religion; however, some believe the company recruits members through behavioral and emotional control.

69. The reason Maxine left Mary Kay was that her husband became a physician and her new social circle (upper-middle class) regarded Mary Kay products as lower class. She was afraid to be viewed negatively by these other women and quit, though at the time of the interview she still believed Mary Kay was a true opportunity for women.

70. *Applause* magazine is provided free to all Mary Kay consultants.

71. Barbara Welter, "The Cult of True Womanhood: 1820–1860," *American Quarterly* 18, no. 2 (Summer 1966): 151–174.

72. Sharon Hays, *The Cultural Contradictions of Motherhood* (New Have, CT: Yale University Press, 1996).

73. If all commissions she earned were 13 percent of retail sales. For 4 percent and 9 percent commissions, she would need even larger sales.

74. Only Elaine was aware that she was "still in the red." She had borrowed money from her husband (from her second marriage) to purchase inventory and was obligated to pay it off but had not yet done so. She was giving money she received from retail sales to her husband each time but was not keeping track of how much she had paid him.

75. Peter M. Blau, *Exchange and Power in Social Life* (Hoboken, NJ: John Wiley and Sons, 1964).

76. Charles Derber, *The Wilding of America: Money, Mayhem, and the New American Dream* (New York: Worth, 2002); Robert D. Putnam, *Bowling Alone: The Collapse and Revival of American Community* (New York: Simon and Schuster, 2000).

77. Hernando De Soto, *The Mystery of Capital: Why Capitalism Triumphs in the West and Fails Everywhere Else* (New York: Basic Books, 2000).

78. International Labor Office (ILO), *Women and Men in the Informal Economy: A Statistical Picture* (Geneva, Switzerland: ILO, 2002), http://www.ilo.org (April 25, 2009).

79. Judith Lorber, "Believing Is Seeing: Biology as Ideology," *Gender & Society* 7, no. 4 (1993): 568–581.

80. Candace West and Don H. Zimmerman, "Doing Gender," *Gender & Society* 1, no. 2 (1987): 125–151.

81. Wayne J. Villemez and John Beggs, "Culture, Opportunity and Attainment: The Impact of the Local Area," paper presented at the annual meeting of the International Sociological Association, Bielefeld, Germany, 1993; L. Susan Williams, "Gender Regimes

and the Prophecy of Place: Micro/Macro Dimensions of Stratification Processes for Young Women," PhD dissertation, University of Connecticut, 1997.

82. Luis Felipe Fernandes, "Comunidades: Hora de Crescer," *Tribuna do Planalto*, October 19, 2007, http://www.tribunadoplanalto.com (April 6, 2008).

83. Kathleen Z. Young, "The Imperishable Virginity of Saint Maria Goretti," *Gender & Society* 3, no. 4 (1989): 474–482.

84. Adam Smith, *An Inquiry into the Nature and Causes of the Wealth of Nations* (Middlesex, UK: Echo Library, 2006).

4

How Marketplaces of Interaction Modify the Party Plan Economy

This chapter explodes the idea of a narrowly defined party plan economy. That is, the party plan economy incorporates more than the obvious. The first three chapters of the book spotlight a fairly strict interpretation of gender parties—products such as cosmetics, purses, and kitchen goods sold through home-based direct marketing venues referred to as parties. The party plan economy has gone global, with direct marketing giants such as Avon now in 140 countries, Amway in eighty countries, and Mary Kay in thirty-five, implying that the party plan economy transports easily into many contexts. However, as Avon China illustrates, the transition from US-based models to other cultures is far from seamless. This chapter demonstrates ways in which marketplaces of interaction—defining a structure of relations that incorporates both personal and professional connections—reshape and repurpose the party plan economy.

Avon China

Avon, a startup company in 1886, developed into a marketing goliath, quickly expanding internationally. Growing like gangbusters, the company had moved into China by the late 1980s. A decade later China halted all direct-selling initiatives. Other party plan companies such as Amway and Mary Kay also experienced botched attempts to move their Americanized economic strategies into foreign markets.

Among the factors (some political and legal) that barred the party plan economy from immediate success in China, one that loomed large was a serious misunderstanding of the Chinese concept of *guanxi,* which places a premium on harmonious connections and relationships. As such, guanxi represents a quality of marketplaces of interaction, one that cannot be assumed as universal yet demonstrates the power to undermine an economic giant. The competitive, sometimes aggressive US custom of encouraging sales and bookings from mere acquaintances or even strangers did not mesh well with the Chinese social scene, quickly halting the advancement of Avon products into the potentially massive market. Avon and other corporations now effectively embrace guanxi, using ideals of social harmony, such as building relationships with government officials and local businesses, to maneuver around the cultural roadblocks that impede direct selling.

Still, gender as a relational social construct remains understudied and undertheorized as a major driving force in the party plan economy.

Beyond Products

The party plan economy sells more than products. A dominant ideology—a way of gathering ideas and attitudes that support the status quo—sells ideas. Participants take part without questioning; ideologies, by definition, are unacknowledged and their proponents unaware.[1] As one example, Pampered Chef founder Doris Christopher speaks of her "one-woman show," describing her story as that of a "small-town girl from Chicago," stressing that "what happened to me can happen to you."[2] These lines mesh perfectly with the American Dream myth—that anyone who works hard can make it to the top. Just pull yourself up by your bootstraps.

Throughout Christopher's book, she emphasizes a higher purpose, including doing God's work,[3] bringing families together,[4] and teaching women to help women.[5] When scrutinized, all these elements contradict the reality of a high-pressure environment in which sales consultants must sell in excess of $800 per party just to break even. After all, Pampered Chef grew into a billion-dollar company, which Christopher sold to mega-capitalist Warren Buffet; it's hard to imagine that profit was a simple byproduct, completely unrelated to her real goals. Further, by her own declaration, Christopher owed much of her success to timing, luck, and the help of her husband and family. None of these are negative elements per se, but they defy the ideology of the bootstrap theories, which mask structural barriers to women's success.

Beyond Parties

The stereotypical 1950s portrayal of women's lives hardly speaks to gender revolutions. Think, for example, of television shows like *Leave It to Beaver* and *Father Knows Best*—these are not pictures of women's liberation. It would be 1963 before Betty Friedan's book *The Feminine Mystique* called into question the idea that women's only path to fulfillment lay through housework, child care, and man-pleasing duties; contrast that idea with Friedan's statement: "No woman ever gets an orgasm from shining the floor."[6] Yet it was in 1952 that Brownie Wise, Tupperware's author of the home party plan, moved into her large, relatively opulent residence in Lake Toho, Florida, complete with indoor pool. Wise, a single mother, became the first woman to grace the cover of *Business Week*; the year was 1954. Clearly, the party plan revolution predated what is regarded as the second wave of the US women's movement.[7]

The interpretation of the word *revolution* depends on one's perspective, and what is seen as progressive by one side is seen as threatening to the other. Earl Tupper did not see Wise's contributions as fully positive but as encroaching on his own territory. In one conversation, as described in *Tupperware Unsealed*, he addressed Wise this way: "Now listen to me, woman, I do the manufacturing and you do the selling."[8] After Wise's marketing genius leveraged Tupperware into a multimillion-dollar company, Tupper edged her out, leaving her with no stock and one year's salary as compensation. Shortly after, he sold the company for $16 million.[9] Revolutions always exact power struggles and never progress in a straight line. A critical analysis of gender parties reveals much of the makeup of gender revolutions and their suppression.

Beyond Boundaries

Once we understand that gender parties are more than parties and products and that the party plan economy is more than economics, other dynamics become apparent. Just as we acknowledge the significance of guanxi, ideology, and power struggles, Chapter 4 demonstrates how the party plan economy reaches far beyond conventional definitions of gender parties. This chapter reveals how the party plan economy opens up space for women, for their relationships with one another, for social and political connections to action and activism, and for the realization of gender consciousness. All those make empowerment possible (though not inevitable).

Gender Dealings:
Moving Between Public and Private Spaces

Space and time are not conditions in which we live; they are simply modes in which we think. —*Albert Einstein*

QUESTION 1: What do the following have in common: US product-based parties, Brazilian street markets, and piecework in the Czech Republic?

ANSWER: Gender dealings, wiggling between public and private lives.

Women often find themselves caught between personal and professional demands, work and family needs, and inner and outer well-being. This chapter looks at the importance of integrating our lives—both public and private—so that we reduce such conflicts and optimize our sense of self.

QUESTION 2: What is a gender dealing?
ANSWER: Transactions that depend upon individuals *doing gender*.

For example, think of the Mary Kay party described earlier in Figure 1.1. (Remember the 1980s photo and the 1980s hair?!) Without women actively participating in primping, chattering, and mirroring one another's look, the party would not happen. The situation demanded that women do gender, and thus gender dealings became both the process and the outcome.

Even though gender dealings are omnipresent, they are seldom evident to the naïve eye. Einstein's claim that space and time are "modes in which we think" reminds us that our most common ways of knowing—those based on shared impressions of the material world—represent a small part of our total existence. We seldom think about the way we do gender, which begins, arguably, in our head but takes form through practice.

Because we are not conditioned to recognize gender dealings, our gender "seeings" fall short of preparing an authentic view of the world. We often fail to see real-world connections (for example, recognizing that much of women's labor is unpaid), while we sometimes see "things" that are not there, like a water mirage. An example of such chimera is the lack of significance behind certain relationships. We may pour great energy into unsatisfying work or a halfhearted educational choice or an overeager attempt at pleasing others—only to find that nothing of substance exists at that road's end. Many such troubles are rooted in gendered expectations but have real consequences. Once we acknowledge gender dealings, they become visible and thus malleable to negotiation. Awareness is power.

Similarly, the nexus between public and private spaces represents a contrived distinction, one that unnecessarily splinters parts of women's everyday lives. This chapter focuses on ways in which gender parties blur the boundaries between public and private spaces in modern-day life. In particular, women find common ground through everyday experiences such as motherhood or singlehood or economic position; finding commonalties promotes individual and sometimes collective empowerment. Case studies in this chapter illustrate how empowerment may happen, how women in different regions of the world bridge what is traditionally seen as the separate venues of public and private spaces.

In this book, the idea of gender regime—an inventory of gendered structures—provides a frame for understanding the significance of spaces. Certainly, space alludes to many meanings, including intellectual, political, and emotional openings in various social configurations. We also use physical space as a metaphor to understand power, and we continue this chapter by reviewing how *knowing strategies,* and in particular women's ways of knowing, incorporate spatial references to both control and resistance. The next section discusses *bifurcated consciousness.* Bifurcated consciousness refers to a segmented existence, and the concept is instructive in analyzing how ideology becomes embedded in the public/private concept, fragmenting women's lives. The final section (before the case studies) looks briefly at the idea of common space, which lends promise to reformulating women's individual lives and connecting women across the globe.

Knowing Strategies

How do you learn? What are your strengths and limitations? When you say you "just know," where does that knowledge come from? William Perry, an educational psychologist, is credited with identifying how college students "come to know" the world around them (circa 1970). He documented a process in which young people progress from dualistic (that is, black/white) thinking to relativist (shades of gray) cognitive processing, developing a pattern of knowing strategies.[10] Reminiscent of Lawrence Kohlberg's theory of moral development, Perry's work was based primarily on a male model and men's experiences, a method that was heavily critiqued, most adamantly by Carol Gilligan in her 1982 book, *In a Different Voice.* Gilligan argued that girls and women develop an alternative sequence of maturing, which she describes as an ethic of care. Gilligan's work generated two decades of scholarship based on the idea that women have a unique "way of knowing."

In response to Perry's and Gilligan's theories, psychologist Mary Field Belenky and colleagues studied female college students' knowing strategies, culminating in the book *Women's Ways of Knowing.*[11] These authors conducted 135 in-depth interviews with women about decisionmaking and moral dilemmas, finding that the trajectory differed significantly from Perry's results with young men. Perry defined a progressive set of stages for men's moral development, in which they became more and more nuanced in their decisions. In contrast, Belenky and her colleagues' work with women identified positions, not stages, which varied from fewer options to greater options, depending on their life situations. The five positions, or strategies for knowing, consisted of silence, received knowing, subjective knowing, procedural knowing, and constructed knowing. Think of the little girls at the Mary Kay party in Figure 1.1 (silent knowing) or adult women processing and constructing not only techniques but also the need for a bucket full of cosmetics.[12]

Arguably, women's ways of knowing grow out of the artificial construction of public and private spaces. The symbolism of space chronicles women's experiences over time; I'll mention just a few. Charlotte Perkins Gilman's nineteenth-century story "The Yellow Wallpaper" artistically portrays the stark reality of confinement of women's time and talent. The protagonist is a woman whose husband (a physician) confines her to a solitary room, windows barred and doors gated against the outside world. She eventually descends into madness, seeing herself as living behind the patterns of the wallpaper. This important early feminist work signified the curtailment of women's physical and intellectual selves as they were excluded from public space.

Virginia Woolf's book *A Room of One's Own* is a series of essays first published in 1929, centered around a fictional sister to William Shakespeare, Judith. The aim was to illustrate that women's gifts were denied the same opportunities as men's, blocked from realization by the larger society. Woolf argued that women must have their own space (and resources and freedom) in order to develop their full potential.

A contemporary use of spatial reference may be more familiar to younger generations of women. "Take back the night" activities represent a resistance movement by women, begun in the 1970s with increased knowledge about the prevalence of violence against women. The movement continues today, typically through organizations on college campuses that organize marches through public streets, symbolizing the ability of women to unite and "take back" public space that has been denied them or proclaimed as "too dangerous" for women. For many decades, even centuries, women have been denied freedom of movement. These marches draw attention to women's collective power to resist such restrictions.

Finally, shedding light on a specific personal space may be instructive to understanding many women's dilemmas. My (few) women colleagues and I (Sue) work in a male-dominated space: science and academia. This may surprise you. Chances are, you remember many female teachers, certainly in your early educational years. Probably most of you had women as instructors in high school and in selected postsecondary classrooms. However, consider this: In public universities across the United States, women constitute minorities in upper administration, with only 15 percent of public university presidents being female. The numbers are even lower at private institutions, where women hold only 9.5 percent of presidencies, many of them at women-only colleges.[13] In 2000, of full-time faculty at institutions that accept federal student loans, women made up only 21 percent of full professors, with the percent falling to 14 percent at doctorate-granting institutions. In a country where it is prohibited to discriminate according to gender in education, and despite the growth in the number of women completing PhDs (over half of higher degrees were received by women), only 31 percent held full-tier tenured positions.[14] Certainly, many women are instructors and junior (untenured) faculty. Those positions, although more visible, are also the least well-paid. As rank and salary increase, the proportion of women decreases.[15]

Why is this important to our discussion? Because women like me (and millions of others) face a high degree of conflict between our public and private selves that is foreign to most men. Throughout my work life, I have experienced abrupt shifts between my private and public selves. I recall working at the local Sears catalog store I operated (while running another business, a household, and a family of five). It was one of those catalog-plus-appliances stores that were common in small towns in the 1970s and 1980s. Once school let out for the day, afternoons were extremely busy: customers (mostly women) would come by to browse, place orders, pick up orders, and ask questions about the thousands of items in the Sears catalog. Women, as you probably now realize, are the designated shoppers for the entire family—the ultimate consumer that capitalism depends on. I can't tell you how many times (though my daughter may have kept score!) that my mind became so inundated by the after-school flurry that I totally lost track of time. Finally, glancing at my watch, I would realize I had left her waiting at school yet again—sometimes for an hour. In a panic (though this was a different time and place), I dashed for the nine-passenger 1980 family van, sped with beating heart to find her playing with pebbles or doing her homework on the curb. Aaarrgghh! For all those years, I felt a huge disconnect between my private and public selves, each seeming to demand 100 percent.

Today is a bit different. I no longer have children at home. I don't cook or clean much, though I do have to pick up dry cleaning; shop for groceries; pay bills; have the car serviced; buy and deliver gifts; gather items for class; arrange for meetings; remember birthdays, anniversaries, and holidays; and attend many functions both social and professional. I mostly focus on my career, but I don't feel that work is 100 percent a place that belongs to me. I am still a woman in male-dominated space, an outsider.

So, rather unconsciously, I've tried to bridge. Looking around my office, I see a dual-screen high-powered MacPro computer setup, more powerful than that of most of my colleagues, male or female. I have a nice laser printer, twenty file drawers of research projects, and about 1,500 books. All these are marks of the ultimate professional. But I also have photos of the entire family scattered about, a clock I was awarded from those early Sears days, a basketful of Mardi Gras beads from my days at Louisiana State University, eight national championship posters of University of Connecticut basketball teams, a plate with my grandchildren's handprints, Elvis memorabilia (a lot!), a Ouija board, a peace sign colored by a small child visitor, a Texas license plate, bronze horse bookends, a charcoal impression of women's fragmented lives (by a former student), a photo of my friend Dena and myself at Julia's wedding, and another of my daughter Kimber and Sister Helen Prejean. There is much more, but you get the idea. This is my life. I don't feel as if I fully belong to the academy, so I surround myself, in this little space of my professional life, with symbols of my private life. I shouldn't have to see them as separate. But I do.

As students and other visitors enter my office, they usually remark about

Figure 4.1 A bookshelf in coauthor Williams's university office. *(Dr. Sue's Photos)*

my bookshelves, asking about one or another of the odd collection of items. I started noticing other offices. My male colleagues' offices are not as personalized, but female colleagues' offices look similar to mine, with several personal tokens having taken up residence.

This casual observation of the public/private split is reflected in literature; scholars regularly debate it, with varying positions about the continuing degree and usefulness of dualism as an area of study.[16] Feminist scholars generally agree that a hierarchy of separate spheres still exists, with women's access to public (and therefore sociopolitical and economic power) remaining abridged.[17] Although both men and women bear the cost of separate spheres (consider the costs for men in limiting what is "acceptable" in one's office space), the balance of disadvantage lies with women's struggle to balance home and work.[18] For example, in *The Meaning of Wife*, Anne Kingston describes the "new Wife economy," in which women are increasingly touted as unshackled from tradition while simultaneously being told to "'dress for success,' to get on the 'mommy track,' to get off the 'mommy track,' to become more aggressive, to become less aggressive, to not marry or have children if we want to succeed, and, finally, just to throw in the towel and make wife a career."[19] One could get whiplash from the dizzying messages that dictate how to navigate the public/private divide.

These observations offer interesting implications for our study of gender parties. The party plan economy represents a space different from traditional workplaces, wedging itself between formal and informal, visible and not, and between public and private places. Gender parties offer an intriguing look into spaces that defy conventional categories. Given that the public/private divide persistently disconnects pieces of women's lives, do women really exhibit different knowing strategies for each sphere, and does the study of gender parties speak to that question? Do gender parties occupy a space totally different from other venues—both as work and as party? The concept of bifurcated consciousness lays an instructive foundation for that discussion.

Bifurcated Consciousness

At first glance, my story of leaving little daughter Kimber on the curb seems like evidence of misplaced priorities, bad mothering, or perhaps temporary insanity. But millions of mothers face the same dilemma—how do they choose between being a good career woman and a good mother/wife/partner/daughter/granddaughter? Dorothy Smith writes that the relations of ruling (formal and informal rules and practices that organize power) reside in "government, law, business and financial management, professional organization, and educational institutions as well as the discourses in texts that interpenetrate the multiple sites of power."[20] She calls these places of residence "extralocal" modes of ruling. That is, they exist outside the local spaces of individuals' everyday and personal lives, so the public takes dominion over the private.

The separation of public/private spheres has not always been so evident; the advent of industrialization and capitalism removed production from the private realm, and afterward a radical sexual division of labor developed. As capitalism and economic power became the predominant model, at least in the Western world, men's occupation of public space afforded them greater power relative to women. Scholars such as Heidi Hartmann claim that this separation was not "natural" and that capitalism threatened to place women and children into public work, where production would be optimized.[21] Thus, a sexual division of labor, coupled with an ideology of separate spheres, became the patriarchal tools to keep men in power. Similarly, sex segregation of occupations, still very strong today, conveniently keeps women's wages lower.[22]

Contemporary sociopolitical power lives not in local ties of kinship, family, and households, but in the extralocal places just designated, public places, creating "forms of consciousness . . . that are properties of organization or discourse rather than of individual subjects."[23] Ruling and power come through this formal standpoint and are fully segregated from considerations of personal, family, and child care issues. Because separation is attached to power, the bifurcation creates problems for everyone, but not for everyone equally. For the traditional family, in which men are seen as primarily responsible for the rational/economic side of affairs (whether or not this is actually true), men suffer a lesser degree of bifurcation. Men are not regularly called upon to account for their private lives. If "he" has one family photo on his desk, everyone smiles and gets back to business, assuming he is achieving a good balance. For women, the degree of bifurcation is accelerated and often extreme. If "she" has the same family photo on her desk, her professionalism and commitment to work may be questioned; the boss worries that she may take off work to care for the children (or elderly parents), do shopping on her lunch break, and not be able to take that all-important business trip. The harsh reality is that she probably will experience more private/public conflicts than her male colleagues.

In a bifurcated consciousness, the two worlds—pubic/private, personal/impersonal, career/family—cannot coexist. Studies demonstrate that even when we think we are masters of multitasking, we are not.[24] The best we can do is shift from one form of consciousness to another. In the case of small, relatively insignificant or menial tasks, the hop may be relatively easy and interpreted as nothing more than a slight hiccup. But when tasks and responsibilities are intense, serious, and significant, it may become a precarious leap. Moving from one to another takes great effort and, sometimes, great risk. The stakes are high, the costs large.

Common Space

> I have wanted to make an account and analysis of society and social relations that are not only about women but that make it possible for us to look at any or all aspects of a society from where we are actually located, embodied in the local historicity and particularities of our lived world. —*Dorothy Smith*

Smith calls attention to the fact that women everywhere combine their lived worlds. For precisely this reason, the party plan economy presents an optimal study of the amalgamation of gender and business. We now have the foundation to study the merger of the two—gender and work, invisible and visible, public and private—without the artificial separation that plagues our understanding of the sum of women's lives. We start by looking at common space, as defined within the party plan economy.

The party plan economy turns the business model on its head. Business sense bases itself on a male model—rational, cogent, forceful, sound. In such a model, anything associated with the feminine—passivity, weakness, emotion, relations—is shunned, and because masculinity is associated with "neutral," gender becomes invisible, as we just saw in Chapter 3. Outside of a very few disciplines in academia, business is never analyzed as gendered. Enter the party plan economy. Gender parties place gender at the forefront because they deal in a woman's world: cosmetics, jewelry, kitchenware, cleaning products, scrapbooking, toys (to entertain the kids), and sex toys (to entertain the husbands). Could it be that the appeal of gender parties relates to the need for women to resolve their private and public selves?

But the marriage of public and private is tentative, often resulting in the business end of gender parties (and women's work) becoming invisible. The circle completes itself; the worlds of business and worlds of gender remain largely unresolved. Or do they? As we see in Chapter 5, the personal becomes political and vice versa, potentially making boundaries more fluid. The party plan economy gives promise to the possibility of gender revelations and revolution.

In the "From the Field" case studies that follow, Michelle Bemiller provides a study of women's motivations to attend home-based parties—motivations that are firmly embedded in the private sphere, even though the activities ultimately benefit capitalist organizations. Moving to a global front, Karen Kapusta-Pofahl, Eva Kavková, Ivana Šindlerová, and Jana Smiggels-Kavková examine women's search for common ground through shared experiences as they engage in home-based work in the Czech Republic. These studies vividly illustrate the uniqueness of the party plan economy in local and global terms, glimpsing spaces that are neither purely public nor purely private.

From the Field

Using the term *paradox of parties*, Michelle Bemiller illuminates the presence of both exploitation and empowerment within the party plan economy. From individual and group-based interviews with party guests, Bemiller draws attention to women's motivations to host and attend parties. Fun and friendship, obligation, and product interest encourage women to come to the party, which provides a venue for social support, networking, and conversations around issues salient to women. The upshot of party attendance goes well beyond products and individual enthusiasm—through parties, women create a collective awareness and potential for activism. The downside is that the same situation bolsters a consumerist model, masking exploitation of friendships for the sake of capitalist ventures that ultimately keep women (as a group) from positions of real power.

Case Study 4.1
Women Helping Women on the Party Line
Michelle Bemiller

Come to my Cooking Show! Please RSVP . . . and bring a friend.

The quotation above comes from a Pampered Chef invitation. The "bring a friend" request is common to the "party line," playing on a term that pressures loyal members to follow a particular practice or ideology. As applied to gender parties, the strategy is designed to ensure that party attendance is good and product sales are high.

By encouraging women to rely on friends to attend home-based parties—regardless of individuals' good intentions or even idealism by some—the result is that capitalist companies exploit women's relationships in the name of profit. This exploitation is invisible to hosts, guests, and consultants as the boundaries between public and private spaces are blurred at product parties. Women go to parties in their friends' homes (the private sphere) where they buy and sell products made by capitalist organizations (the public sphere). The premise of product parties—fun and friendship—masks the capitalist purpose (profit) behind the US party plan economy. I refer to the disconnect between these two purposes as the paradox of parties.

Capitalism exploits women's labor (and experiences) more often than men's by ignoring their contributions to both paid and unpaid labor while enhancing men's rewards through better jobs, higher pay, and more benefits.[25] At the same time, women believe they experience empowerment by earning money and supporting one another through party attendance. Whether or not capitalist companies purposely take advantage of women's connections and need for empowerment, one thing is certain: bringing a friend optimizes attendance and revenue.

I couldn't help but wonder why women (myself included) would host or attend a party that appears to use women's friendships and consumption patterns to increase profits. What motivates women to attend such gatherings? Is it really about fun and friendship? Do they really want or like the products? Or is there more to this puzzle?

Background
The party plan economy provides an opportunity to understand women's nebulous position as they move between the public and private spheres. These constant negotiations can produce a dizzying effect, making them more vulnerable to exploitation. That women do not recognize such a ploy is unsurprising; it is well hidden behind promises of profits and flexible schedules. To fully understand women's experiences with exploitation, some context is in order.

Microlevel exploitation. Recall that Zschoche referred to the separate spheres doctrine, an ideology that emerged during the nineteenth century, which encouraged women to take care of "domestic duties" while men worked in the public sphere. The ideology was so strongly embraced that when women attempted to find work in the public sphere (most often out of economic necessity), they were denied the opportunity because their place was at home taking care of husbands and children. When women did find work in the paid labor force, they were faced with lower wages than men because it was assumed that they were worth less and that they had a man at home providing for them. Despite such obstacles, many working-class women found low-paying jobs or ways to earn a living in the home (e.g., doing laundry, sewing, taking in boarders).[26] The work remained invisible and undercompensated or unpaid.

Today, women continue to increase their labor force participation, most often to provide for their families. In 2007, 59 percent of US women were part of the paid labor market, a statistic that has remained stable over the past few years. From 1975 to 2000, the labor force participation of women with children increased from 47 percent to 73 percent. By 2004, this number had shifted to 71 percent, where it remained through 2007.[27] Women's entrance into paid labor on a global scale demonstrates similar increases.[28] Still, when women work outside the home, there is an expectation that they will continue their unpaid responsibilities at home.[29]

Since the 1950s, the party plan economy has served as one solution to women's difficulty in navigating public and private life. Party plan companies target women with families, selling the idea that they can make a lot of money and still spend time with their families. This is a tempting proposition, but as you have seen in other field studies in this book, women's labor within the party plan economy is not as flexible and profitable as one might think. A quick perusal of party plan materials illustrates that commissions may be as low as 22 percent of party sales and that women must work long hours in order to be successful, if at all.[30]

Macrolevel exploitation: patriarchal capitalism. Coinciding with women's exploitation in the private sphere, the marriage of patriarchy and capitalism exploits women's labor inside and outside the home by ignoring women's unpaid labor and devaluing their paid labor.[31] Capitalism provides a hierarchy of workers, but it does not dictate who fills the positions within that hierarchy. It is patriarchy that dictates who will occupy the most and least rewarded positions and who will make laws that help shape ideological processes.[32] Men (most often white) own most property, monopolize better jobs, and make laws.[33] Women serve as a reserve labor force, providing labor that is free or cheap and often without benefits, allowing capitalist organizations to take advantage of cheap labor for profit.[34]

The party plan economy provides a potential foil to such a system. Women certainly earn low wages and work long hours within this economy, but party plan workers and guests demonstrate a sense of fulfillment that comes from working with other women, networking, and sharing feminine experiences. Again, the paradox of parties becomes salient in women's lives.

This party paradox contributes to a lack of recognition of oppressive circumstances. Misrecognition,[35] or a sense of false consciousness (to use Marx's terminology),[36] flows from the construction and maintenance of a gendered (or raced, sexed, aged) ideology that legitimates social processes by claiming that equality of opportunity is a reality for everyone, regardless of social position. Misrecognition can be seen in women's reactions to pay differentials between themselves and coworkers; research finds that women agree with procedures that determine payment without recognizing the patriarchal processes that underlie such procedures.

As one illustration of false consciousness, John Jost studied 132 undergraduate students (sixty-eight men and sixty-four women) at Yale University.[37] In this study, participants were asked to fill out inventories that measured self-evaluation and self-payment; women were more likely than men to accept lower earnings and see them as justified. Similar research finds that women are more likely to compare their earnings to those of other women rather than male coworkers. Brenda Major argues that such findings illustrate that social inequality is perceived as legitimate and thus likely to be perpetuated.[38] The result is continued exploitation of women's paid and unpaid labor.[39]

Looking closely at women's participation in the party plan economy, I was able to better understand women's motivations to attend parties that operate under a capitalist agenda. My findings further highlight the paradox of parties—part exploitation and part empowerment.

Methods

The goal of this research project was to better understand women's motivation to attend gender parties. Group interviews seemed an optimal way to collect information about women's experiences at home-based gatherings. Group interviews provide respondents the opportunity to share their own stories and listen to those of others. Women will often relate to what the group has expressed and bring in experiences that dovetail with what other respondents are sharing. I conducted three group interviews to better understand women's motivations to host and attend product parties. In total, twenty-five women were interviewed.

The first group interview took place after a Silpada jewelry party in Ohio. I happened to be visiting when my mother held a Silpada party in her home on a weekday evening. Twenty women between the ages of thirty and fifty were present, five of whom agreed to participate in an interview.

The second interview took place after a class that I was teaching during the spring semester of 2009. Five of the seven college women (aged between twenty and twenty-five) agreed to be interviewed. Men in the class were also given the opportunity to be interviewed but declined.

The third interview took place during an evening meeting with local members of a national service organization.[40] This particular organization consisted of about thirty women who regularly gathered to socialize and participate in organizing community events. Of the thirty members, fifteen were present on the evening of the interview; all fifteen agreed to participate. Their ages ranged from fifty to eighty.

The interviews lasted between twenty and twenty-five minutes and were recorded. After each interview, I transcribed detailed field notes related to the atmosphere, the women's interactions with one another, nonverbal reactions to questions and answers, and my own personal thoughts and feelings while completing the interviews. I transcribed the interviews and completed the analysis using line-by-line coding.

Findings
After analysis of the data, the following themes emerged: fun and friendship, obligation, and consumption. Women's thoughts on party attendance were often contradictory, demonstrating a subconscious grasp of the party paradox. At some points women felt parties were fun and about friends and friendship, but after considering motivations more deeply, they discussed feelings of obligation.

Fun and friendship. Product parties are a bit different than the average informal gathering of friends because consumption is a defining part of this party model. As a result, some women see these gatherings as fun, whereas others dread getting invited. Respondents who saw product parties as a fun opportunity to engage with friends gave that as their real purpose in attending the party. They did at times participate in consumption, but they claimed to attend because they wanted to visit old friends or make new ones.

Liz, a respondent who attended the Silpada jewelry party, fits this profile: "I mean, I can't really afford some of this stuff but I'm going to go because I enjoy talking to people. And seeing people I haven't seen in a while. I like that part." Two other respondents who attended the jewelry party nodded in agreement. Aubrey went on to say, "You can catch up on old memories, you know?"

Like the women at the jewelry party, the students I interviewed agreed that they just wanted to have fun with their friends. According to Lisa, parties are "a blast. They are so much fun. There's always alcohol involved. Everyone is really laid-back and relaxed." Mary agreed with Lisa but also provided insight into why women would want to host or attend product parties instead of an informal gathering of friends: "It makes you aware of new things. It's just a time to get together, have fun, meet new people, hang out, and relax."

Three of the women from the service organization said product parties are enjoyable because they provide an opportunity to try something new.

Statements such as these assume that parties without products would be boring because there would be no opportunity to learn about or try something new.

Not all women wanted to attend product parties. Linda, a Silpada jewelry attendee, is one example of a respondent who did not look forward to invitations to these parties. She said, "I'd rather have a gathering and just eat food . . . and get together to talk. That would be more fun to me." Her lack of interest stemmed from feeling obligated to buy products that she could not afford. Two other women at the jewelry party agreed that purchasing products made the party feel more like an obligation than fun.

Obligation. The fact that Linda (and others) felt obligated to attend parties and purchase products is not unique. The majority of the respondents in this study discussed feeling a sense of obligation at some point during their interviews. In some instances, the women who felt obligated to attend these gatherings discussed their participation in a mutual give-and-take relationship with their friends. This reciprocity often resulted in going to parties they didn't want to attend as a favor to a friend or family member. Some women were comfortable with this expectation, but others were not.

Linda was one respondent who appeared to feel trapped in relationships that rested on obligation. Her obligation was intertwined with a fear that some of her friend(s) would be angry if she did not attend their parties and buy something. She indicated that in many cases party hosts would "have an attitude with you . . . if you don't go to the party." As a result, she felt that she had to go to the party or suffer the consequences. This sense of obligation was so strong for Linda that she purchased products even when she could not attend parties because, "there again, I feel guilty if I don't." Other participants were quick to agree, laughing among themselves about this sense of obligation and their fear of upsetting the hosts of the parties.

Liz shared a story about her years as a Longaberger consultant with this group of women. As a consultant, Liz was encouraged to rely on her friends to increase her sales. She felt uncomfortable when her friends felt obligated to buy baskets from her, so she stopped selling the product. Liz claimed that her awareness of others' feelings of obligation causes her to be careful about what types of home-based parties she agrees to host. "I have Tastefully Simple parties. They're food. I don't feel as bad asking people to come to those parties because some of the things are like $5 or $6, you know? So when I have those parties . . . I don't feel as bad because I know people feel obligated to buy." Patty agreed with Liz: "I know whenever I have any sort of party I tell people, just come. Please don't feel like you have to . . . I know I say that . . . but I don't know that they actually feel that way. I would like to see them and enjoy talking to them." Here, Patty provides one example of a contradictory response. She is aware of the obligation that people feel to attend product parties but sees them as a fun opportunity to talk to friends.

The college women whom I interviewed stated that obligation was sometimes a part of their parties, but not attending a party did not mean the end of their friendships. Mary poignantly stated that obligation comes into play when you have a relationship with the host. "I think that if you know the person, then yes [you feel obligated]. For instance, someone recently invited me to one and I said I wasn't going and they confronted me and asked me why I wasn't attending." Because Mary knew the hostess of the party in question, she felt an obligation to support her in an effort to maintain their friendship. Ally disagreed with Mary's statement: "I don't feel an obligation to go or to buy because people are doing it to make money. That's where the basis started. You are selling things for a profit."

Demonstrating the presence of give-and-take in their relationships, the women stated that attendance is about supporting one another. Kate gives a good example:

> I think it's a personal thing. If a friend was throwing one [a party] then I would want to be there to support them because sometimes you have high expectations . . . and then only three people come. So even if I'm not going to buy anything I should be there for moral support. She came to my party, so then I should go to hers.

Some of the women at the service organization event also felt that when you are friends, you have to support one another by returning favors. "I've had a jewelry party before because a friend of mine used to buy a lot of Longaberger baskets from me. So I told her I would have a party to help her. She supported me so I wanted to support her." As several women nodded in agreement, Lucille articulated how she supports her friends within the party plan:

> I like the products. They always have something that I don't have that I think, "I need one of those." So I can give someone else credit for having the party instead of just calling up and saying I need one of these ordered, put it on so and so's party from three months ago. I wait until someone else has a party and then I say, "OK. Now I'll go and get that other piece that I couldn't afford before."

These similar statements made by respondents clearly illustrate the connection between obligation and product consumption.

Through personal observations I made at the Silpada jewelry party (as well as other product parties over the years), I concluded that product companies know of this connection among women. In fact, Silpada jewelry parties are structured around having fun with friends, which ultimately results in women feeling obligated to purchase products as a way of showing their support. Consultants do not do a formal product demonstration. Instead, women are encouraged to try on jewelry. The consultant and other guests compliment women on how they look in the product, and the result is increased product consumption and profits for the company.

Consumption. As noted, oftentimes women's feelings of obligation coincide with consumption. As a result of the combination of obligation and consumption, some women were not excited about buying expensive party products. Both Linda and Karen worried about being able to afford purchases at the jewelry party. Liz also worried about the price of the products, but seeing friends took center stage for her, so her worries about buying were alleviated once she started visiting with her friends. Mimi, a respondent in the service organization interview, also talked about the expense of the products: "You look at it and the expense is just . . . Fifty dollars is too much."

Other women looked forward to buying products. Berta, a service organization respondent, stated she knows what she wants before she even goes to the party. "I went to Silvia's Pampered Chef party because I needed a cutting board and I like their products." Nina agreed, "Yeah. I want everything in the catalog but I can't afford it all. I always like the products."

The college students I interviewed claimed that consumption played only a small part in their motivation to attend parties. They were adamant that when they do purchase products, it is due to a genuine interest, and that there is no pressure to buy because "we're all poor college students." Ally says, "If my friend was throwing a Mary Kay party I'd be like, 'I'm not going.' . . . I'm not going to spend my money or my time if I'm not going to buy." This statement resembles some of the contradictory statements made by respondents earlier. At the beginning of the group interview, Liz said that parties are about fun with friends. If they are truly about fun, couldn't she go and just visit with the women in attendance without buying anything? It seems that she really does feel an obligation to buy if she is in attendance and, therefore, would rather not go if she does not want to buy the products—obligation to buy trumps friendship and fun.

Conclusion

As the data indicate, the motivations to attend product parties varied for women partygoers. One unexpected variable that seemed to influence motivation was the age of the respondents. College-age women tended to emphasize fun with friends more than the other two groups. In addition, they felt that they did not have to purchase products in order to maintain their friendships. This group, however, also made more contradictory statements surrounding motivation (e.g., parties are just fun . . . but sometimes I feel obligated to go to help a friend).

Women at the jewelry party interview (ages thirty to fifty) spoke about fun and friendship at parties, but most of their interview centered on obligations not only to attend parties but also to buy products. This obligation was not discussed as a reciprocal form of obligation but instead as an uncomfortable feeling that not adhering to the "party line" of attending and purchasing products might result in loss of friendships and negative social encounters. Unlike college-age women, this group of women might not have a large friendship pool. As a result, they may feel the need to protect the friendships they do have through attendance and consumption.[41]

The service organization women (ages fifty to eighty) spoke of obligation as well, but in a different manner. They saw obligation as a form of positive support. Like the college-age women, they claimed that nonattendance would not negatively affect their friendships. In addition to this finding, these women were more likely to enjoy buying products at the parties.

These age differences indicate that the motivation to attend such gatherings varies with the structure of friendships at different stages in life. Many college-age women interact with large groups of friends. They tend to have fewer responsibilities and do not depend on one another as much as women who work and have children. Working mothers might rely on their friends a great deal for assistance. For these women, friends provide social support for one another that they do not want to compromise. Loss of a friendship means loss of this inner circle that is so necessary. Older women, however, may be at the point in their lives where friendships are so solidly in place that they need not worry about failing to attend a party.

In all these age groups, social class certainly plays a role. I did not, however, inquire about the social class of these women. Based on statements made in the group interviews, it appeared that the college-age women and the jewelry respondents had less disposable income to purchase products. The women in the service organization, however, regularly attended one another's product parties and almost always purchased something.

Themes discussed by the respondents were not mutually exclusive but were simply meant to highlight some of the women's key statements. Several contradictions and overlapping motivations are due in part to the party paradox. Women experienced empowerment through interacting with friends and providing social support to one another at home-based gatherings. At other times, women spoke of feeling an obligation to attend such gatherings to maintain their friendships—an uncomfortable feeling that connected more to exploitation than empowerment. Through the women's discussions, it became clear that their interpretations of motivation connected intimately to the private sphere. Fun, friendship, reciprocity, obligation, and social support are feminine experiences centered within the private sphere.

Some women admitted feelings of discomfort that centered on obligation, yet they still saw this obligation as central to friendships. What they failed to recognize was how inviting friends to product parties supports the capitalist mission of increasing sales. Women become entrenched in the private sphere, making it difficult to recognize how relationships are manipulated by product companies in the name of profit. Blurred boundaries between public and private spaces contribute to the invisibility of such exploitation by shifting women's attention to one another and away from the capitalist agenda.

By highlighting the paradox of parties, I do not mean to imply that product company officials are behind closed doors conspiring to use women's friendships to encourage consumption. Nor do I want our lasting impression of women at parties to be that of social dupes who are coerced into going to parties and buying products. Certainly the party plan has its exploitative side (as do other capitalist ventures), but women also have some level of agency within these structures. As some participants indicated, the choice to attend parties is sometimes due to a genuine interest in products they can only purchase at product parties. Other women really wanted to take advantage of the party to interact with their friends.

It is easy, however, for women to miss the capitalist motivations (i.e., profit) behind product parties. As women get caught up in friendship and fun at product parties, they miss the real point of these gatherings—making money. It is important to raise women's awareness of such processes. Collective awareness of these structural arrangements may result in women banding together to encourage better pay and working conditions for women who rely on the party plan for all or part of their income.

Encouraging women to note the positive aspects of their relationships with one another may also serve as an empowering force. Relying on one another for help—even if that means showing up at a party or buying a pair of earrings—is part of the social glue that binds women. But this bonding does not always have to happen through consumption.

Linda declared that all she really wanted was to see her friends and to have them over to her home to enjoy one another's company without having to buy unwanted products. As women recognize the motivations of companies who sell party plan products, perhaps we will see the advantages of emphasizing fun, friendship, and support without supporting capitalism. Hopefully, that will be the new party line.

A major strength of this book, and particularly the following contribution, is its focus on connections among segments of a global system of work that sometimes empowers and other times exploits women. In the following field study, situated in the Czech Republic, Karen Kapusta-Pofahl, Eva Kavková, Ivana Šindlerová, and Jana Smiggels-Kavková examine women's home-based work as an emerging facet of globalization. These authors examine women's search for common ground through shared experiences as they consistently struggle to balance the public and private spheres of their (whole) lives. This case study demonstrates how the party plan economy has gone global. In this case, just as in US-based gender parties, we glimpse spaces that are neither purely public nor purely private, yet these conflicting aspects work in concert to control women's seemingly "free" choices.

Case Study 4.2
Womanhood and Home-Based Work in the Czech Republic
Karen Kapusta-Pofahl, Eva Kavková,
Ivana Šindlerová, and Jana Smiggels-Kavková

> It's some kind of natural phenomenon that the man comes home and he sprawls on the bed. He can't understand that after a whole day with two kids, I'm more tired than if I had worked in peace. . . . I'm half emancipated, half not. —*Věra, a home-based worker and mother of two*

Imagine a woman in her thirties with two small children. Her husband works full-time, and she stays home with the kids. Before having children, she worked outside the home but now cannot find a spot at a day care center, or is unable to work long hours, or simply believes her proper place as a mother is with her children. Her husband became the breadwinner of the family. Perhaps his income alone cannot make ends meet, or perhaps she finds herself in need of intellectual stimulation or a feeling of financial independence. One day, she hears that she can get paid to work from home and decides to give it a try.

The promise of home-based work is flexibility. Proponents claim that it allows someone to meet her financial goals while caring for children or elderly family members. Or it might provide an avenue for personal or financial self-fulfillment to someone who is unable to participate in the formal labor market due to disability or ill health. Very much like Tupperware or Mary Kay, companies that utilize home-based workers capitalize on the desires of women, telling them they too can "have it all."

However, the markets of interaction within which these Czech home-based workers are embedded have features that distinguish them from those in the United States. In the following pages, we discuss the findings of our research team within three broad thematic areas: the historical context of women and work in the Czech Republic, institutional constraints on the participation of women (especially mothers) in the formal labor market, and ideological tensions regarding a gendered division of labor that challenge the desirability or feasibility of "work-life balance."

This case study analyses the ways in which a sample of women in the Czech Republic conceptualize and express their decision to undertake home-based work (also called "homework").[42] Although Věra and other respondents with children seek to combine work and motherhood by working at home, this seeming compromise often fails to provide a satisfactory resolution. We have found that when respondents are unsatisfied with labor arrangements, they usually attribute their inability to find work-life balance to structural incompatibilities between workplace and caregiving obligations or grand narratives about human nature.

The tension between the public and private offers a critique of the oft-touted notion of work-life balance grounded in everyday experiences of real women. This case study represents the first such study of home-based workers in the Czech Republic and as such not only provides valuable insight into the everyday lives of Czech home-based workers but also provides a more complete understanding of home-based worker practices worldwide.

The Research

The parent study was conducted by the European Contact Group (EKS), a Prague-based nongovernmental organization, as part of an ongoing project to map the conditions of home-based workers, particularly of women, in the Czech Republic.[43] It is a qualitative study of twenty-two women who fit set criteria for the definition of home-based work.[44] Recruited respondents participated in a semistructured interview that lasted between one and a half and two hours. Interviews were conducted at various locations as dictated by the individual respondents.

Respondents ranged in age from twenty-five to sixty years of age. Fifteen were married, three were divorced, one had a live-in partner, and two were single.[45] Thirteen respondents had a secondary education, two had completed higher vocational school, five had a university degree or were university students, and two had a primary education. Nine respondents lived in Prague, the capital city; one lived in a regional capital; eight lived in mid-size towns around the country; and four lived in villages. Seventeen of the respondents had one or more children.

Fifteen respondents were classed as manual homeworkers, and seven were classed as knowledge-based homeworkers.[46] Manual work consists of producing or assembling part of a material product, such as a child's toy or a necklace. Typically, home-based work is only one of many steps leading to a completed product. For instance, a Czech worker will receive boxes of already dyed swatches of hair and already assembled empty hair swatch catalogues and must insert the swatches into the catalogues, then send them to be packaged or labeled. Manual workers use specialized tools and materials in completing their tasks. By contrast, knowledge-based work consists

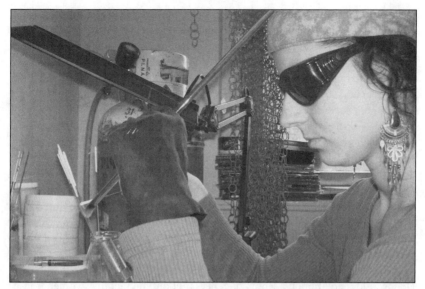

Figure 4.2 A woman in her "natural" place. A highly skilled glass-blowing artisan works at her home-based job. *(Karen Kapusta-Pofahl)*

of tasks completed solely by the worker, such as the translation or proof-reading of documents. This type of work resembles what has been called "telecommuting" or "e-work."

Czech Women and Work in Historical Perspective

When she claims that she is "half emancipated, half not," Věra is calling upon a number of rhetorics about the proper role of women in Czech society. Women in the Czech Republic have historically had a different relationship to work than their US counterparts. US women had to mount a social movement in order to convince the government that they had the right to enter the labor force, whereas the Czechoslovak Communist Party compelled women as well as men to enter the workforce.[47] In other words, during the socialist era (1948–1989), the state required Czech women to work outside the home.

In the heavily industrialized planned economy touted by the Communist Party, it was crucial that the female half of the population participate in the formal employment sector. In the 1950s, state propaganda encouraged women to help "build socialism" by driving tractors on collective farms and handling machinery in factories. Women, the early rhetoric went, were as capable as men of contributing to the socialist future through workforce participation. In the 1960s and beyond, however, falling birthrates prompted party officials to increase the discursive emphasis on motherhood as a socialist prerogative, without abandoning the emphasis on workforce participation.

Attempting to resolve conflicting socialist ideals with a sagging economy, the state modified its rhetoric to emphasize the value of women as "worker-mothers," backing up this ideal with policies designed to raise the birthrate while still requiring women to participate in the workforce. The government subsidized child care centers, for example, which could be used by working women. When they came home from work (not to mention before work and over their lunch breaks), however, women's work was not finished. They had to take care of their children, tend to their husbands, wash the clothes (often without the aid of a washing machine), make dinner (often after having stood in numerous long lines to acquire this food), clean house, iron clothes, and do dishes.[48] Thus the Communist state pressured women to do both productive *and* reproductive labor. In response, many women found themselves attempting to be superwomen as they juggled the double burden of employment and motherhood.[49]

The double burden is similar to the "second shift" concept that Hochschild made famous. Both concepts point out the fact that women do not simply work outside the home *or* do domestic work, but rather find themselves coming home from work only to begin domestic tasks. Furthermore, neither the male partners of women on the second shift nor those experiencing the double burden attempted to contribute equally to household and child care duties.

A key difference between the double burden in socialist Czechoslovakia and the second shift in the Reagan-era United States, however, has to do with some big social and political factors. In the United States women had to fight to gain equal employment and protection under the law, but in Czechoslovakia the ruling Communist Party integrated women into the labor market by decree. Women in the United States who pursued careers in the 1980s did so in hopes of "having it all" and enjoying the gains of the feminist movement, but women's participation in the Czech labor force during the 1980s and previous decades was generally considered to be a government imposition rather than a feminist victory.

After the fall of the socialist regime in 1989, Czech women faced rising prices and increased workplace discrimination in the wake of the transition to capitalist neoliberalism. Amid a general repudiation of anything associated with Communist Party priorities, women were the subject of debates among (mostly male) politicians as well as the public at large about the best "place" for them in the postsocialist era. The prevailing sentiment at the time, which in great part persists to the present day, was that women were "natural" mothers and as such should prioritize childrearing over career advancement. In reality, however, a single breadwinning income was economically infeasible for many families.

Despite the widely held sentiment that mothers should devote them-selves to full-time care of their children, many women were unable or un-willing to give up paid employment. As we hope to demonstrate in this case study, however, mothers who need to work do not escape conflicting ap-praisals of their situation. Respondents mentioned several institutional bar-riers to managing both productive and reproductive work.

Institutional Barriers to Formal Employment
As a consequence of postsocialist market capitalism, Czech women seeking to combine productive and reproductive labor face a number of institutional challenges. Some are formal constraints, such as a lack of affordable child care options that coincide with working hours, employer expectations of long hours or frequent travel, or even lack of public transportation to a job site. Informal barriers are no less powerful, such as (illegal) discrimination in hiring on the basis of age, sex, and/or parental status.

Although nearly all respondents had chosen to engage in both produc-tive labor and carework, their motivations for home-based work differed. One group of women, mostly made up of manual homeworkers, were driven by the need to make ends meet. The other group, consisting mainly of knowledge-based homeworkers, explained their decision as a desire to prioritize carework while remaining financially active. Regardless of their motivations, both groups of women found themselves unable to obtain or maintain work in the formal labor market that met their need for financial remuneration *and* allowed them to meet their obligations outside the em-ployment sector.

Constraints and discrimination. Home-based work was not the first choice of employment for several respondents. Rather, they turned to it after expe-riencing barriers to formal employment due in large part to their status as mothers. When these women attempted to "flex" their work schedules to accommodate child care obligations, they found themselves faced with un-tenable rigidity. Absent a comprehensive network of affordable day care centers and extended-hours preschools, flex scheduling is unfeasible for many. Lea, a married manual worker in her mid-twenties with one child, explaines her conflict with child care availability: "I can't go to work and take care of my child at the same time, because the working hours start be-fore the kindergarten opens."[50] Furthermore, as Lea found out, an em-ployee's desire to flex her schedule is only as effective as her employer's willingness to allow her to do so. She goes on: "Basically, I [suppose] no-body will ever give me a job in catering, which is my field, as I can't do morning shifts or twelve to fifteen hour shifts because of my child."

Silvie, a married knowledge-based worker in her mid-thirties with two children, expressed similar constraints: "In a regular company, you can't say no when there is an assignment and you must work overtime, at night and [on] weekends. Nobody cares if your children are sick." In workplaces where overnight trips or ten-hour days are expected, workers with child care responsibilities find themselves unable to successfully harmonize the two roles.

A small number of respondents described situations in which they experienced direct discrimination from employers because they had small children. Hana, a married manual worker in her forties with four children, explained how this sort of discrimination occurs: "I've had a lot of experience with job hunting. But they often want to know who takes care of my children when they're sick, and they turned me down, saying that I would frequently be absent from work. I felt I was discriminated against for having young children. Then I gave up and only looked for home-based work." Hana's potential employers refused to hire her because she was the primary caretaker of her children, reasoning she would be an unreliable worker. Although discrimination in employment on the basis of parental status is illegal in the Czech Republic, it is nonetheless widely practiced.

Implicit constraints: opting out of the workforce. Other respondents explained their undertaking of home-based work not as a forced choice but as a flexible means of financially supporting their decision to be primarily responsible for domestic and child care tasks. In particular, a number of respondents explained that they were unwilling to obtain employment that required them to commute to a workplace while they were caring for small children. Wanda, a married knowledge-based worker in her forties with four children, explains:

> I wanted a home-based job to fit in with my family responsibilities. . . .
> I used to work full-time and had three children, and it was the worst time of my life. . . . If you looked at our home, you could tell I worked 7 a.m. to 5 p.m. I always lagged behind with my housework, I would put the ironing and the cleaning off until the weekends, and my weekends were for housework. Instead of spending my time with my family, I did household chores and cooked, and I didn't like it. Spending time with my children is my priority. It was impossible for me to balance work and family. Although I loved my job, my fourth maternity leave was a great relief. Family comes first. If we had enough money I wouldn't work at all.

Gita, a married manual worker in her thirties with three children, explains: "I work at home and don't have to leave the children. I can organize my time and combine work and cooking. Stringing rosary beads leaves no mess, so I can work wherever in the house without needing a workroom." Silvie concurs: "Home-based work is an ideal solution for me. I don't have to go back to work, I can be with my family and I have more freedom. . . .

When I work at home, I set my own limits and my children and family are a part of my work." Wanda, Silvie, and Gita all cite their desire to combine work and child care, which requires an amount of flexibility that can be a barrier to undertaking employment outside the home. Each woman explained that home-based work allows the flexibility to determine working hours, as well as the amount and type of work, in order to spend the desired amount of time carrying out child care or household duties. Even though they frame their exit from the formal labor force positively, an underlying incompatibility between employer demands and carework duties and a basic lack of infrastructure supporting flexible work schedules are implicit in their comments.

Although all the respondents report having to navigate a series of institutional barriers to formal employment, these constraints were not brought up by the majority of respondents as the main reasons why they chose home-based work. Instead, what arose was a popular belief among the women that a mother's "natural" place was at home with her children, whereas men belong in the workforce—a gender ideology that shaped many respondents' worldview.

Embracing a Gender Ideology
The respondents did not unanimously share the belief that productive work (in any form) is a valuable thing for women to undertake. Rather, women's ideal roles are firmly associated with domestic tasks and child care. These associations, as well as men's inability to competently share domestic duties, were expressed by several respondents as natural. Women's province is necessarily the home and children, and men's is "naturally" the workplace. Furthermore, several respondents imply that although it is possible for a woman to become "emancipated" and work for remuneration, if her work takes her away from her children, it is in fact regressive and unnatural rather than empowering. The relative inflexibility of the "natural" roles of women and men also serves to reinforce the idea that it is neither valuable nor practical to encourage men to take up "women's tasks"—they simply are not naturally suited to it.

Motherhood: a natural priority. Our research team found that both manual and knowledge-based homeworkers generally subscribe to a division of family labor within which women are primarily responsible for child care and housework and men are financial breadwinners. Within this worldview, women's income is considered to be supplemental, whether or not she also cites financial need as a reason for undertaking the work. Their explanations for the reasons behind their assumption of the role of homemaker tend to rely on notions of the "natural" as well as the perception that men are incapable of doing such tasks well. Hana, for instance, states her view suc-

Figure 4.3 A mother and daughter sharing home/work space.
(Karen Kapusta-Pofahl)

cinctly: "I take care of the children. That's what a mum is supposed to do."
Although Hana also acknowledges in the interview that she has been discriminated against in hiring because she is a mother, she nonetheless es-
pouses the view that, working or not, child care is her primary maternal
obligation.

Šárka, a knowledge-based worker in her forties, explains this view in
more depth: "We have divided our roles the natural way. My husband
leaves family and household care up to me. . . . Everybody should know
what their role is. . . . Naturally, mums are meant to take care of children,
and the man can join in. . . . My home comes first, then I can think about
self-actualization." In Šárka's view, individual self-fulfillment is a luxury to
be indulged in only after a woman fulfills her natural role. Silvie expresses
this gender ideology in starker terms:

> It's me who takes care of the children most of the time, even though he
> realizes he should spend more time with them. The father role is about
> being the ultimate idol, an authority figure safeguarding values, the one
> who leads the way and opens new horizons. The mother ensures every-
> day life and a happy home. . . . The woman takes care of the children and
> the household and the man earns money and organizes the balance be-
> tween work and family time.

In other words, it should not be up to women to attempt work-life balance. Rather, this is something that men should have to contend with—how to be breadwinners while still spending some quality time with their families.

Other respondents felt that even home-based work detracts from a woman's natural duties. Gita, for instance, explained that becoming a home-based worker does not eliminate the problems that accompany outside work: "When you work at home, your work clashes with child care and family responsibilities. The children suffer when the mother works. And the older children need much more attention. If mothers on maternity leave received at least as much as the minimum wage, they wouldn't have to look for jobs." Gita believes that even home-based work remains work, which detracts from a woman's core duty to her family. Perhaps the children suffer less, she suggests, but they still suffer. Gita then calls upon the state to provide a higher maternity leave allowance in order to lessen what she sees as the negative impact upon children of working mothers, at home or otherwise.

As a counterpoint to this prevailing view, a few respondents suggested that they turned to home-based work partly to defy the monotony of full-time carework. For instance, although Šárka believes that she and her husband "have divided our roles the natural way," she nevertheless has turned to home-based work not only as a means of supporting her desire to stay home with her children but also as a respite from those same duties:

> I started looking for a home-based job actively between the birth of my first and second children. I needed to get in touch with day-to-day reality after being isolated at home with my child for a relatively long period of time. After the birth of my third child I did the same. . . . So my main motivation was getting back in touch with people again.

Although she expresses a strong view that the gendered division of labor is natural and right, Šárka has found that remaining at home to care for her children was also less fulfilling in practice than in the ideal.

Incapable men. Regardless of whether they espouse a clear gendered division of labor or wish their male partners would help more around the house, a number of respondents explained men's minimal involvements in domestic life as an inevitable aspect of their nature. Alena, a manual worker in her fifties with three grown children, puts it this way: "Guys are lazy by nature and it's hard to make a man take part in housework." Silvie expressed her views on men's ability to participate in domestic tasks by telling a brief anecdote: "The usual housework is my responsibility. My husband thinks a lot of it is pointless. When I'm not at home, he has his own way of dealing with the situation: he asks his mother to come over and take care of the household." Věra expresses frustration with her role as domestic caretaker:

> My husband says he helps with the household, but he could do more. . . .
> I never sleep, not even on the weekends. . . . Today's guys are weak; a
> woman can take much more. I can see it all around me. . . . It's some kind
> of natural phenomenon that the man comes home and he sprawls on the
> bed. He can't understand that after a whole day with two kids, I'm more
> tired than if I had worked in peace. . . . My husband takes care of the kids
> sometimes. But he's unable to do it all day. He can mind the children,
> but it's me who has to dress them and cook for them. . . . I appreciate
> men who control themselves and don't complain. . . . My husband says
> he can't work properly if he hasn't slept and eaten well. But when do I
> sleep and eat in peace? My man says that women are just made that way.
> . . . I'm half emancipated, half not.

Věra explains her husband's lack of sustained involvement with child care
and household tasks in terms of his "natural" disposition. She further cites
her perception that women can "take much more" physical discomfort and
her husband's justification for his prioritizing his own needs for rest above
hers as a matter of being "made that way." However, she does not seem to
be wholly comforted by this recourse to nature.

Home-Based Work as an Imperfect Solution: Concluding Thoughts
Respondents were often ambivalent about their roles as mothers *and* home-
based workers. For many, work-life balance is a compromise rather than a
goal. As was evidenced in Šárka's responses, even women who believe that
it is natural and proper for women to devote the bulk of their waking hours
to child care and domestic tasks may be dissatisfied with the claims of flexibility that proponents of home-based work promise. Silvie acknowledges
that although she is generally satisfied with home-based work, things are
not perfectly balanced.

Moreover, others have found even the practicalities of home-based
work to be difficult to balance with carework. Zdena, a married knowledge-
based worker in her late thirties with two children, argues that even at home
she is not able to find sufficient time to work to her satisfaction: "I never
work longer than a short while. . . . I must interrupt it whenever I am disturbed. I don't have enough space or my own table where I can leave work
all the time."

Respondents also discussed the need to drive long distances across the
city or into different towns to acquire materials, long unpaid idle periods
when another worker along the production line is behind on her duties, or
abrupt changes in the terms of employment. In short, although it has recently been recognized by the International Labour Organization as real
work worthy of protection under the law and is touted by the European
Union as a viable means to achieve work-life balance, home-based work remains an imperfect solution.

When seen from the perspective of the political and historical contexts surrounding women's experiences of home-based work in the Czech Republic, the notion of "work-life balance" seems more like a double burden or second shift than a happy medium. As women negotiate their interpersonal relationships with their partners and children, including obligations, desires, and expectations, some turn to home-based work with the hope that it will help them successfully navigate these choppy waters. The findings of our research team suggest, however, that often women retain the feeling that things are just not balancing the way they should. Věra's proclamation of being half emancipated, half not reflects their ambivalence.

Beyond the Party

The bifurcation of public and private space is a structural reality, but it is nonsensical to think that we experience two separate lives—one public, one private. The reality is that individuals simultaneously navigate the public and private. Anyone who has a family knows that many times we bring our personal lives to work with us. Think of mothers and fathers who must peel off crying children at day care so as not to be late for work. The image of this child may linger in the parents' minds as they go about their workday. Similarly, anyone with a friend or family member fighting terminal illness cannot reasonably be expected to check those concerns at the door as they punch in at work.

In the same vein, when we go home, we are never truly away from our public lives. Cell phones, the Internet, and home offices ensure that we still participate in work—or at least think about work—while at home. Again, public and private spaces are interlaced. The bottom line is that separating public and private lives is virtually impossible. Yet, we are encouraged, or required, to do so, resulting in a contrived distinction between these spaces.

The division between our public and private lives has consequences at the individual and structural levels. These outcomes were demonstrated in the two field studies in this chapter, illustrating that the artificial division between public and private space occurs locally but is shared with locations across the globe.

Reaction to such a division, however, varies. In research by Kapusta-Pofahl et al., we learned that, historically, all Czech women were expected to participate in the public sphere. After the fall of Communism, women were encouraged to prioritize children. While some Czech women were satisfied to be at home with their children, not working in paid labor was not economically feasible. In an effort to combine work and family, Czech women in Kapusta-Pafahl, Kavková, Šindlerová, and Smiggels-Kavková's case study opted to work from home. As a result, they were able to benefit economically from the public sphere while also spending time with their children in the private sphere. However, as demonstrated in studies of the second shift, combining family work and for-pay work is never without its costs, psychologically, emotionally, and physically.[51]

The intersection of public and private space is also illustrated in Bemiller's case study of women's attendance at home-based parties. Women in the United States go to home-based gatherings that occur in the private sphere (the home) but are infiltrated, even dictated, by the public sphere (capitalist product companies). Such attendance is motivated by emotions connected to the private realm—obligation, reciprocity, and love of friends—while women buy products from companies connected to the public realm.

At first glance, the intersection of public and private space is easily identified in both studies. Yet, participants' recognition of this intersection differs. Czech women are cognizant of the fact that they must participate in two spheres that do not work in tandem. The result is the meshing of home and work. Awareness of the division between public and private space resulted in Czech women finding a solution to their public/private dilemma, but that solution accomplished little to advance women's overall position in the economy.

The party participants in Bemiller's study, however, lack recognition of the party plan's structural position between public and private spaces. As a result, capitalist organizations manipulate women's relationships and consumption patterns for the sake of profit. All the while, party participants see only what is happening in the private sphere; this lack of awareness means that capitalism exploits friendships and purchasing power. In the meantime, women may come together as friends, but they remain unaware of their part in an exploitive system.

In both cases cathexis affected how women navigated public and private spaces.[52] The Czech women's decision to work at home was motivated by relationships with family, while the women in Bemiller's study were motivated by friendship. These emotional attachments influenced women's thoughts and actions as they took part in the party plan economy. Relationships are important: once awareness emerges, they provide impetus for recognition and change within the local and global party plan economy.

Despite differences in awareness of the public/private divide, women in both studies experienced some level of empowerment within the party plan economy. In Bemiller's study, personal empowerment may have occurred as women supported one another by attending home-based parties. The Czech women experienced economic and personal empowerment as they fulfilled work and family obligations, creating a satisfying lifestyle. However, little evidence suggests a raising of consciousness about women's collective identity and related social issues.

To have a true "economy," there must be exchange. A shipwreck survivor alone on an island doesn't constitute an economy. The party plan economy comes into its own only when we consider interactions between its participants. Unlike formal work environments, where the private sphere enters mainly by discussing home life with a coworker, the party plan economy openly welcomes the private sphere into the exchange. But awareness is a prerequisite.

Variation in the levels and types of empowerment experienced by women within the party plan economy are important to note and can be revisited by going back to the table and chart in Chapter 1 of this book.

Notes

1. Jeffrey Reiman, *The Rich Get Richer and the Poor Get Prison: Ideology, Class, and Criminal Justice,* 8th ed. (Boston: Pearson/Allyn and Bacon, 2006).
2. Doris Christopher, *The Pampered Chef: The Story of One of America's Most Beloved Companies* (New York: Doubleday Business, 2005), 4.
3. Ibid., 4.
4. Ibid., 40.
5. Ibid., 120.
6. Joan Walsh, "Feminism After Friedan," *Salon*, February 6, 2006, http://www.salon.com (June 6, 2009).
7. Walsh, "Feminism After Friedan."
8. Bob Kealing, *Tupperware Unsealed: Brownie Wise, Earl Tupper, and the Home Party Pioneers* (Gainesville: University Press of Florida, 2008), 119.
9. *Tupperware!* The Film and More, "Timeline: Women, Work, and Plastics History," *The American Experience,* PBS, December 11, 2003, http://www.pbs.org (June 8, 2009).
10. William G. Perry, *Forms of Intellectual and Ethical Development in the College Years* (New York: Holt, Rinehart, and Winston, 1970).
11. Mary F. Belenky et al., *Women's Ways of Knowing: The Development of Self, Voice, and Mind*, 10th ed. (New York: Basic Books, 1997).
12. K. Taylor, C. Marienau, and M. Fiddler, *Developing Adult Learners: Strategies for Teachers and Trainers* (San Francisco: Jossey-Bass, 2000), 345–349.
13. Judith Glazer-Raymo, "Gender Inequality," in *Women in Higher Education: An Encyclopedia,* ed. Ana M. Martinez Alemán and Kristen A. Renn (Santa Barabara, CA: ABC-CLIO, 2002), 226.
14. M. S. West and J. W. Curtis, "AAUP Faculty Gender Equity Indicators 2006," American Association of University Professors, 2008, http://www.aaup.org (May 25, 2009).
15. Susan K. Dyer, ed., *Tenure Denied: Cases of Sex Discrimination in Academia* (Washington, DC: American Association of University Women, October 2004).
16. Joan B. Landes, "Further Thoughts on the Public/Private Distinction," *Journal of Women's History* 15, no. 2 (Summer 2003): 28.
17. For example, see Myra Marx Ferree, "Beyond Separate Spheres," *Journal of Marriage and the Family* 52 (1990): 866–884; Judith Lorber, *Paradoxes of Gender* (New Haven, CT: Yale University Press, 1994); Jackie Guendouzi, "'The Guilt Thing': Balancing Domestic and Professional Roles," *Journal of Marriage and Family* 58 (2006): 901–909; Scott Coltrane, "Elite Careers and Family Commitment: It's (Still) About Gender," *Annals of the American Academy of Political and Social Science* 596 (2004): 214–220.
18. Heidi Hartmann, "Capitalism, Patriarchy, and the Subordination of Women," in *Social Class and Stratification: Classic Statements and Theoretical Debates,* ed. Rhonda Levine (Lanham, MD: Rowman and Littlefield, 2006).
19. Anne Kingston, *The Meaning of Wife: A Provocative Look at Women and Marriage in the Twenty-First Century* (New York: Farrar, Straus and Giroux, 2006), 23–25.
20. Dorothy Smith, *The Conceptual Practices of Power: A Feminist Sociology of Knowledge* (Boston: Northeastern University Press, 1990), 3.

21. Heidi Hartmann, "The Unhappy Marriage of Marxism and Feminism: Towards a More Progressive Union," *Capital and Class* 8, no. 2 (1979): 1.

22. Institute for Women's Policy Research, "Fact Sheet: The Gender Wage Gap by Occupation," April 2009, http://www.iwpr.org (June 8, 2009).

23. Beth B. Hess and Myra Marx Ferree, *Analyzing Gender: A Handbook of Social Science Research* (Newbury Park, CA: Sage, 1987).

24. American Psychological Association, "Is Multitasking More Efficient? Shifting Mental Gears Costs Time, Especially When Shifting to Less Familiar Tasks," August 5, 2001, http://www.apa.org (June 30, 2009). University of Michigan researchers explored whether multitasking was a more efficient way to accomplish multiple tasks. They found that with all types of tasks, whether simple or complex, subjects lost time when having to switch between them. If a task was particularly complex, significantly more time was needed to complete that task. See also, Winifred Gallagher, *Rapt: Attention and the Focused Life* (New York: Penguin, 2009).

25. Heidi Hartmann, "Capitalism, Patriarchy, and Job Segregation by Sex," *Signs* 1, no. 3 (Spring 1976): 137–169.

26. Irene Padavic and Barbara Reskin, *Women and Men at Work,* 2nd ed. (Thousand Oaks, CA: Pine Forge Press, 2002).

27. US Department of Labor, Bureau of Labor Statistics, "Women in the Labor Force: A Databook," December 2008, http://www.bls.gov (June 1, 2009).

28. In 2003, 1.1 billion of the 2.8 billion workers worldwide (40 percent) were women. This is an increase of almost 200 million women in the past ten years. See International Labor Office, "Global Employment Trends for Women, 2004," March 2004, http://kilm.ilo.org (June 15, 2009).

29. Arlie Russell Hochschild, *The Managed Heart: Commercialization of Human Feeling* (Berkeley: University of California Press, 1983).

30. Pink Lighthouse, "What Can We Learn from Mary Kay's Company Information?" April 10, 2008, http://www.pinklighthouse.com (June 15, 2009).

31. Hartmann, "The Unhappy Marriage."

32. Under patriarchal capitalism, individuals experience power and subordination differently based not only on gender but also on race, sexuality, age, and so on. The intersections of our different social locations affect where we sit within social hierarchies.

33. Lorber, *Paradoxes of Gender*.

34. Allan G. Johnson, *The Gender Knot: Unraveling Our Patriarchal Legacy* (Philadelphia: Temple University Press, 1997); Gayle Rubin, "The Traffic in Women: Notes on the 'Political Economy' of Sex," *Feminist Anthropology* (2006): 87–106.

35. Pierre Bourdieu and Loic Wacquant, *The State Nobility: Elite Schools in the Field of Power* (Palo Alto, CA: Stanford University Press, 1989).

36. "'False consciousness' is a concept derived from Marxist theory of social class, referring to the systematic misrepresentation of dominant social relations in the consciousness of subordinate classes. . . . Members of a subordinate class suffer from false consciousness in that their mental representations of the social relations around them systematically conceal or obscure the realities of subordination, exploitation, and domination those relations embody." See Daniel Little, "False Consciousness," University of Michigan, http://www-personal.umd.umich.edu (June 19, 2009).

37. John Jost, "An Experimental Replication of the Depressed-Entitlement Effect Among Women," *Psychology of Women Quarterly* 21 (1997): 387–393.

38. Brenda Major, "From Social Inequality to Personal Entitlement: The Role of Social Comparisons, Legitimacy Appraisals, and Group Membership," *Advances in Experimental Social Psychology* 26 (1994): 293–355.

39. John Jost, "Negative Illusions: Conceptual Clarification and Conceptual Evi-

dence Concerning False Consciousness," *Political Psychology* 16, no. 2 (June 1995): 397–424.

40. This group of women belongs to a nationally recognized service organization that members refer to as a sorority.

41. Claude S. Fisher and Stacey J. Oliker found that as women's lives progressed, friendships decreased in number and intensity. More specifically, women with children were less likely to have close friends than married men with children. Along the same lines, working mothers were less likely than working fathers to have close friendships. See Fisher and Oliker, "A Research Note on Friendship, Gender, and the Life Cycle," *Social Forces* 62 (1983): 124–133.

42. The focus of this case study is on the ways in which home-workers conceptualize and negotiate often competing facets of womanhood in contemporary Czech society. As a result, this case study represents only a portion of the data that was collected in this project.

43. Research team members were Jana Smiggels-Kavková, Ivana Šindlerová, and Eva Kavková. More information on EKS can be found online at www.ekscr.cz. All the methodological information and data discussed are taken from the report, Ivana Šindlerová, "Women and Home-Based Work in the Czech Republic: Home-Based Work: A Precarious and Underpaid Occupation Concealed Within the Walls of the Home, or a Flexible Option Ensuring Life-Work Balance?" The full report upon which this case study is based can be accessed in English online at http://www.ekscr.cz (June 17, 2009).

44. "The definition of home-based work that was used in this study is based on ILO Convention 177 (1996) and expanded to take into account aspects of the Czech labor market: Work carried out at home for remuneration, other than common everyday housework; work carried out by persons who do not have employee status and do not enjoy employee rights; work which is not registered as self-employment and is carried out by persons who do not have any regular income; work that is carried out informally and within a formal employment relationship." Ivana Šindlerová, "Women and Home-Based Work in the Czech Republic."

Two of these twenty-two respondents provided only answers to a written questionnaire, and five of the 20 remaining interview transcripts were drawn from an unpublished pilot study on HBW conducted by EKS in 2002 (ibid.).

45. Researchers did not ascertain respondents' sexual orientation or ethnic identity, with the exception of two respondents who identified themselves as "foreigners" or as not having Czech citizenship.

46. Manual home-based workers undertook the following activities: making and assembling hair color swatch charts; lampworking; assembling adjustable date stamps; making rosaries; making jewelry and costume jewelry; making glass chandeliers; making hospital uniforms, sleepwear, and bed linens; cooking or preparing vegetarian meals; arranging and sealing greeting card gift boxes; decorating Christmas tree ornaments; inserting/pasting inserts in foreign magazines; assembling baby pacifiers; decorating tin miniatures; assembling promotional toy cars; and designing and making shoes. Knowledge-based work includes administrative work (accounting), real estate management support, editing, electronic library and website administration, research and technical translation, graphic design, and artwork (making coloring books and other items for preschool-age children).

47. Czechoslovakia split into two countries (the Czech Republic and Slovakia) in 1993.

48. You may notice that there is no mention of a double burden for men. In fact, men were not targeted by the state as "worker-fathers." They were instead simply "workers." Of course, men also participated in some domestic duties, such as car maintenance and

household repairs. Child care, however, was widely considered by men and women alike to be the chief concern of women.

49. Chris Corrin, ed., *Superwomen and the Double Burden: Women's Experience of Change in Central and Eastern Europe and the Former Soviet Union* (London: Scarlet Press, 1992). This was a common trend throughout socialist Europe, Russia, and Eurasia.

50. Children are not required to go to school until six years of age. As a result, working parents with children under six must rely upon for-fee child care services from state-run or private centers, or nanny care.

51. Arlie Russell Hochschild, *The Second Shift* (New York: Avon Books, 1989).

52. Raewyn Connell, *Gender and Power: Society, the Person, and Sexual Politics* (Palo Alto, CA: Stanford University Press, 1987).

5

When Consumption, Markets, and Movements Meet

I (Michelle) recently received the products that I ordered through my Pampered Chef party. Imagine my surprise when I noted that the majority of the products that I ordered were made in China. In the name of profit, many US-based companies are guilty of hiring low-wage labor (often located overseas) to produce goods and services. Sometimes we are unaware of the use of such labor, and at other times we simply do not pay attention.

On exceptional occasions, people have come together and raised awareness of these processes. One recent example can be seen in the uproar that occurred when students learned that logo apparel for some colleges was being produced in sweatshops. As a result, university students, in coordination with United Students Against Sweatshops (USAS), embarked on a grassroots movement. Through campaigns and protests, students increased public awareness about poor working conditions and poverty wages paid to sweatshop workers. To date, the movement has resulted in the mobilization of resources to create a national network that demands fair pay and safe working conditions for workers.[1]

The work of USAS illustrates what happens when consumption, markets, and movements coincide. This relationship is explored further in this chapter through original field studies by Leigh Fine and Summer Lewis. The studies investigate the unique nature of the party plan, both in the United States and worldwide, clearly demonstrating how gender parties take us beyond a formal, rationalized understanding of consumption and marketplaces.

Consumption, Markets, and Movements

Consumption, markets, and movements merge within the party plan economy. Consumption refers to the purchase of goods and services by individuals to satisfy needs.[2] This definition applies as we discuss gender parties, where goods and services are bought at US home-based gatherings and within similar global contexts, but there is much more to the connection between gender parties and consumption. In addition to the consumption of material products, consumption within the party plan economy occurs as women encounter less tangible "products" such as friendship, knowledge, and ideas.

Consumption takes place within a particular niche, differing from formal, rational structures that we tend to think of when we hear the term *market*. It would be inaccurate to say that gender parties do not include some elements of a formal market (e.g., public gatherings, buying, selling), but it is important to focus on the distinct nature of marketplaces of interaction.[3] These marketplaces incorporate both professional and personal associations that guide economic transactions and incorporate friendship, reciprocity, and loosely structured social networks.

Within the marketplace of interaction, opportunities abound for women to join together in various ways to participate in consciousness-raising movements. You may be thinking, "How can a makeup party lead to a movement?" Admittedly, much of the potential for such movements is subterranean because of the emphasis placed on consumption at these gatherings. Nevertheless, I demonstrate the possibility in this chapter.

The Political Is Personal

As consumption, markets, and movements coalesce for women within the party plan economy, we turn "the personal is political" (the mantra of the second wave of the women's movement) on its head; we look at what happens when women's personal politics (that is, ideology) influences their personal *and* professional lives.

As you read in Chapter 2, ideology can be defined in several ways, ranging from heavy-handed, even oppressive, conditions that dictate thought to a set of cultural ideals that convey positive self-persuasion and motivation. Ideology drives our everyday experiences in many contexts, including religion, family, and politics. In this chapter, we address capitalism[4] and compulsory heterosexuality[5] as ideologies that influence women's experiences within the party plan economy.

Capitalist ideology supports the notion that anyone can be successful if s/he works hard enough. If you are not among the wealthy, then it is your own fault.[6] Of course, this ideology does not take into consideration the structural inequality that exists within capitalist societies. Instead, it breeds classism and extreme competition—a winner-take-all philosophy. The party plan economy sometimes operates under a capitalist mentality but at other time resists capitalism.

The second ideology addressed is compulsory heterosexuality, the assumption that men and women are innately attracted to one another. Although it is typically studied as a form of natural sexual behavior, heterosexuality is really a highly regulated, ritualized, and organized practice tied to particular rules and behaviors. Such rules and behaviors direct women's allegiances to men, working against a shared consciousness of sex-based inequality.[7] Much like the negative ramifications of capitalism, compulsory heterosexuality, because it is privileged as normal, remains invisible and leads to rampant sexism.[8] However, as active agents within the party plan economy, women may negotiate strategies to challenge capitalism and compulsory heterosexuality.

The Political Is Personal:
When Personal Ideology and Markets Collide

I was proud to be running as a woman but I was running because I thought I'd be the best President. But I am a woman . . . and I know there are still barriers and biases out there, often unconscious. . . . I ran [benefited by] opportunities my mother never dreamed of. I ran as a mother . . . who wants to lead all children to brighter tomorrows. To build that future I see, we must make sure that women and men alike understand the struggles of their grandmothers and mothers, and that women enjoy equal opportunities, equal pay, and equal respect.
   —*Hillary Rodham Clinton, Concession Speech 2008*

As consumption, markets, and movements collide, individuals connect with issues and experiences that are both personal and political. The personal and the political are instrumental in understanding the possibility for collective action within the party plan economy. "The personal is political" means that women's conditions are the product of systematic oppression. This phrase illustrates what happens to women when their personal lives are affected by structures outside their control.

Betty Friedan helped to bring this notion to the forefront during the women's movement of the 1960s and 1970s in her pivotal book, *The Feminine Mystique*.[9] In this classic, Friedan highlights an unrealistic image of femininity—what she terms the feminine mystique—that women have been socialized to accept. According to Friedan, women's confinement to the roles of housewife and mother results in the denial of opportunities to them to receive educations and find fulfilling careers, leading to women's dissatisfaction with their lives. *The Feminine Mystique* became a household name because it brought to the forefront what millions of women felt and experienced everyday.

Using a more contemporary example, the excerpt above from Hillary Clinton's concession speech provides an example of how the personal is political for one woman. Clinton discussed how her reasons for running for the Democratic

Figure 5.1 A 1950s happy housewife.
(Flickr Creative Commons and Seattle Municipal Archives, #20947)

nomination were connected to her personal experiences as a daughter and a mother. Clinton subverted the dominant patriarchal political system when she chose to run for president of the United States. The personal is political.

As a teacher, I (Michelle) can relate to Clinton's story of the personal becoming political. I teach a family violence course at Kansas State University in which it is not uncommon for at least one woman to share her story of victimization at the hands of a male partner during the course of the semester. Each time this has happened, I've spoken with the woman about her choice to share her story, and each time the answer is the same: while difficult to do, the women see sharing their stories as an opportunity to increase awareness for other women.

Our understanding of the personal as political often works from the bottom up. We look at women's individual experiences (e.g., intimate violence, rape, unequal pay) first and then argue that such experiences are political because they affect more than just one woman. Using my Pampered Chef party as an illustration, I focused on the individual women in attendance at the party (i.e., the personal), but our actions and experiences were really influenced by—and continued to maintain—a particular gender order (i.e., the political).

This bottom-up approach has especially made sense at particular points in history as we attempt to bring women's subordination and oppression to light. Look at the image of the 1950s housewife. Is she really happy? Is cooking that much fun?

According to Stephanie Coontz, the smile on these housewives' faces masked a sadness hidden from public view.[10] Our naïve understanding of 1950s-type families led us to believe that this decade was a time of happiness and contentment in the family, as opposed to the divorce and violence against women and children we see now. In reality, the 1950s mirrored what is happening in our families today—we were just better at hiding these problems fifty years ago. With time, the personal as political proved to be useful for analyzing this period because it pulled women's stories into the public eye and resulted in an increased awareness of numerous political issues that affect women.

Within this chapter of *Women at Work,* we discuss how the political is personal in our everyday lives and, more specifically, within the party plan economy. As Katherine Viner notes, it is easy to agree that equal pay for equal worth has an important effect on women's everyday lives.[11] It is less obvious that our personal actions have political grounding. The political is personal.

By turning this concept around and focusing on how the political becomes personal, it should not be assumed that the personal as political is no longer important. It is. But, as we researched and wrote this book, it became clear that political issues surround us.

Turn on the television, read the newspaper, go online—the political is everywhere, bombarding us with numerous messages about sexuality, family ideals, consumption, gender, and so on. What we choose to embrace politically is very personal. With so many important issues, how do we choose which to take on? We choose what is most personal to us—what is having an impact on us in the here and now.

My own experience as a working mother provides a clear example. I moved to Manhattan, Kansas, with my husband and five-month-old daughter in the spring of 2006. This was a huge adjustment since neither my partner nor I had ever lived away from our families, and now we only had each other for support.

One of the biggest difficulties we (along with many other parents) faced was finding affordable, quality day care in a town where infant day care is limited. We immediately got on wait lists, hoping for a slot for little Riley. Finally, a spot opened up at the university day care. We were thrilled—until we found out about all the safety hazards present in the building. We loved the teachers and the programming, but the building structure left much to be desired. I took the bull by the horns and became a member of the center's advisory board as well as the parent's organization.

In both capacities, I began advocating for the university to take the conditions at the day care center seriously. K-State families needed a new facility immediately. With several other concerned parents (mostly mothers), teachers, and administrators, I worked to raise awareness of this issue on campus and in the community. Two years after we started on this journey, success was ours. The new center should be up and running in 2011.

Figure 5.2 Coauthor Michelle Bemiller and daughter Riley and others march in the St. Patrick's Day parade, representing the K-State Center for Child Development to raise awareness for safe child care. Using the theme, "Keep the Music Alive," children played homemade instruments while marching. *(Michelle Bemiller)*

Reflecting on this experience, I see that day care as a social issue existed before I had a child and moved to Manhattan. It was out there, looming large, but I had not paid much attention to this issue because it did not affect me personally until Riley came into this world. It was then that the politics of child care rained down on me, resulting in a personal connection to this issue.

This tends to be the case for most of us. We work toward what we know and care about at the moment. We push back against structures that have a negative effect on ourselves and people we care about. I followed in the footsteps of many women before me who fought to bring attention to the issue of child care. In Australia, first-wave feminist activists were concerned with women's economic vulnerability and its effect on their material lives. In light of these concerns, feminists strove to draw attention to the need for child care facilities and free kindergarten.[12] At the end of the nineteenth century, North American feminists also focused their service and social action efforts on developing child care facilities. More recently, child care providers have started to unionize in an effort to secure increased public investment in child care and improve working conditions for providers.[13]

Such examples serve as one demonstration of how women subvert the political through everyday resistance (though not always in a straightforward path) as they push back against the confines of oppressive systems. This top-down approach—seeing the political as personal—is also useful for understanding women's participation in the party plan economy. Gendered expectations that coincide with dominant gender ideology influence women's experiences as producers, distributors, hosts, consultants, and guests at gender parties.

Remember my discussion of the Pampered Chef party that I was gearing up to host? Invitations were sent, I bought food and drinks, the consultant prepared food, and the guests mingled with one another. We all behaved like good women should, having fun (or pretending to have fun) and buying gendered products. Even though I told myself I wouldn't do it, I even cleaned my house (at least the parts my guests would see). That night, we all experienced the political as personal, without even recognizing it as such. What a lost opportunity to raise awareness.

Awareness and Resistance

Paying attention to how the political becomes personal allows for the possibility of awareness within the party plan economy and the larger gender order. Such awareness contributes to our ability to solve collective problems for women (e.g., violence against women, reproductive choice, and equal pay for equal worth).

Women often ignore or make light of their common experiences. As a result, efforts at consciousness raising are not simple. It is much easier for women to see differences between one another, but in order to be successful in their personal and public lives women must recognize how political ideologies affect personal experiences. This disregard of commonality is not an individual, calculated practice; it is instead shaped by relations of ruling (people, usually men, in positions of power in society) that women have tried to uncover and dismantle for almost a century.

In the nineteenth century during the first wave of the women's movement, for example, individual women worked to gain the attention of women as a collectivity in an effort to gain the right to vote. Early on in this movement, women came together as one voice, regardless of race or social class, to support the abolitionist and women's movements. In fact, both Elizabeth Cady Stanton and Susan B. Anthony regarded the abolitionist movement and the women's movement as inseparable.[14]

During the second wave of the women's movement in the 1960s and 1970s, women drew attention to important issues such as violence against women, inequality in pay, and reproductive rights by protesting in the streets.[15] "The personal is political" became the mantra of this movement, and one of its most important goals was passing the Equal Rights Amendment (ERA), which states: "Equality of rights under the law shall not be denied or abridged by the United States or by any state on the basis of sex." Many women during this time saw the ERA as essential for providing a constitutional foundation to protect women from gender inequality. Today, the ERA has still not been ratified.[16]

By the time the third wave of the women's movement emerged (during the early 1990s), women focused on individual expression, articulating that women should be allowed to express themselves in whatever way they choose. Women who are part of this movement have worked toward dismantling categorical thinking among women that emphasizes an "us versus them" mentality (e.g., stay at home moms versus working moms; women who wear makeup versus those who do not).[17] Purporting a more inclusive feminism, third-wave feminists work toward understanding women's activities on both a local and global scale.[18]

At each point throughout history, women have been scrutinized in terms of gender expectations. During the first wave, women were treated negatively for going outside the home, causing trouble in the streets as they protested and fought for equal rights. During the second wave, women's important successes were overshadowed by the supposedly radical methods they employed to reach their goals. Some third-wave women experience criticism for violating perceptions of appropriateness (e.g., rocking out in punk bands), whereas others are seen as following expected paths of femininity (e.g., wearing makeup, acting "girly").

I use these historical examples because it is easy to forget the individual and collective resistance that led to increased rights and freedoms for women today. If we pay close attention, we see that pockets of resistance still exist. Young women today, for example, are still resisting the age-old double standard surrounding sexuality that reveres young men with multiple sex partners as "studs" while young women with multiple sex partners are "whores."[19] Sound familiar?

Taking a page out of a script from the very popular HBO series *Sex and the City*, young women are experimenting with their sexuality more now than ever. In informal discussions with our young female students, we have heard stories surrounding dating and sexuality. These women discussed parties with sexual undertones as well as their collective viewing of pornography—but they were very clear that this pornography was only pornography that placed women in a powerful or equal position with their male partners.

Through these actions, young women weaken ideological constraints put on sexuality, leading to attitude changes that encourage women to express their wants and desires. Such resistance illustrates women's agency within an oppressive system.

Outside sexuality, beauty norms also create barriers for young women. Notions of beauty are socially constructed and historically situated. Violating the standards of one's culture leads to negative appraisals. In Western culture, beauty is generally seen through a white, middle-class, heterosexual lens.[20] Femininity is emphasized, for example, through one's body shape and one's hair. Pattie Thomas discusses fatness as a cultural struggle that most activists have not taken head on. Activists pay attention to eating disorders, and dating services provide opportunities where fat people can meet each other, demonstrating a rejection of the ideal that only certain people are beautiful. But developing a more inclusive beauty aesthetic rarely finds its way on to the agenda of activists.[21]

Encouraged by the media and the modeling industry, women are socialized to believe that in order to be seen as attractive they must conform to a particular image. They must be young, slender, and have large breasts. If a woman does not possess these characteristics, she must find a way to become this perfect woman by using surgery or Botox or other expensive treatments; some women develop eating disorders because of this social pressure.[22] Not all women, however, support such notions of beauty. Some women resist these raced and gendered notions of attractiveness by embracing a full, natural figure.[23]

Long hair also represents the ideal beauty standard for young women. One might even go as far as to say that long blonde hair represents beauty. Yet women opt for other hairstyles. Rose Weitz argues that choice of hairstyle serves as a cultural artifact that women use in an effort to assert power.[24] Some women accommodate expected beauty norms in an effort to be successful, but other women resist these standards for the same reason.

Weitz notes examples in which women use their hair to assert independence and to make political statements—both examples of resistance to subordination. Such resistance is not easy. One of my young female students stated that she knew all too well the penalty for not adhering to appearance norms. This student cut her hair very short not to resist gendered expectations but to be practical— it gets very hot during Kansas summers. After cutting her hair, my student became painfully aware of the gendered nature of hair. She felt as if everyone was staring at her new 'do. To compensate for the perception that she looked less feminine, she increased the amount of makeup she wore.

Similarly, Betsy Lucal, using her body as an object of research, discusses expectations associated with body type and appearance.[25] A larger woman with short hair, Lucal describes herself as a gender bender. Going into car dealerships and other stereotypical male spaces, Lucal demonstrates how her appearance affects the way in which she is treated. As a woman with a somewhat masculine look, Lucal is accorded privileges not provided to stereotypically feminine women. Lucal's resistance is not completely a matter of choice (she did not choose her body type but did choose her hairstyle), yet her appearance goes against feminine expectations. She discusses how this unintentional deviation from the norm affects her on a daily basis.

Other women subvert systems of oppression by severing the tie between womanhood and motherhood. Women who opt not to have children resist assumptions that every woman wants children. Women who do have children often resist dominant notions of the "good" mother. In other words, not all women participate in mothering strategies that consistently place their children's wants and needs above their own, and not all mothers see it as necessary to forever be in the physical presence of their children.

Working mothers provide one example of resistance to dominant norms of motherhood. As mothers who work outside the home, these women must navigate taking care of children and succeeding in their careers. Because they are unable to spend all their time with their children (one of the many mandates of "good" mothering), they are discussed as mothers who fall outside the dominant discourse of motherhood. This ideology of the good mother is based on the experience of white, middle-class women, yet women of other social classes and sexualities are aware of this ideology and are still, to a degree, affected by its strictures.[26]

Unconventional sexual preference also subverts systems of oppression. Lesbianism is a perfect illustration of how the political becomes personal. Lesbians counter patriarchal expectations connected with what Adrienne Rich terms compulsory heterosexuality—the demand to meet society's conventional standards for sexuality or face serious, even dangerous, sanctions. Because heterosexuality is viewed as natural and unchanging, it is privileged as normal, and other forms of sexuality are devalued.

Being in a same-sex partnership is one example of resistance to patriarchal notions of heterosexual intimate relationships. Homosexual couples who have children add another layer of resistance, often becoming double resistors. Jenny Wald, for example, views lesbian mothers as resisting institutionalized motherhood by having/raising a child outside the confines of a heterosexual relationship. Ellen Lewin, however, sees lesbian mothers as both accommodators and resistors, stating that when lesbians become mothers they accommodate gendered expectations of womanhood. At the same time, becoming a lesbian mother means overcoming the equation of homosexuality with unnaturalness. By doing so, lesbian mothers resist gendered constructs of sexuality.[27]

The Pain and Promise of Resistance

As we have already noted, this resistance to dominant ideologies is not easy. Women who go against the grain may experience indirect and direct costs. As a result, women (and men) often follow what Allan G. Johnson calls "the path of least resistance."[28] We "go along to get along," supporting and maintaining the status quo because it is comfortable.

In terms of gender, we do what is defined as appropriate as a woman or man. Using the division of household labor as an example, women cook and clean—what Arlie Hochschild defines as "upstairs work"—whereas men do "downstairs work," maintaining cars and mowing the lawn.[29] Women also maintain the status quo in the public sphere. Recent scholarship finds that by neglecting to negotiate starting salaries for their first jobs, women may sacrifice as much as half a million dollars in earnings by the end of their career.[30] Women often do not feel entitled to ask for more than they have already received, whether in pay or the division of household labor.

The above examples provide two instances of going along to get along—there are many more that demonstrate how individuals consciously and subconsciously participate in their own subordination and/or oppression (e.g., laughing at a joke targeted at women or racial minorities when we did not find it funny, agreeing to do work activities that we see as stereotypically male or female). We have all gone along to get along because resistance to these expectations is uncomfortable.

Going along to get along presents itself in a variety of forms within the party plan economy. Women who host parties may do so because gendered expectations surrounding politeness and women's obligations as friends tell them that it is the right thing to do. They may not want to host the party. They may, in fact, be dreading the event. They go along with gendered expectations. The same can be said for women who attend such parties.

At other times we subvert the system, either indirectly or directly. Within the party plan economy, this subversion may occur as women network during gatherings, resulting in the development of new friendships or business endeavors. Not long ago I read an article about two women who had met at a child's birthday party (not the kind of party that we are discussing here, but I'm simply trying to make a point about networking). One of the women was a stay-at-home mother; the other worked in a high-profile corporation. During their conversation, the stay-at-home mother's educational and professional qualifications became part of the dialogue, resulting in an interview with this company. Imagine the possibilities at home-based parties!

Pockets of resistance, when they happen, create circumstances in which change is possible (and sometimes even probable). It is not always easy, and women's strategies of resistance may not always be successful. But resistance demonstrates consciousness of oppressive circumstances. The political becomes personal.

From the Field

Leigh Fine's study of lesbians at sex toy parties offers a fascinating look at what happens when consumption and sexuality intersect. Through interviews with lesbian party attendees, Fine provides valuable information about party motivation, consumption, and strategies for navigating a heterosexist event. The women's stories point to the presence of a double bind—lesbian guests feel that they must either act as if they are heterosexual (which requires a great deal of emotion management) or disclose their sexual preference during the party (which may risk stigmatization). In either case, the political is personal as these women challenge heterosexist notions that contradict their personal experiences of sexuality.

Case Study 5.1
Sex Toy Parties, Compulsory Heterosexuality,
and "Being" in Community
Leigh E. Fine

> Silly lesbian, dicks are for (straight) chicks. —*Leigh E. Fine*

Sex toy parties, a relatively recent adaptation of in-home party market-ing, are gatherings of women in a private home where a professional saleswoman attempts to sell vibrators, creams, lotions, and other sex-re-lated products to the hostess's friends and guests.[31] Though vibrators have been sold in mail-order catalogues since the early 1990s, the sex toy party has brought vendors of dildos and other intimate products directly into homes across the country.[32] Although catering almost exclusively to women, the sex toy industry still has a fundamentally male-oriented view of women's sexuality.[33] This, of course, presents a problem not only for heterosexual consumers, but also for several consumers who do not in-clude men in some or all of their sexual activities. For example, borrow-ing from Pat Kirkham's notion of the gendered object, many sex toys resemble phalluses—objects that may not be of interest to a lesbian.[34] Heather Findlay's "lesbian dildo debates" illustrate that the sex toy in-dustry still has a charge to "demystify what women want"—particularly queer women.[35]

Before we set out to demystify what queer women might want, articu-lating a sociological and feminist theoretical framework is necessary. In her work, Dorothy Smith frames "the everyday as problematic" using the lens of gender.[36] To Smith and many other feminist scholars, the interactions and institutions women encountered in their everyday lives continued to re-inforce the mechanism of gender that held women as "less than." In essence, "the personal is political," meaning that the grand social models of privilege and oppression are reproduced at the individual level on a smaller scale, contributing to the greater social structure of oppression.[37] Smith, Carol Hanisch, and other prominent second-wave feminist scholars ques-tioned the status quo and how gender operated covertly and at its most in-sidious: in the context of everyday interactions.

As noted earlier in this chapter, Rich's model of compulsory heterosex-uality holds that society assumes everyone straight until proven gay—and enacts several rituals and governs interactions to uphold this assumption on a societal level. As a result of these forces, sexual minority women often find their voices silenced as they attempt to make sense of their experiences and oppression.

Gender itself has been defined by feminist scholars as a presentation—something one "does," and labor and power are divided accordingly along these lines.[38] However, for lesbians, performing gender is not as straightforward as it may seem. The performance may be influenced by the intersection of sexual identity and gender, as Rich points out. Using Patricia Hill Collins's notion of intersectionality, a woman's unique identities give her a unique experience and a unique perspective on the "everyday as problematic."[39] Feminism has made great strides, but the concerns of certain subgroups of women, particularly queer women, still struggle to find their way to the forefront of scholarship and political attention. To improve the conceptualization of Black women's experiences, Collins first described the concept of intersectionality as the mutual influence of two or more social identities on how one experiences the world. However, the concept is also useful in understanding how lesbians "do" gender. The difference in queer women's experience necessitates its integration into current scholarship on gender issues. The sex toy party is one such environment, where the desires and experiences of queer women and the resulting impacts of such experiences have yet to be empirically studied.

The role of sexual minority women in gender parties is almost uncharted territory. This hole in the literature demonstrates the need for a thoughtful exploration of how queer women interact with this environment, make meaning of these experiences, and reproduce the mechanism of gender. Sex toy parties are a fascinating milieu in which to investigate the role of compulsory heterosexuality for sexual minority participants. Any gender party is an environment of gendered space, but the nature of a sex toy party brings issues of sexual identity to the forefront for all participants.[40] Though some research has been done on women at gender parties, compulsory heterosexuality is again a consideration. The women in these studies are presumably straight. Where, then, are the voices of lesbians and bisexual and gender-queer women, and a critical examination of their experiences?

Many studies of party work employ a Marxist approach, examining how women use one another for commercial gain as opposed to examining the relationship-building and other experiences of women at parties.[41] In modern society, women's sexuality has enjoyed recent freedom—and recent commercialization.[42] There is still an overall ambivalence regarding women's sexuality that promotes consumption and exploration on the one hand and abstinence on the other.[43] This new burgeoning industry, although seemingly celebrating the emancipation of women's sexuality in the Western world, could also be omitting the experiences and desires of queer women.

Mirroring how the queer woman's experience has been ignored or lumped together with the experiences of all women, the few studies conducted on gender parties, not to mention sex toy parties, analyze the situation from a marketing or economic perspective. Similarly, studies on queer women and sex toys ignore the social experience of interacting with other women in the gender party environment.[44] Specifically, I am interested in how the sex toy party uses women's relationships and camaraderie at the event to reproduce Rich's model of compulsory heterosexuality. That is, to what degree does the gendered party and gendered market recreate a mechanism that perpetuates the assumption that everyone is—and should be—heterosexual? How do queer women "do" gender at these parties, and how do the participants construct meaning of their experiences? To answer these research questions, a qualitative research design was created to hear these women's experiences and investigate the existence of compulsory heterosexuality and the experience of it in the environment of the sex toy party.

Methods
Originally, direct observation of sex toy parties was planned. However, interviews were determined to be a more appropriate course of action, allowing respondents to engage in the research process at a level they felt comfortable. Additionally, as the emphasis in this study is on making meaning, interviews afforded the respondents the ability to describe how they interpreted their experiences, as well as how they defined compulsory heterosexuality in the party context.

This research project used a paradigm of feminist qualitative research with an emphasis on making meaning.[45] That concept emphasizes how research participants actively construct their own reality through experiences and worldviews. From a feminist standpoint, an investigation of compulsory heterosexuality in sex toy parties would be best unearthed through the words of the participants themselves, who could best explain their experiences at sex toy parties and how they interpreted them in a greater social context.

Participants were solicited using a preliminary online survey to gauge some basic attitudes toward sex toy parties and the potential presence of heterosexism. Requests for respondents were sent via email listservs to several higher education institutions and LGBT community organizations across the country, initially asking for lesbians interested in participating in a study of their experiences at sex toy parties. The initial survey screened respondents on the basis of their sexual identity, whether or not they had attended a sex toy party, and their desire to speak to a researcher about their experiences. Twenty-three women responded to the initial survey, with fifteen women completing at least three-fourths of the items. Of these fifteen, five women both met the screening criteria and indicated a willingness to participate in a phone interview with the researcher to discuss their experiences.

The final set of qualitative interviews was conducted with these five self-identified women. Of the women, three identified as lesbian and two as bisexual. All respondents were white. Four of the respondents had either completed or were completing postgraduate work, and the other respondent had completed a bachelor's degree. Geographically, one respondent lived in Kansas, one in Oklahoma, one in Ohio, one in New York, and one in California. All five women indicated being "out" in their normal lives, though one participant mentioned that others at the sex toy party she attended did not know she identified as a lesbian. The interviews were semistructured in nature. Though there was a list of formal questions and points for discussion to be utilized during the interview, the emphasis on making meaning in this study prompted me to follow up on points of interest brought up by the respondents that may not have been included on the original list of questions. General themes for discussion included the respondents' interest in participating in the interview, interactions with other guests, interactions with the saleswomen, perception of the products being marketed, and overall impressions of the sex toy parties, as well as specific experiences of interest to the respondents.

Results and Discussion

The perceived existence of compulsory heterosexuality was affected by others in attendance. With regard to the other women present, interviewees reported varying levels of heterosexist behavior and comments. Many of the women were out at the parties they attended, resulting in fewer heterosexist comments from the participants. Other respondents discussed the sex toy party as a very liberating environment, particularly parties where there were other queer women in attendance.

However, on the other end of the spectrum, Chris was initially not out to anyone at the sex toy party she attended:[46]

> A lot of the things that lesbians would be talking about at a sex toy party are quite different. I was a little intimidated or a little bit afraid to talk about some of the things that were being presented . . . I had a pretty good time if I didn't focus on the lesbian stuff. . . . But I did feel uncomfortable when it came to thinking about lesbian issues.

Later Chris talked about being the object of derision at the party:

> Being the token, open lesbian, . . . I got some jokes from some people. . . . I think they tried to weird me out, actually. The other girls there were

focused on what . . . their husbands or boyfriends wanted . . . and I just thought, "Oh my God." And I guess they just tried to catch me off guard. . . . To be honest, I couldn't believe I was there. It was . . . really different to sit there in a room where you're the [only] lesbian and they're talking about those sorts of things.

Chris believed that the party she attended would not have been accepting of her lesbian identity. Though she did come out to the party about halfway through the event, she mentioned how she still felt uneasy about discussing her unique sexual desires at the sex toy party. She also felt singled out because of the nature of her desires.

Kelly, too, had an interesting experience with her friends, who went to a sex toy party with her: "I think I'm a minority being gay. So, obviously, it would just be me in the room or just another one of my friends who are gay. And so when something would be passed around and someone might make a comment like, 'Oh, you don't need to use this.'" When asked how that exchange made her feel, Kelly replied: "Umm, I guess since it was my friends, it was okay, so I made some remark, like, 'I'm glad I don't have to use it' sort of thing?" Kelly felt singled out based on her sexual identity.

Based on the interviews, there are three broad classes of responses. Some women interviewed felt that the sex toy party was either liberating or did not affect their sexual identity. Chris and Kelly, though, commented on how the environment of the parties they attended made them uncomfortable because of their sexual identity. The salience of compulsory heterosexuality, in the form of behaviors and comments from other women in attendance at the parties, seemed contingent both on the sexual identity makeup of the other attendees and the outness of the women themselves. Respondents who were attending parties with other queer women—who, also, were the respondents who were more vocal about their sexual identity with others at the party—did not report hearing heterosexist comments or witnessing heterosexist behavior.

This pattern of compulsory heterosexuality left respondents such as Chris and Kelly feeling like the sex toy party environment was not welcoming. In a space with the potential to bring women together to discuss intimate matters, these women encountered subtle forces that left them questioning their role in this gendered context and their visibility as queer women. This unpleasant experience on the personal level is representative of political forces: the valuation of heterosexuality in the milieu of sex toy parties over other forms of sexuality.

Products and saleswomen typically were judged to be heterosexist, perhaps to achieve the end of selling the most products possible. Although the perceptions of heterosexism on the part of fellow participants varied, four respondents mentioned heterosexist behavior from the saleswomen, and all five respondents discussed how they believed the products were not marketed to queer women.

Kelly discussed how she didn't feel included in the saleswoman's pitches. The use of heterosexist language (i.e., "boyfriend" instead of "partner") was a cue to Kelly that heterosexism was assumed. Because of Kelly's perception that the "whole thing . . . is staged for heterosexuality," she felt uncomfortable engaging with the saleswoman.

Chris, too, felt uncomfortable with the heterosexism displayed by the saleswoman at her party. Chris acknowledged that the saleswoman made an effort to be inclusive but also realized that "she was catering to how she was going to make the most money." Chris talked further about her interaction with the saleswoman:

> I think someone else brought [up that I was a lesbian] first . . . and it was kinda put out there . . . and the woman who was putting on the party said she had done parties with a lot of lesbian women before, so she started saying things about lesbian stuff, but I didn't really feel she was overly accurate about her perceptions of lesbians, so I thought, "Maybe it's the types of lesbians that go to these parties, and I'm just different?" But she had some crazy ideas about what I would like or want. Some crazy stuff related to bisexual activity. Two different things that emulated a penis? Stuff that I thought, "Now why is that specific to lesbians?"

The saleswoman went so far as to make conjectures about her sexual preferences—a powerful demonstration of the personal being political. In the end, these conjectures were attempts, based on the saleswoman's perceptions, to promote the sales of as many products as possible.

Capitalism as a justification for heterosexism was a point brought up by another respondent. Angela, who has done training for organizations and educational institutions on sexual and gender identity issues, described the heterosexism she believes exists on an institutional level within the sex toy party industry:

> I tried to work with [this company] to help train their staff members to be more LGBT inclusive in how they'd talk about people's partners and what types of body parts they might use it with and things like that. And I talked with their staff and we worked really well together, but then they came to the conclusion that, "There weren't going to be enough queer people at these parties. Forget it." So then I even tried to plant queer people at their parties who would buy things, and it still didn't work. So it looked like one avenue where heterosexism was always going to win.

The company Angela consulted for had taken a capitalist stance on enforcing compulsory heterosexuality. She had encountered staff who, after determining that meeting the needs of queer customers would not be as profitable as catering to the majority, decided to forgo being inclusive in their sales methods. Angela saw compulsory heterosexuality affecting the highest levels within the company—and, therefore, the customers as well.

One respondent, Toni, did attend a sex toy party where she felt the saleswoman and products were inclusive of queer women. But even though the party she herself attended was inclusive, she is running into difficulty finding other saleswomen like the one she met to bring to her LGBT group on her college campus:

> Trying to schedule something with the campus now, I've looked at stuff online, and the comments are very vague as to what people actually talk about, so [I don't know] if the person identifies as queer or not or what their experiences are in working with queer people. . . . I don't want them to get here and not be able to talk to my target audience, which would primarily be the LGBT community, so that's been kind of a challenge, 'cause I haven't seen anything that's like, "I'm queer-friendly!"

Products, too, were not recognized by the respondents for their marketability to queer women. Kate thinks about what was being sold at the party: "There isn't a lot that's actually marketed toward lesbians, per se. The brochures, if they have a picture, it's probably going to be a man and a woman." Angela, too, noticed a heterosexist slant in the product marketing:

> At any party I've been to where they're selling [a particular product], they always say, "Wouldn't this be a great way to get him in the mood?" And I never understand. So I ask. And I always say, "I don't understand. Are you talking about me trying to get a man aroused, or are you talking about me leaving it around for a man to get me in the mood?" It doesn't make any sense to me.

All the women interviewed talked about their perception of the saleswomen, products, and product marketing as inherently heterosexist. With the exception of one party, few statements inclusive of queer customers were made, and those that were made were an afterthought. The women also discussed how they believed the products were designed primarily with heterosexual women in mind.

The women's perception of a capitalist motivation for preserving compulsory heterosexuality may be a valid one, in line with assertions by Debra Curtis and Martha McCaughey and Christina French concerning the commodification of women's sexuality.[47] These researchers discuss how the new sex toy industry is yet another milieu in which women can be financially exploited by one another, much like other gender parties. The respondents' experiences seem to indicate that compulsory heterosexuality may be intimately tied into this commodification, promoting the maximum consumption of goods. Because queer women make up a smaller segment of the overall population, it appears that saleswomen and companies see little financial return on adopting more inclusive sales practices. However, for the queer women who attend these parties, the personal again becomes political when lesbian and bisexual women's desires are not represented—or not represented accurately—by those in power.

Social bonding with other women about sex, regardless of the perception of compulsory heterosexuality, was important. A surprising theme emerged from the simple preliminary question, "Why were you interested in attending a sex toy party?" It was assumed that the presence of compulsory heterosexuality at sex toy parties would leave the queer women interviewed upset, angry, saddened, or frustrated by their experiences. However, throughout the interviews, the queer women gave consistent responses to this question that seemed to run opposite to this conjecture. In the words of Kate:

> It's of interest to me 'cause I really like sex toy parties. I like them because I'm pretty comfortable with my sexuality, and, therefore, an environment like that seems to free women up, and it's nice to talk about sex for once in a free environment. . . . It takes a minute to break the ice with the women, but everybody gets to pass the toys and get to talking, and, I don't know—it's just a nice social opportunity, I guess. When you go to a sex toy party, things start to become a little more intimate between people, because sex is an intimate thing, and you start talking about things that are more personal to you. So it kinda gave us more of a bond—"I feel like I'm better friends with this person."

For Kate, the sex toy party was a freeing environment where connections with other women could be made and celebrated. Although she felt there were no products marketed specifically to queer women and she noticed the relative invisibility of her lesbian identity, she discussed at length the enjoyment she derived from talking about sex with the other women in attendance.

Toni, who attended a more queer-affirming sex toy party, also talked about the importance of the environment and social connection:

> I think it was great, seeing as I was coming from an undergrad institution where I wasn't really out, so to have a community where I felt like I could be myself and I felt like I wasn't being judged for being bi, and there weren't those stereotypes of, you know, having to choose between parts of my identity. . . . Just being who I am—to talk about what I like about being with men and with women, it was wonderful. I loved the support I felt in that particular environment.

Even Chris, who discussed primarily the negative experiences she had at the party she attended, acknowledged her desire to form social bonds with other women:

> I probably would not attend another [sex toy party] unless I knew there would be other bisexual or lesbian women there. . . . The toys there were not necessarily meant for lesbian women, . . . but there was no really catering to a lesbian woman or a bisexual woman, so there's really no other reason why I would go except to hang out with my friends and see how crazy they are. [Laughs]

Chris indicated she would prefer an environment with other queer women in attendance, but she also mentioned several times the enjoyment she received by seeing how "crazy" her friends would get. Although the sexually charged environment coupled with apparent heterosexism made Chris nervous, she talked about how interesting it was for her to see women she was close to behave in such a liberated manner.

For these women, the sex toy party was an environment where issues of sexual identity had to be weighed, considered, and deliberated. Compulsory heterosexuality manifested itself in the actions and words of the saleswomen and other participants, as well as in the products being marketed. However, when asked why they wanted to attend a sex toy party in the first place, the women were all able to discuss their desire for closeness and platonic intimacy with other women.

Initially, I did not design this study to investigate the importance of the connections with other women at sex toy parties short of the influence of compulsory heterosexuality. As the study continued, though, all five respondents talked at length about the positive experiences they had connecting with other women. Undoubtedly, this was a large part of their understanding of the party.

There are some notable limitations to my study that deserve mentioning. First of all, I interviewed only five respondents. Qualitative work can be written about sample sizes of one (i.e., case studies), but it would have been preferential to obtain more respondents. Because all my respondents are white, I can say little about the impact of the intersections of race and sexual identity in this work. Along the same lines, no respondents identified as transgender or gender-queer, meaning I am unable to discuss their experiences.

Although these limitations must be mentioned, I believe my study makes an important contribution to furthering our knowledge about gender parties and lesbian/bisexual women's experiences there. Future research could build on the findings I have elaborated here and address some of these limitations and unexplored variations.

Conclusion

Originally, I set out to explore issues of compulsory heterosexuality at sex toy parties. In that respect, I made some discoveries that suggest the sex toy party is an environment where compulsory heterosexuality is replicated and enforced. Respondents indicated that the sales staff in particular made several heterosexist assumptions. No interviewees could recollect a product specifically designed for or marketed to queer women. Participants were subjected to heterosexist comments or behaviors from other women at the party as well, whether they were out to others or not. From a Marxist perspective, the mechanism of compulsory heterosexuality may be used to fuel the consumption of goods at these parties, reinforcing the heterosexist structure that does not investigate the concerns or desires of queer women. If the end goal, after all, is to market the available goods most effectively to the most people, then the minimization of lesbian desire becomes a vehicle for both economic exploitation and compulsory heterosexuality.

However, a second, important finding emerged from this study's data: all the queer women interviewed indicated they valued the sex toy party for the bonding it permitted with other women. Regardless of the level of disclosure of sexual identity or the sexual identities of the participants, all five women interviewed mentioned that their interest in attending sex toy parties stemmed from a desire to join a community of other women. Though compulsory heterosexuality manifested itself in some fashion in every participant's account, even the interviewees with more negative experiences at sex toy parties recounted the joy they derived from sharing the experience with other women. This indicates that although compulsory heterosexuality was generated and contributed to heterosexism, there may be positive social and interpersonal benefits of attending a sex toy party, even for nonheterosexual women.

The experiences of these lesbian and bisexual women at sex toy parties are a powerful illustration of the personal becoming political. Through routine exclusion by sales staff and the heterosexually oriented milieu of the party, these sexual minority women found themselves in situations that communicated to them that their forms of sexual expression were not normative. Based on their gender, however, these women found a sense of community that allowed them to be sexually expressive in an alternate manner. Although this form of sexual expression may not have allowed the integration of these women's sexual identities, all the subjects interviewed still made meaning of the sex toy party as a liberating space. This tension between sexual identity and gender identity at the gender party may be similar to the tension experienced by women of various social identities. These women may be asking themselves questions such as, "How will I manage my identity?" "What identity is at the forefront in this context?" "How are my other identities being negated?" As a sociologist, it is important to explore the consequences for women who are forced to ask such questions of themselves, as compared to those who are not.

In line with Smith's paradigm and Rich's description, the sex toy party proved to be a milieu through which the mechanism of compulsory heterosexuality—the social mandate that heterosexuality is the only appropriate expression of women's sexuality—was reinforced, creating "the everyday as problematic." The research demonstrated that participants experienced the phenomenon of compulsory heterosexuality during a sex toy party. The sex toy party seems to be a fun, rambunctious, "everyday" environment where women come together to explore sexuality. Yet there continue to be judgments as to what is "normal" embedded within this "everyday" occurrence. Nevertheless, the queer women involved were able to forge bonds of community that made their experience a memorable one. This ray of hope provides support for researchers investigating the lives of queer women while simultaneously encouraging future research into the lives of queer women and the unique performance created at sex toy parties.

Expanding upon the political as personal, Lewis draws attention to Guatemalan women's resistance of Westernized notions surrounding gender, individuality, and consumption. As participants in the fair-trade movement, the women in Lewis's study support interdependence, sustainability, and the eradication of inequalities worldwide. Fair-trade markets subvert dominant expectations connected with Western economic structures by encouraging interdependence—a deeply humanistic objective. Besides illustrating how the political becomes personal within the fair-trade movement, this case study serves to encourage critical thought related to materialism and exploitation of women worldwide.

Case Study 5.2
Challenging the Global Economy Through Home-Based Labor
Summer Lewis

> We were working with women who needed to earn a living yesterday, not six months hence. And so in three hours they needed to be trained to actually work—after three hours they should be able to make something that they could earn from.
> —*Pushpika Freitas on the founding principle*
> *of MarketPlace Handwork of India*

As part of an international volunteer team in 2004, I met a cooperative of women weavers in the Guatemalan highlands. This organized group of women—part of the informal economy—invited our team to learn about their weavings and their lives. Another team member and I decided to help find more extensive markets for the lifework of these women. Through this relationship with the Guatemalan women's cooperative and my academic work in women's studies and sociology, I developed a passion for grass-roots economic organizing and made a commitment to learn about the individuals and groups often overlooked by global capitalism.

Beyond an Imbalanced Economic System:
Alternative and Fair-Trade Networks
Our current system of global capitalism continues the historical legacy of colonization through economic means. Globalization of the economy involves "an unprecedented penetration of all regions of the globe and all areas of life by the logic and practice of capital accumulation, epitomized as 'global free trade.'"[48]

Fair trade is a response dedicated to challenging the inequalities of conventional trade and ultimately changing the global economy as we know it. According to the World Fair Trade Organization:

> Fair Trade is a trading partnership, based on dialogue, transparency and respect, which seeks greater equity in international trade. . . . Fair Trade is more than just trading: it proves that greater justice in world trade is possible. It highlights the need for change in the rules and practice of conventional trade and shows how a successful business can also put people first.[49]

In the United States, alternative trade organizations (ATOs)—businesses with the goal of helping artisans and small-scale producers from developing countries—were instrumental in starting the fair-trade movement following World War II. These organizations started as mission-driven businesses marketing cultural products in a socially responsible way.[50] Over the years, awareness of global issues relating to trade and development—poverty, child labor, trade policy, and development aid—increased interest in "alternative trade."[51] The mid-1980s saw the formation of businesses such as Equal Exchange and MarketPlace Handwork of India, as well as associations to facilitate networking among the growing number of ATOs.[52] The first fair-trade label for a product (Max Havelaar coffee) was launched in 1988 and introduced a wider group of consumers to fair-trade products. Other labeling initiatives around the world began to certify products as "fair trade," and eventually these labeling initiatives were organized under an umbrella group, the Fairtrade Labelling Organizations (FLO), to set a standard for fair-trade certification.[53] FLO takes into account current market prices and producer input in order to set a fair-trade minimum price.[54] Beyond paying a fair price, certification requires that producers and traders adhere to a number of principles, including developing long-term, transparent relationships, promoting gender equity, providing healthy working conditions, and promoting environmental sustainability.[55]

Handicrafts, Fair Trade, and Women
In developing countries, informal wage labor has served as a buffer against economic crises—downturns in which women make up the majority of casualized workers. As Swasti Mitter has observed, "Informalisation . . . occurs when women, in the absence of job opportunities in the formal sector, take up self-employment as a measure of survival."[56] This self-employment is often carried out in the home and may include "the production of handicrafts . . . propagated to poor rural and urban women in Third World countries to 'supplement' their meager incomes."[57] Many experts see craft marketing in the developing world as a way to generate income as well as effect social and cultural change. As Julian Morris puts it: "Artisans are not going to disappear in the new millennium and neither will their contributions to our daily lives and culture. The time has come to rethink their position."[58]

Both men and women participate in craft production in Third World countries; however, gender distinctions also present themselves in these artisans' activities. "Year-round, day-to-day constancy typifies the lives of women artisans. Craft production occurs around household tasks of cooking, gathering water, caring for children, and gardening."[59] Men, in contrast, are often responsible for agricultural production, which, occurring on a seasonal cycle, allows them longer periods of time to work in a centralized craft workshop. Additionally, "As artisans commercialize products for external markets, production often shifts from household to workshop venues."[60] Thus, there is the possibility for women artisans and their household production to be overlooked in a more formal craft economy not based in the home.

One way organizations have addressed this situation is by seeking out and partnering with women's home-based artisan groups worldwide. I will cover a profile of the Ixoq aj Kemool Women's Textile Cooperative in Guatemala, a group of indigenous women who weave in their homes and struggle to sell their textiles for a fair price, and the story of MarketPlace Handwork of India, an example of how women sewing and embroidering in their homes in India are collectively challenging economic and social injustice.

Encountering Those Overlooked by the Traditional Economy:
The Women Weavers of the Ixoq aj Kemool Textile Cooperative
My volunteer work in Guatemala with the indigenous women of the Ixoq aj Kemool (Women Who Weave) Textile Cooperative awakened me to the impact of US trade and foreign policy and the experiences of women outside the United States. Our team visited twenty-five cooperative members in

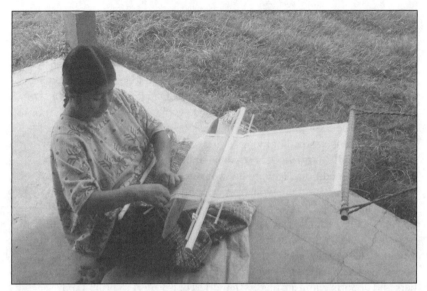

Figure 5.3 An Ixoq aj Kemool artisan weaves on a backstrap loom in Tactic, Altaverapaz, Guatemala. *(Summer Lewis)*

their homes, wrote the first socioeconomic profile of the women and their families, and created marketing materials (a brochure with photos).

Composed of twenty-eight Poqomchi' women weavers aged seventeen to sixty, the cooperative was founded in 1991 as a means of organizing casualized workers. It is managed through a general assembly; each of the twenty-eight active members possesses one vote in electing administrative positions, which are held by active members. The cooperative operates out of a small, two-room building. One room is used for meetings and training; the other displays weaving materials and textiles for sale.

The women weave on traditional backstrap looms for an average of six hours a day. Although the *huipil* (blouse) is the most traditional weaving, the Ixoq aj Kemool also produce *chalines* (shawls), *manteles* (tablecloths), and *individuales* (placemats). Although geared toward a Western market, the work incorporates traditional Mayan designs, such as *venados* (deer), *pacayas* (palm leaves), and *arcos* (arcs), with innovative patterns.

The Ixoq aj Kemool Textile Cooperative will not sell to market vendors who fail to adequately pay the weavers for their work. Therefore, over the course of its existence, the cooperative has had to sustain itself through selling weavings in boutique shops that market to tourists, even though such shops are in larger cities many miles away.

Nearly every woman in the Ixoq aj Kemool Cooperative has a family and home that she manages. While serving as an *ama de casa* (homemaker) and caring for children, collecting food, preparing meals, and doing household chores, the women find time to weave. Male partners of weavers earn, on average, 25 Guatemalan quetzales (approximately $3.11) a day, often working as day laborers for nearby landowners. Even though the Guatemalan minimum wage for agricultural workers is set at Q56 ($6.95) per day, the US Department of State writes, "Noncompliance with minimum wage provisions in the informal sector [is] widespread" and "the minimum wage [does] not provide a decent standard of living for a worker and family."[61]

Additionally, farm work is seasonal and may not be steady due to climate or crop conditions, leaving the weavers' male partners without work. Thus, the income from the women's weaving is essential for food, children's school supplies, and other expenses.

As women's studies students, a fellow volunteer team member and I were intrigued by the weavers. We decided to center our upcoming Senior Seminar class around the central concern of the Ixoq aj Kemool Cooperative: a more extensive, far-reaching market for their textiles. Co-op members and cohorts enthusiastically supported our project to bring Ixoq weavings to the United States. Through sales and presentations at local events, we were able to share the stories and textiles of Women Who Weave with women in the United States.

In an attempt to partner with the cooperative and support the weavers' search for fair prices and markets, our project aligned with the goals of the fair-trade movement. After working with the Poqomchi' women, I firmly support the idea of women's cooperatives and home-based production as a subversive act in today's capitalist world.

Women Who Needed to Earn a Living Yesterday: MarketPlace Handwork of India

MarketPlace Handwork of India was founded in 1986 by Pushpika Freitas. Pushpika's progressive parents raised their six daughters to be independent and resourceful. The combination of her upbringing and background in social work led Pushpika to the firm belief that "women were going to make the change, make the difference."

This led Pushpika and Lalita Monteiro to help form Support the Handicapped's Rehabilitation Effort (SHARE), a cooperative made up initially of three women from the Mumbai slums. In the beginning, Pushpika and Lalita told the women, "If you cannot put food on the table, you do not have a voice." Eventually, more women joined the cooperative "because the need was really there." The women did not have sewing machines in their homes, but they did know how to do basic sewing by hand. According to Pushpika, "that's how handwork and hand embroidery became such a hallmark for MarketPlace."

Additionally, in order to care for their children and manage household duties, the women needed to be able to do work at home. In response, Pushpika determined, "We really had to bridge the gap between what was needed in the marketplace and what they could do." Beautiful hand-sewn quilts, which required basic sewing skills, were the first products. "Basically we said we were working with women who needed to earn a living yesterday, not six months hence. And so in three hours they needed to be trained; after three hours they should be able to make something that they could earn from."

Sales were dismal at the first quilt exhibition in India, and Pushpika and Lalita realized they needed to move into apparel production and focus on marketing the products. On a trip to the United States in 1982, Pushpika featured apparel made by the women's cooperative at a home party. The women who attended the party identified with the Indian women producers: "There was a woman-to-woman connection there." The women attendees loved the products. "We pretty much sold everything we brought."

Although another party a year later was also successful, Pushpika realized that for the business to be sustainable, it could not depend on someone bringing two suitcases to the United States and having a home party. The seeds of MarketPlace India were sown with these two early parties, and the nonprofit was incorporated in 1986. The board consisted of four women and two men who did community organization, paperwork for incorporation as a nonprofit, and liaison work with Catholic Relief Services. As Pushpika remembers, "The board was very much a working board; they would organize home parties and do a lot of the organizing."

The path of a MarketPlace product begins as an idea at the MarketPlace office in Evanston, Illinois. Here Pushpika and colleagues manage marketing needs, determining what seasonal colors and designs to use. These decisions are communicated to SHARE in India, currently made up of 180 women in six sewing and design cooperatives in the Mumbai area. Fabric is printed and dyed by small, rural producers using indigenous techniques and is sewn into basic garments. Intricate design work is then done by representatives from the SHARE sewing cooperatives at design workshops that last two to three weeks. The embroidery and embellishment on the garments are done at this time in a collaborative way as the women discuss their ideas of how they want to do things. This partnership is about "acknowledging that both sides have something to put in to make it work."

Economic empowerment is one of the benchmarks of the work. As a member of the World Fair Trade Organization, MarketPlace is a mission-driven organization committed to upholding fair-trade principles. The artisans are collectively challenging inequalities not just in India but also globally. According to Pushpika, they are "doing social change."

We are way more than just fair wages. . . . We have a very close relationship with the groups we work with. It's really social change that is happening with them. Anybody who has been to India and has visited the MarketPlace artisans will say, "You know, you walk down the street and you can really tell the difference between the women who you see on the street, [and] the women who are part of the MarketPlace artisan groups."

Examples of this empowerment include an artisan being able to "retire" from her work with enough money to live comfortably. Additionally, in the past five years (2004–2009), no artisans' children have dropped out of high school, and there have not been any child marriages, an amazing accomplishment for a country where almost 36 percent of girls drop out of school.

In Pushpika's words, MarketPlace is unique because of the "connection between the customers here [in the United States] and the artisans in India." MarketPlace products are primarily geared to a gendered market. Consumers (mostly women) are able to purchase fairly traded textiles through a catalog, online, and at various sales and events. Consumers can go beyond purchasing items and get involved in hosting a fair-trade fashion show, a fundraiser, or a church sale or in volunteering with Market-Place. Additionally, home party kits are available. These events offer an alternative to conventional products at most home parties and encourage hosts and attendees to consider the connection between the product, the producer, and themselves.

The Personal Is Global

Many Western women and men find it hard to admit that their material quality of life comes as a direct result of the exploitation of women and men from the Third World. If a person is to admit this truth to themselves, in order to continue working toward equality for all, that person would have to drastically change her life. In M. Jacqui Alexander's words: "Our standard of living, our very survival here, is based upon raw exploitation of working-class women—White, Black, and Third World—in all parts of the world. Our hands are not clean."[62] Alexander's bold and true statement forces us all to critically examine the social, political, and economic structures we participate in everyday.

As a woman in the United States studying, working with, and promoting fair trade, I have been connected with women artisans in Guatemala, India, and countless other countries. I have heard their stories, seen their handiwork, and come to a better understanding of the different privileges we enjoy or the prejudices we face based on our sexuality, class, race/ethnicity, age, and geographic location.

In the midst of these intersecting inequalities is the home. Sometimes considered "stifling" and "confining" by Western women, the home is one of the places through which women worldwide are challenging the global economy. Pushpika Freitas illustrates the reality for the women artisans in India: "You do it in your home, you do it while you're looking after your kids . . . women should have the opportunity to work at home, to do everything else that they're responsible for and to just earn a living."

The timeless feminist slogan, "the personal is political," reminds us that the inequalities an individual woman faces are not isolated problems; rather, these issues are the result of a system of oppression that affects all women. Taking this a step further, I have found that "the personal is global." It is our responsibility to examine the privilege, power, and influence we wield in the world so we can challenge inequalities and work toward social justice. In observing our own consumer habits, in supporting the fair-trade movement and small-scale producers, and in seeking to find connection with other women and men globally, despite geographic, economic, and social distance—we can make change. No matter who or where we are, in a global society such as ours, we can be part of this movement.

Beyond the Party

The intersecting relationship between consumption, markets, and movements within the party plan economy anchored this chapter of *Women at Work*. Our immediate image of parties within the party plan is that of women having fun buying products at a home-based gathering. Such an image recognizes the presence of "fun and friendship," as well as consumption patterns, but ignores the global nature of such parties and their potential for resistance of dominant ideologies. By ignoring opportunities for resistance, we shut down the potential for social action within (and beyond) the party plan economy.

In an effort to bring women's resistance to the forefront, this chapter highlighted instances in which women resisted dominant ideological frameworks—particularly capitalism and compulsory heterosexuality—and exerted agency within the party plan economy. These individual-level examples show how the political becomes personal in women's everyday lives and within the party plan economy. The studies by Fine and Lewis underscored this message.

The political became personal for the women in Lewis's study as women's participation in fair-trade movements challenged capitalist ideology that supports competition and profit seeking by any means necessary. The fair-trade movement has really taken hold and demonstrates significant potential for ideological change surrounding the production and distribution of goods. In addition, as women embraced the opportunity to work from home, supporting themselves and their families, they took advantage of opportunities for individual empowerment. The end result may be a real challenge to capitalism as more people support the principles of interdependence and sustainability.

Individuals are beginning to see buying products through fair-trade marketplaces as win-win situations. We can still buy the products that we consume within capitalist organizations, but by supporting fair trade we help to dismantle an oppressive system that subordinates women and other minorities.

The lesbians in Fine's research resisted compulsory heterosexuality at sex toy parties, mingling with heterosexual guests and consultants. By participating in these gatherings, lesbians helped to dismantle an "us versus them" mentality that often surrounds sexuality, as homosexual, bisexual, and heterosexual women bonded, having fun, around sex. The women challenged the notion that only heterosexual women are interested in sex toys, increasing understanding of all sexualities and of systemic inequality within capitalist corporations. An unanticipated outcome of the parties was women's connection to their own sexuality and enjoyment of sex. The opportunity to express oneself as a sexual being, in the presence of like-minded women, served as a source of empowerment for party participants.

One example of empowerment could be seen as some of the lesbians in Fine's study educated party consultants and sex toy companies about the importance of being inclusive. Some might say that these women were not successful (think back to Angela's statement) since the companies ultimately determined that the queer sex toy market was too small to warrant attention. But the reality is that small attempts at change chip away at the status quo. The potential for a full-blown movement of lesbians at sex toy parties may be less obvious than the potential of the fair-trade movement, but it is present. The catalyst for the movement to take hold lies in women's ability to see beyond their differences to their commonalities, joining together to resist the confines of compulsory heterosexuality.

Part of the reason that fair-trade workers are more likely to bring about change has to do with the structure and function of fair-trade marketplaces. In order for women at sex toy parties to have similar success, a structure and collective consciousness must take form at these get-togethers. (For a more detailed examination of empowerment and collective consciousness in the party plan economy, see Figure 1.2 in Chapter 1.)

Recognizing pockets of resistance and the potential for change is essential to overcoming oppression. When these pockets of resistance are recognized, opportunities for women to come together increase, and change becomes a possibility. For example, had other lesbian and heterosexual women recognized the opportunity that Angela presented when she encouraged the sex toy company to take lesbians' wants and needs seriously, they could have joined together, forcing the company to take this issue more seriously.

Pockets of resistance provide opportunities to make change happen. Successful, enduring change requires collective action from both women and men.

Our commonalities are much more important than our differences. The next chapter of *Women at Work* explores how the party plan economy reaches beyond products, resulting in increased potential for collective action through consciousness raising.

Notes

1. United Students Against Sweatshops, "History and Formation of USAS," http://www.studentsagainstsweatshops.org (June 14, 2009).

2. John Benson, "Consumption and the Consumer Revolution," *ReFresh* 23 (Autumn 1996): 5–8.

3. The word *market* can be defined as a public gathering place where people buy and sell merchandise; see Murray N. Rothbard, "Free Market," in *The Concise Encyclopedia of Economics*, ed. David Henderson (Indianapolis, IN: Liberty Fund, Inc., 2007). The formalized nature of markets is further explained in Chapters 1 and 3.

4. *Capitalism* is a set of social relations in which production takes the form of turning money, things, and capital into capital. See Ellen Lewin, *Feminist Anthropology: A Reader* (Malden, MA: Wiley-Blackwell, 2006).

5. *Compulsory heterosexuality* assumes that women are innately attracted to men. See Adrienne Rich's critique, "Compulsory Heterosexuality and Lesbian Existence," *Signs* 5 (1980): 631–660.

6. For a recent discussion of the American dream ideology, see Isabel Sawhill and John E. Morton, "Economic Mobility: Is the American Dream Alive and Well?" Economic Mobility Project, 2007, www.economicmobility.org (June 15, 2009).

7. Chrys Ingraham, *White Weddings: Romancing Heterosexuality in Popular Culture* (New York: Routledge, 1999).

8. Judith Butler, *Gender Trouble: Feminism and the Subversion of Identity* (New York: Routledge, 1990); Chrys Ingraham, "The Heterosexual Imaginary: Feminist Sociology and Theories of Gender," in *Materialist Feminism*, ed. R. Hennessy and Chrys Ingraham (New York: Routledge, 1997), 275–290.

9. Betty Friedan, *The Feminine Mystique* (1963; reprint, New York: W. W. Norton, 2001).

10. Stephanie Coontz, *The Way We Never Were* (New York: Basic Books, 2000).

11. Katharine Viner, "The Personal Is Still Political," in *On the Move: Feminism for a New Generation,* ed. Natasha Walter (London: Virago Books, 2000).

12. Nonie Harris, "Radical Activism and Accidental Philanthropy: The Impact of First-Wave Feminist Activism on the Later Construction of Child Care Policies in Australia and the United States of America," *Women's Studies International Forum* 31 (2008): 42–52.

13. Child Care Providers Together, "National Women's Law Center Reports on Child Care and Early Education," 2007, http://ccptmn.org (February 12, 2010).

14. These women worked long and hard to support antislavery and the right of women and African Americans to vote. In the end, the Fourteenth Amendment was ratified. After its ratification, Anthony and Stanton were upset about the inclusion of the word "male" in the amendment—the first time that this word had been inserted into the Constitution. It became clear that a Fifteenth Amendment was necessary to ensure that Black men had the right to vote. Anthony and Stanton lobbied for the inclusion of women in this amendment. They were turned down. Even their Black male allies told them to step aside, that it was much more important that Black men have the right to vote than

women. As a result, these women denounced Congress for supporting Black men and ignoring women. This racism alienated many of the women who had been their allies in the movement, resulting in a schism in the crusade for women's rights. See Lynne Olson, *Freedom's Daughters: The Unsung Heroines of the Civil Rights Movement from 1830 to 1970* (New York: Scribner, 2002).

15. In 1968 women who were part of the second wave rallied outside the Miss America Pageant in one of the first public protests for women's equality. The women chanted, put on theatrical productions, and planned to burn bras and other symbols in a Freedom Trash can that demonstrate constraint on women's movements, but could not get a fire permit in time. See Chicago Women's Liberation Union, "No More Miss America!" 2005, http://www.cwluherstory.org (June 15, 2009).

16. Margaret Andersen and Dana Hysock, *Thinking About Women: Sociological Perspectives on Sex and Gender*, 8th ed. (Columbus, OH: Allyn and Bacon, 2009).

17. Leslie Haywood and Jennifer Drake, *Third Wave Agenda: Being Feminist, Doing Feminism* (Minneapolis: University of Minnesota Press, 1997); Susan Magarey, *Passions of the First Wave Feminists* (Seattle: University of Washington Press, 2002); Linda Nicholson, *The Second Wave: A Reader in Feminist Theory* (New York: Routledge, 1997).

18. R. Claire Snyder, "What Is Third Wave Feminism? A New Directions Essay," *Signs* 34, no. 1 (2008): 175–196.

19. Emily W. Kane and Mimi Schippers state that attitudes surrounding gender and sexuality are often biologically based, resulting in the assumption that men are naturally more inclined to want and/or need sexual gratification than women. As a result, women who go against assumptions of feminine passivity risk being viewed as sexually promiscuous while men are perceived as acting as proper men. See Kane and Schippers, "Men's and Women's Beliefs About Gender and Sexuality," *Gender & Society* 10, no. 5 (1996): 650–665.

20. Sharlene Nagy Hesse-Biber, *The Cult of Thinness* (New York: Oxford University Press, 2007).

21. Pattie Thomas, *Taking Up Space* (Nashville, TN: Pearlsong Press, 2005). See also Esther Rothblum and Sondra Solovay, *The Fat Studies Reader* (New York: New York University Press, 2009).

22. One example of embracing a fuller figure can be seen in research that examines Black women's body image. See C. S. W. Rand and J. M. Kaldau, "The Epidemiology of Obesity and Self-Defined Weight Problems in the General Population: Gender, Race, Age, and Social Class," *International Journal of Eating Disorders* 9, no. 3 (1990): 329–343.

23. Marisol Perez and Thomas E. Joiner, "Body Image Dissatisfaction and Disordered Eating in Black and White Women," *International Journal of Eating Disorders* 33, no. 3 (2003).

24. Rose Weitz, "Women and Their Hair: Seeking Power Through Resistance and Accommodation," *Gender & Society* 15 (2001): 667–686.

25. Betsy Lucal, "What It Means to Be Gendered Me: Life on the Boundaries of a Dichotomous Gender System," *Gender & Society* 13, no. 6 (1999): 781–797.

26. Patricia Hill Collins, "The Meaning of Motherhood in Black Culture and Black Mother/Daughter Relationships," *Sage* 4 (1987): 3–10; Anita Garey, *Weaving Work and Motherhood* (Philadelphia: Temple University Press, 1999); Angela Hattery, *Women, Work, and Family: Balancing and Weaving* (Thousand Oaks, CA: Sage, 2001); Carolyn Morrell, *Unwomanly Conduct: The Challenges of Intentional Childlessness* (New York: Routledge, 1994).

27. Ellen Lewin, "Negotiating Lesbian Motherhood: The Dialectics of Resistance

and Accommodation," in *Mothering: Ideology, Experience, and Agency*, ed. Evelyn Nanako Glenn, Grace Chang, and Linda Renney Forcey (New York: Routledge, 1994), 333–354; Jenny Wald, "Outlaw Mothers," *Hastings Women's Law Journal* 8 (1997): 169–193.

28. Allan G. Johnson, *The Gender Knot: Unraveling Our Patriarchal Legacy* (Philadelphia: Temple University Press, 1997).

29. Arlie Russell Hochschild, *The Second Shift* (New York: Avon Books, 1989).

30. Linda Babcock and Sara Laschever, *Women Don't Ask* (New York: Bantam Books, 2007).

31. Debra Curtis, "Commodities and Sexual Subjectivities: A Look at Capitalism and Its Desires," *Cultural Anthropology* 19 (2004): 95–121; Martha McCaughey and Christina French, "Women's Sex-Toy Parties: Technology, Orgasm, and Commodification," *Sexuality and Culture* 5, no. 3 (2001): 77–96.

32. Rachel P. Maines, *The Technology of Orgasm: "Hysteria," the Vibrator, and Women's Sexual Satisfaction* (Baltimore, MD: Johns Hopkins University Press, 1999).

33. Danusia Malina and Ruth A. Schmidt, "It's a Business Doing Pleasure with You: Sh! A Women's Sex Shop Case," *Marketing Intelligence and Planning* 15, no. 7 (1997): 352–360.

34. Pat Kirkham, *The Gendered Object* (Manchester, UK: Manchester University Press, 1990); Heather Findlay, "Freud's 'Fetishism' and the Lesbian Dildo Debates," *Feminist Studies* 18 (1992): 563–579.

35. Malina and Schmidt, "It's a Business," 358.

36. Dorothy Smith, *The Everyday World as Problematic* (Boston: Northeastern University Press, 1987).

37. Carol Hanisch, "The Personal Is Political," in *Notes from the Second Year: Women's Liberation: Major Writings of the Radical Feminists,* ed. Shulamith Firestone and Anne Koedt (New York: Radical Feminists, 1970), 76–78; Marilyn Frye, "Oppression," in *Politics of Reality: Essays in Feminist Theory* (Trumansburg, NY: Crossing Press, 1983), 1–16.

38. Raewyn Connell, *Gender and Power: Society, the Person, and Sexual Politics* (Palo Alto, CA: Stanford University Press, 1987); Deborah L. Tolman, "In a Different Position: Conceptualizing Female Adolescent Sexuality Within Compulsory Heterosexuality," *Rethinking Positive Adolescent Female Sexual Development: New Directions for Child and Adolescent Development* (2006): 71–89.

39. Patricia Hill Collins, *Black Feminist Thought: Knowledge, Consciousness, and the Politics of Empowerment* (Boston: Unwin Hyman, 1990).

40. Susan Vincent, "Preserving Domesticity: Reading Tupperware in Women's Changing Domestic, Social, and Economic Roles," *Canadian Journal of Sociology and Anthropology* 40, no. 2 (2003): 171–196; Catherine Egley Waggoner, "The Emancipatory Potential of Feminine Masquerade in Mary Kay Cosmetics," *Text and Performance Quarterly* 17 (1997): 256–272.

41. For example, Alison J. Clarke, *Tupperware: The Promise of Plastic in 1950s America* (Washington, DC: Smithsonian Institution Press, 1999); McCaughey and French, "Women's Sex-Toy Parties"; Rex Taylor, "Marilyn's Friends and Rita's Customers: A Study of Party-Selling as Play and Work," *Sociological Review* 26, no. 3 (1978): 573–594.

42. Feona J. Atwood, "Fashion and Passion: Marketing Sex to Women," *Sexualities* 8 (2005): 392–406; Curtis, "Commodities," 95–121.

43. Beth Montemurro, "Sex Symbols: The Bachelorette Party as a Window to Change in Women's Sexual Expression," *Sexuality and Culture* 7, no. 3 (2003): 3–29.

44. See, for example, Findlay, "Freud's 'Fetishism,'" 563–579.

45. S. D. Walters, "Sex, Text, and Context: (In) Between Feminism and Cultural Studies," in *Revisioning Gender,* ed. Myra Marx Ferree, Judith Lorber, and Beth B. Hess, 2nd ed. (Thousand Oaks, CA: Sage, 2004).

46. To protect the respondents' confidentiality, pseudonyms are used in this work.

47. Curtis, "Commodities," 95–121; McCaughey and French, "Women's Sex-Toy Parties," 77–96; Taylor, "Marilyn's Friends," 573–594.

48. Maria Mies and Veronika Bennholdt-Thomsen, *The Subsistence Perspective: Beyond the Globalised Economy* (London: Zed Books, 1999), 35.

49. World Fair Trade Organization, "What Is Fair Trade?" February 9, 2009, http://www.wfto.com (April 23, 2009).

50. Mary Ann Littrell and Marsha Ann Dickson, *Social Responsibility in the Global Market: Fair Trade of Cultural Products* (Thousand Oaks, CA: Sage, 1999), 4.

51. Marlike Kocken, "Where Did It All Begin?" World Fair Trade Organization, February 9, 2009, http://www.wfto.com (April 23, 2009).

52. Focus on Fair Trade: Scholarly Anthology Series in Fair Trade Studies, "Fair Trade Timeline," 2009, http://www.fairtradestudies.com (March 4, 2009).

53. Marlike Kocken, "Fair Trade Organizations and Fair Trade Labelling," World Fair Trade Organization, February 9, 2009, http://www.wfto.com (Path: About Fair Trade; 60 Years of Fair Trade; Fair Trade Organizations and Fair Trade Labelling) (April 23, 2009).

54. Fairtrade Labelling Organizations International, "About Fair Trade," 2006, http://www.fairtrade.net (April 23, 2009).

55. Sustainability involves the conservation and reuse of natural resources in addition to the generation of ways of living that restore ecosystems and global human relationships. See Katrina Lewis et al., "Pedagogical Innovations in Sustainable Development: Fair Trade in the Classroom," paper presented at the Leading Kansas in Sustainability Conference, Kansas State University, Manhattan, KS, January 23, 2009, http://krex.k-state.edu (April 25, 2009); Equal Exchange, "Fair Trade," 2009, http://www.equalexchange.coop (April 25, 2009).

56. Swasti Mitter, "On Organizing Women in Casualised Work: A Global Overview," in *Dignity and Daily Bread: New Forms of Economic Organizing Among Poor Women in the Third World and the First,* ed. Sheila Rowbotham and Swasti Mitter (New York: Routledge, 1994), 16.

57. Maria Mies, *Patriarchy and Accumulation on a World Scale: Women in the International Division of Labour* (London: Zed Books, 1998), 134.

58. Quoted in Littrell and Dickson, *Social Responsibility,* 41.

59. Ibid., 42.

60. Ibid.

61. US Department of State, Bureau of Democracy, Human Rights, and Labor, "Guatemala," March 8, 2006, http://www.state.gov (April 23, 2009).

62. M. Jacqui Alexander, "Remembering *This Bridge,* Remembering Ourselves: Yearning, Memory, and Desire," in *Sing, Whisper, Shout, Pray! Feminist Visions for a Just World,* ed. M. Jacqui Alexander, Lisa Albrecht, Sharon Day, and Mab Segrest (Fort Bragg, CA: EdgeWork Books, 2003), 4.

6

When the Party Reaches Beyond Products

This chapter marks a significant departure from previous chapters of this book. We turn from our focus on the importance of products and consumerism (though we review its significance) and shift to underlying messages and possibilities of gender parties.

The party plan economy still runs in the background; it skulks around, existing as scaffolding that loosely binds women together worldwide. But now we turn to the ways in which gender structures—revealed here through parties and marketplaces—reveal fault lines in the (universal) gender order. It is useful to think of these spaces, or openings, in the gender order as "structural holes," or opportunities for displacement. We argue that structural holes potentially undermine entrenched patriarchal arrangements by allowing space for women and men to consciously connect to one another. Through necessity, individuals (especially those in marginalized positions) who traverse the public and private, the pragmatic and the ideological, often discover survival mechanisms by relying on their common experiences and goals. This chapter first reviews the enticement of gender structures, specifically through gender parties and other similar meeting places, and then illustrates how groups make use of structural holes in the party plan economy to accommodate their own purposes.

First, let's take a step back and look at how ideology works through gendered products. As coauthors, we focused on our own fascination with party plan events—which we immediately dubbed gender parties—and all their accoutrements. As earthly inhabitants, subject to our own material culture, we are (as Madonna proclaimed) "material girls/women/people." Thus, the first gender element to draw our attention was products: we saw gendered products everywhere, most with gendered names and gendered colors. Think of pink razors (are they more useful than navy blue ones?) or the pink Tasers illustrated in Williams's field study in Chapter 3. Why are ties reserved for men and skirts for women? Ever notice the overwhelming pink in the girls' section of toy stores and the dark blues and browns in the boys'? (Or, why we have sex-segregated toys at all?) We drew upon our own experiences to watch gender parties and products through an analytical lens. We spotted gender everywhere.

To illustrate, we recently looked at an ad on the Mary Kay website, featuring a flawless woman, Carol, who is dubbed a "global beauty." All we need to get Carol's look, according to the ad, is Moonstone Mineral Eye Color, Dusty Lilac Mineral Eye Color, Precious Pink Mineral Eye Color, Denim Frost Mineral Eye Color, Navy Eyeliner, the NEW! Limited-Edition Mary Kay Coastal Colors Mineral Eye Color Palette (using Blue, Brown, Green), the NEW! Limited-Edition Mary Kay Coastal Colors Eyeliner Pencil in Tahitian Gold, Cherry Blossom Mineral Cheek Color, Pink Porcelain Mineral Highlighting Powder, Neutral Lip Liner (what's the point?!), and NEW! Limited-Edition Mary Kay Coastal Colors Lip Gloss in Caribbean Coral.

We assume that this list does not include the various anti-aging/moisturizing cleansers, night creams, day creams, and sun care products we also need; nor the concealers, foundations, and powders we need; nor the collection of brushes, applicators, and facial highlighting pens necessary to achieve Carol's look. If I (Sue) am still delusional enough to believe that I, a worn, overweight, aged, wrinkled grandmother, can achieve Carol's look, I can always buy the "trend wave" collection, which was "inspired by ethereal layers of sky, a sparkling ocean and a silky beach," together with the mineral powder foundation and brush set. Upon completing these purchases, which total upward of $400, we are promised a FREE makeup bag. (I think Target has the same one for $3.99.) Moreover, we can make "HIM" feel loved with a MK High Intensity gift set, and if we want to "really score points with him," we can add Domain Cologne Spray to his gift set. Apparently this consumption strategy works so well that we are immediately taken to a webpage that demonstrates the NEW Bridal Feature! (we assume HE has proposed in the meantime), where one can "choose your new makeup artist looks, hairstyles, veils, jewelry and more!"

The point is this: products are gendered through an elaborate ideological packaging scheme. The product is actually not the pink razor, it is the *idea* that women need and must have it. In the United States, the target audience for the ideological scheme is a white, middle- to upper-class heterosexual world of pretty people.

So, we can see how gendered products carry messages. But the combination of products and marketing is only half the story—the structural, or prearranged, element of the equation; interaction is also necessary. The good people at Mary Kay are busily selling a gendered lifestyle, though individuals fail to recognize their own involvement in perpetuating gendered structures. Meanwhile, the rest of us shore up "the system" through parties, consumption, and interactions. The interactions can take many forms within the party plan economy, as we have seen in field studies of women workers from Brazil to Guatemala to the Czech Republic. Keep in mind that this chapter addresses how the party plan economy provides a loosely defined network that carries along gendered interactions throughout "the system."

"The system" refers to the interface between capitalism and patriarchy, a roughly coordinated arrangement that, although rooted in history and structure, is sustained through practice. It is individuals who practice gender through interaction, and they do so within the constraints of gender relations (which depends, as you will recall, on a structure of power). Gender as a system of power guides interactions, while interactions reinforce system boundaries. Although most people do not know exactly how to talk about gender power, Raewyn Connell points out that there is a "sense of something that people fetch up against."[1] Once aware, most people can feel those constraints.

It is this "fetching up" that snags women (and men in somewhat different ways) into double binds. If we don't use the cosmetic products described above, we have no hope of "getting Carol's look." Even though I know, rationally, that I can never achieve Carol's look, nevertheless, as a good woman/citizen, I must try. Otherwise, I deny my womanliness and risk alienating my friends, coworkers, family, and Mr. or Ms. Right. If I emulate Carol's look, however, I risk criticism from my womanist/feminist colleagues who may view me as a sellout, my students in Sociology of Women who may perceive that I am considerably less than a strong role model, and friends my age who may see me as trying to one-up them. Such double binds mark the contradictions of a very unnatural (not biological) system, one that employs sex categories and consumer-based trends to exploit women as a group.

Nevertheless, a social system is never perfect. Exceptions occur, power occasionally is disrupted, and shifts occur. The capitalist-patriarchal system survives. It remains incredibly resilient over time, but it does not go unchallenged or unchanged. This chapter first explicates the concept of structural holes, identifying fault lines in the system, and then explores how such niches reveal potential for a global women's movement. We demonstrate how the party plan economy, shaped and reshaped by women's marketplaces of interaction, reaches far beyond mere products. Now we see how gender parties need not be about products at all. They are about friendship and feelings, spirit and strategy; they embrace risk, rewards, and activism.

Four case studies illustrate the distinctions between and commonalities among various forms of gender parties, even those set in quite dissimilar situations. Underlying each, deep within the party plan economy, is the potential for lifting us beyond the material aspect of parties and products.

The Promise of Parties, the Gender of Markets

In my dissertation days at the University of Connecticut, I talked to, observed, and wrote about teenage girls in two very different communities. The girls engaged in a tentative process I called "trying on gender."[2] I drew the analogy of little girls trying on their moms' shoes—red shoes, blue shoes, sparkly shoes, dotted shoes, and brown boots—experimenting with gender within the confines of the world offered them. As more and more options unfolded, their world stretched.

The notion is that gender is action-based, ongoing, never complete; doing gender is never done. Gendering is a local experiment; individuals slot into and sometimes defy conventions around them. Spotlighting the local milieu in the Connecticut study required that I examine the resident gender regime in terms of norms, cultures, and opportunities. What I found was shocking. In two communities, twenty minutes apart, girls tried on gender in significantly different ways. Some standards crossed over: the girls mostly complied with larger gender order demands such as paying homage to appearance, cultivating relationships, and testing sexual boundaries. But the ways in which they experimented with gender depended on local expectations and prospects. Most significant, the extent of their trying on and resisting gender standards depended on what I called "structural holes"—cracks in the gender system that allow a peek at possibilities for change.

The aim of this chapter, indeed the ambition of this book, is to expose the everyday working mechanisms of a gender order, as revealed in the party plan economy. Two concepts in this section—trying on gender and structural holes—provide tools for grasping how the party plan economy works, in turn giving rise to the potential for change. First is a brief synopsis of how gender parties present the prospect, at least, of structural holes in the gender order. Next, this chapter utilizes a particular event, Michelle's party, as a metaphorical device for analyzing "the secret seduction," illustrating the concept of trying on gender. Awareness of the seduction process gives rise to consciousness raising, the first step in producing gender consciousness and wholesale change. Three other subsections outline a pathway toward gender change: Tools of Recognition, Partying with a Purpose, and Marketplaces of Meaning. The chapter concludes with the section, Beyond the Party, highlighting the promise of alternative forms of gender parties and the potential for raising group consciousness. From Indian women's kitty parties to Black women's book clubs to drag queen gatherings, we review the promise of gender parties.

Gender Parties and Structural Holes

First of all, gender parties offer wiggle room. Just as Brownie Wise recognized, gender parties enable us to take advantage of structural holes. Set within the party plan economy (which is designed to escape the constraints of a fully regulated market), gender parties are positioned to accommodate unconventional gender "tryings-on." Sometimes trying-on, as a practice, plays into gender traditions (like trying to achieve "Carol's look"). But it also pushes boundaries and moves walls, as illustrated in Leigh Fine's passion party study in Chapter 5 (in which lesbians repurposed heterosexist passion parties) and Adryanna Siqueira's work on street market strategies in Chapter 3 (in which women utilized street booths for networking and stepping stones). These local conditions represent structural holes, opportunities to loosen constraints on gender conventions.

Second, gender parties fly under the radar. It is likely that you, as a reader, now recall (only a short time ago) when you never considered the concept of gender parties, much less recognized these events as promoting a universal gender order. Various field studies illustrate the invisibility and undervaluing of work that takes place under the party guise. Who knew that purse parties could make or break a friendship, shore up or negate social status, or land the sellers in jail, all the while contributing to a very large underground economy? But structural holes often hide in just such discreetness, while no one watches.

Third, gender parties offer promise. Thus far, *Women at Work* has brought an awareness of the pitfalls (investing in a long-shot scheme), pain (sacrificing a sense of self), and exploitation (playing upon women's relationships) linked to the party plan economy. But gender parties also give rise to the hope of change. Marketplaces of interaction, forged by women at the local level, incorporate the trying-on nature of gendering, often reshaping thin slices, at least, of the party plan economy. Gender parties can bring women together (as in Michelle Bemiller's telling study of women helping women in Chapter 4), and gender markets allow creative bridging between public and private lives (demonstrated beautifully by Karen Kapusta-Pofahl et al. in Chapter 4) and personal and political issues (as poignantly told by Summer Lewis in Chapter 5). These locally gendered stations bring structural space. Becoming aware and taking advantage of such structural holes can be extremely constructive. This chapter now turns to strategies for optimizing those prospects.

The Secret Seduction

I recently attended a Pampered Chef party, which turned out to write this section for me. Perhaps I went because I was seduced, but at the time it seemed that I went out of friendship. In fact, it was the party hosted by none other than my colleague and coauthor, Michelle.

Michelle decided to give a party just days before the first manuscript deadline, chirping to me, "Oh, it'll be fun!" I stared at her in rapt disbelief. Here we were, furiously writing away about the exploitative, costly (in so many ways) character of gender parties, ramming right up against the brick wall of manuscript deadline, and she was giving a party. Again, a stare-down. "Oh, well, you have to eat sometime, and you don't have to buy anything . . . just come by," she said. Lunacy, I thought.

But, as you must already know, I went. Because that's what friends do, I told Michelle.

In this brief scenario, we glimpse the secret seduction of gender parties. But first, a brief foray into another story illustrates the strength of seduction. Anne Kingston, in *The Meaning of Wife,* opens with an elaborate description of herself as a young professional, watching the wedding rituals of Lady Diana Spencer and Prince Charles.[3] Kingston, about the same age as Diana, was like many women of her generation. She was the consummate young professional woman: educated, well-trained, and independent, who, practically speaking, saw marriage as an option, not a mandate. Yet, she confessed, she carried a dark, secret obsession with the *idea* of Princess Diana.

Kingston saw herself as far removed from the world of Princess Diana, and she consciously resisted that transparent lifestyle that seems designed for outward show. "Even so," she proclaimed, "fairy tales, even manufactured ones, can exert a narcotic effect."[4] Kingston identified with the idea of Diana. Kingston was trying on a particular vision of gender, if only in her head.

In much the same way, all of us at Michelle's house that evening (myself included) participated in the seduction ceremony of gender parties. Because the writing of this book was so fresh, I could not ignore the story unfolding before me. Note the various actors and the roles they play, for they will be instructive as we analyze this party.

Michelle played the perfect contemporary host, with a house in the suburbs. She scurried about, making sure everyone understood that she did *not* spend hours cleaning or cooking or removing toys from the living room. She did, however, keep wine glasses filled and confided to me later that she worried no one would come and that the consultant would be "upset" for having driven a long distance for naught. She even concocted an elaborate scheme to save face and counter negative fallout.

A page taken more from *The Princess Bride* rather than from Diana, Princess of Wales, Michelle and her husband Griffin nevertheless tried on gender; they portrayed the ideal of a modern-day couple.[5] Griffin, the only male in the house, played the supporting role, performing small cleanups and watching the children. Michelle kept referring to the fact that "he" does virtually all the cooking, and that were it not for the simplicity and saving grace of Pampered Chef, she would not be able to produce food at all. The idea of gender equality and women's liberation loomed large in the background, like a neon sign: *Trying on gender, updated version*, I thought.

As the party consultant, Jackie, cheerfully bounced around the kitchen (now cluttered with 100-plus gadgets), the "fun and friendship" Michelle promised manifested before our eyes. About a dozen women politely posed questions and then moved to animated chattering, some even bursting into laughter. Some offered their assessment of various Pampered Chef products (usually at prompts by Jackie), while others recommended recipes or helpful kitchen hints. *Emphasized femininity everywhere.*

I felt I was watching from my observation tower. (Well-meaning, Michelle even told me she had reserved the recliner as my "throne." This added to my sense of being the watcher, but also to my own insecurities as one of the oldest women at the party.) From my observation eyes, the gathering turned into more than a party. From my vantage point, Michelle's kitchen was converted into a gender party stage; everyone played her own respective part, which seemed to correspond with individualized, serviceable roles.

For example, Sarah, a university administrator (who as a person and as a role player is valued for making connections), ensured that everyone was included in the conversation while whispering to me the latest news about university business. Jill, the realtor, relayed to everyone (with a huge smile) the upbeat factors of home purchases in a down market. Meanwhile, Michelle pointed out to me that Mary gets large external research grants (always a plus in our business). Cheryl, sitting next to Mary, perhaps was intrigued by the same tidbit, as she engaged in an intense one-on-one exchange. All around me, it seemed the party turned into rather self-serving (though unconsciously so) swaps.

Other exchanges were only slightly less obvious. Pat exclaimed a few times how great it was to get away from the kids for a couple of hours, while Darla, the day care provider, nodded with deep empathy. Sarah asked someone, anyone, to demonstrate how the can opener worked. Marla, who apparently had been to hundreds of Pampered Chef parties, was only too glad to demonstrate her skill; Marla also won every game we played and assisted Michelle with every host duty. Not to be diverted, Jill's mom, Annie, busily filled out her order form, overexplaining that this is how she shops for gifts.

The point is this: we all played our parts, but the real gender story runs like a sharp undercurrent. Gender is not the role. Gender is much more endemic. Gender sucks you in like quicksand.[6]

Every single one of us—all educated, professional, relatively sophisticated, and strong women—cooperated, seemingly willing to buy the *idea* of a lifestyle that aligns with the "little woman." She is an individual who finds value in an image (not our real selves); who finds fulfillment through urbane, overpriced spatulas and knives that we'll seldom (if ever) use; who gathers recipes we'll never construct; who imagines dinner parties we'll never throw.

Me too. I bought a pastry sheet, pastry cutter, pastry roller, and pans for pies I'll never bake. I already own what it takes to bake pies (good old glass pans and a wooden roller). But I spent $100 on stuff. And I imagined in my daydream that people raved over my coconut cream pie, as if that's what matters. In a surreal turn of events, I became a true participant-observer to the party plan economy underbelly, as it worked its spell. I had taken part in just such rituals many,

many times in my life, playing virtually every role there: the host, the consultant, the obligated friend, the opportunist, the consumer, the gift giver, the supporter, the pretender. Playing up to and within these roles reinforces gender, leaving the gender power structure untouched. But this time, I wore new eyes. I became conscious, even if only for a little while.

I first used the concept of trying on gender in Connecticut as a phenomenon that best describes earlier stages of gendering in girls' and young women's lives. Michelle's party underscores the fact that as adults (both women and men), we still try on gender but become more and more comfortable in our gender shoes, so to speak. That is, we slip into gendered conventions, most often without consciously understanding (1) how embedded we become in the superficial roles we play; and (2) the potential to redirect and reshape deeper gendering processes that tend to keep us vulnerable.

Once individuals become gender-conscious and resist gendered seductions such as those just illustrated, possibilities for gender change pop up like the meringue on my coconut cream pie.

Tools of Recognition

As just demonstrated, consciousness raising is crucial to true recognition. In Chapter 4, Bemiller wrote of misrecognition and the pitfalls it brings to the gender party trap. Unless women acknowledge the deep gendering connected to the party plan economy, there is little hope for redirection. Bringing women together is the first step to true recognition and true consciousness, the ideological elements of the equation. This brief section identifies pragmatic tools of recognition. Three examples are event networks, exchange episodes, and relational contracting.

Event networks. Laurids Hedaa and Jan-Åke Törnroos define events as "temporally specific outcomes of performed acts by the actors," focusing on the relationships formed around such events.[7] "Event networks may appear as streams of interconnected events."[8] The event is the building block for gender parties; several terms in event-based discourse delineate the characteristics of the structure and those who participate.

Network exchange, for example, refers to the idea that bringing together a heterogeneous group of people extends everyone's network resources. At Michelle's party, I knew some of the attendees very well, others I had met briefly, and some I had never met and never would have, if not for the Pampered Chef party. Stations ranged from student to professional to retiree, and ages ranged from eighteen to around seventy-five. From our research, parties typically constitute a fairly heterogeneous group with regard to age and social roles. Once we were all in one room, the potential for network expansion grew rapidly.

Exchange episodes. The concept of exchange episodes emphasizes an important feature of gender party arrangements, the two-way transaction. Each transaction may be over in a flash or longer lasting, but all occurrences wax, wane, and change; none remains the same. Further, as with all social relations, a web of linkage fast becomes complex and intertwined.

Exchange episodes focus on how human relationships are variable and sometimes unpredictable, yet they also have scope and permanence—reminiscent of the concept of cathexis. As Hedaa and Törnroos point out, "Relationships have life courses." In particular, these authors focus on the temporal influence. "The role of time in order to establish, enhance, strengthen and develop relationships is . . . crucial."[9] Certainly, time creates a diversity of opportunities for networking, leading to network evolution and the idea that mutual adaptation among individuals and relationships is necessary for survival. Gender party women, in whatever situations, play to the strength of relationships while also facing challenges and human frailties of competition and outside influences. Recognizing and studying this confluence of cathexis-type features adds value to network exchanges, whether pragmatic, social, or emotional.

Relational contracting. Relational contracting presents a useful way to conceptualize the give-and-take, and sometimes the mutual benefit, that exemplifies women's social and business networks. Malcolm Gladwell, in *The Tipping Point,* identifies three categories of people who serve specific roles in exchange episodes; he calls them connectors, market mavens, and salesmen.[10] According to Gladwell, connectors are people with a "special gift for bringing the world together." It's not hard to imagine how important connectors are to gender parties and the party plan economy. At Michelle's party, Michelle was an obvious connector, but so was Sarah.

Another category is *market mavens,* who are knowledge gurus. You know the kind—they add bits of information to every topic of conversation that comes up, and they almost always win at trivia games. From the party scene described above, it should be perfectly clear that Marla was the market maven at Michelle's party. Mavens are the information specialists, gathering bits of data like relentless street sweepers at Disney World.[11] It's not just the number of people whom connectors know that matters, but the kinds of people they know. And we need access to mavens.

Aside from the fact that Gladwell uses the outdated misnomer of sales*men* (for shame!), the idea has instant appeal for thinking about the importance of persuaders in the gender party market. Whereas market mavens are data gurus and connectors are social glue, *persuaders* (let's bypass the outdated term *salesmen*) are the real people-people. Persuaders are eternal optimists, love what they do, and are workaholics—they never give up. Jackie holds the title of persuader at Michelle's party; she just never gave up, continually dancing around the kitchen with yet another spectacular product.

Although the overuse of categories should be discouraged (it misses the mark of great variety among humans), these three ideal types characterize the various roles that women play in the party plan economy. The larger point is this: each of the tools of recognition presents an opportunity to see a break in the gender system. Each of us, armed with awareness and knowledge, can redirect the party plan economy.

Partying with a Purpose

Following the line of logic in this chapter, becoming aware of the seductiveness of gender parties (and the larger gender order) marks the launch of empowerment, followed, ideally, by learning tools of recognition. Once these ideological and practical devices are in place, groups of individuals may actively engage in collective accomplishment. That is, they can party with a purpose.

The field studies presented in this book hint at partying with a purpose. Consider again Figure 1.2 in Chapter 1. Units in the party plan economy are depicted as engendering different kinds and levels of empowerment. Note that the example of a "consciousness-raising partier," as an ideal type, scores zero on economic empowerment (though there can be exceptions) but very high on both individual gender empowerment and collective gender empowerment. Again, as an ideal type, this designation represents the pinnacle of what we believe is possible for women.

Specific examples are instructive. Despite its undertones of gender exploitation, Bemiller's "Women Helping Women" (Case Study 4.1) undeniably displays a tension between exploitation and fun through fellowship, which in turn gives ample opportunity for consciousness raising. The sex toy party described by Fine (Case Study 5.1) undoubtedly brought together like-minded women who recognized their common challenges, whereas Lewis's work (Case Study 5.2) considered a particular pushback against mainstream capitalistic ventures. All these studies direct us toward this chapter and its message: structural holes within the party plan economy deliver space for partying with a purpose, one that reaches far beyond economic goals.

Thus far, the focus has been on recognizing preexisting fissures in the system. Moving beyond these existing structural holes, the concept of trying on gender demonstrates that human collectives can actively inject additional space into the gender order. At the interactional level, it becomes easier to see potential for human intervention. Structures are hard, stable, and enduring; human agency gives rise to movement. Stemming from the relationship of individuals to social institutions (such as religion, family, education, consumerism), it is possible to now see time and space as fluid and ongoing processes, as existing in the past, present, and future. It is this "future-loadedness" that gives hope for collective empowerment.[12] It is the trying-on of gender that centers efforts on transforming the existing gender order.

As Connell reminds us, these tryings-on (agency) take place at the local level.[13] A few examples, both historical and contemporary, illustrate how parties can incorporate more than simple material goods.

As Sue Zschoche documents in Case Study 2.1, women have always come together for pragmatic and ideological reasons, even when they fall short of both. My grandmother and her generation met in private homes and church parlors, the only public spaces available to them. Historically, women have met in quilting parties, which were arranged partly for craft and partly as a feminine space in which women could share social experiences and practical information.[14] As documented earlier in this book, home parties organized around consumption and products did not enter the landscape until the era of burgeoning capitalist ideals following World War II.

The classic example of partying with a purpose, however, rests with the second-wave women's movement. Coming on the heels of gender-based legislation and the publication of Betty Friedan's *The Feminine Mystique*, a nationwide social movement was organized and perpetuated through small gatherings in women's homes, referred to as consciousness-raising parties.[15] The aim was to encourage women to recognize their commonalties as women and to engage in political activity, ultimately changing the gender culture of society. An excerpt from a 1972 publication of the Cape Cod Women's Liberation organization explains:

> A women's group ideally supports rather than negates a woman's identity. By sharing feelings and experiences, we find what we have in common and feel less weak and less alone. However, the aim of coming together is not to adjust each other to the way things are. We don't believe that we have trouble being "good women" or "fulfilled women" because we're neurotic. We believe there's something wrong with those roles we're supposed to spend our lives acting out. A feminist believes that it isn't the case that we're too stupid or too inept to live up to our programming, but that the programming is destructive.[16]

The overarching success of the second wave of women's liberation in the United States is attributed in large part to these small consciousness-raising parties, in which women gathered for the sole purpose of sharing their gendered experiences *as women,* encouraging a sense of collective identity. Many believe that third-wave feminism has focused only on individual empowerment and an expanding definition of femininity, but it is so much more.[17] In fact, consciousness raising as a strategy[18] may be experiencing a renewal, as evidenced by a 2008 article published on the Feminist Law Professors blog.[19] Citing "cake parties," young female law students talk about their sexuality, careers, politics, and other women-based issues openly, advocating that consciousness raising is "an atrophied feminist method that we should reinvigorate."[20]

Another contemporary example of partying with a purpose is Taser parties. Recall that Kimber Williams, at the end of the "Power of the Purse" (Case Study 3.1), describes parties she discovered in Arizona in which young women pick out their favorite color in Taser C2s, a stun-gun-type defense mechanism designed especially for women. Though some states ban personal ownership of Tasers, the T-parties are spreading to states outside Arizona, with women sometimes crossing state lines to purchase theirs. Though Taser parties revolve around a product, their ideological and emotional basis is fairly obvious. The parties resonate with many young professional women who are concerned with their personal safety; Taser parties become an outlet to protect and empower themselves.

Marketplaces of Meaning

This book began on the foundation laid by Dorothy Smith in *The Everyday as Problematic*, claiming that scholarship by and for women must be conducted from the standpoint of women's everyday lives. *Women at Work* provides just such a focal point. Further, feminist epistemology demands that women, all women, must be included as knowers. Third-wave feminists brought an added awareness of intersectionality and a larger net of knowers, focusing on the richness of experiences within a global community of women. With each wave of movement, the circle of inclusivity widens.

Marketplaces of meaning, as a concept, frames a set of ideas for which we have no words of precision. Marketplaces of meaning widens the gender party net.

Extending marketplaces of interaction. As Chapter 1 of this book claims, marketplaces of interaction refers to the organization of relations. In particular, we have focused on friendship ties, economic transactions, reciprocity and obligation, and various roles that actors take on (such as connectors, mavens, persuaders, and so forth). Marketplaces also encompass a space, physical, digital, or even emotional, within which to conceive a set of loosely organized rules and regulations.

As we near the end of this work, *marketplaces* must now handle multiple meanings and interpretations and also resolve the changing, ongoing character of gendered processes. Trying on gender attempts to address that idea. In other words, the *idea* of marketplaces now encompasses a model in which actors (whether individuals or groups or organizations) are interconnected (however tightly or loosely) to construct meaning. The construction of these meanings is embedded within the process of interaction. Gender parties, as a concept, has served this function well. However, marketplaces must take us further.

Marketplace as medium. Martin Grieger's review of electronic marketplaces offers language that is useful for thinking of the architecture of marketplaces.[21]

Obviously, interactions are of utmost importance in the party plan economy, but it becomes more difficult to think about the form that guides interaction. Marketplaces constitute an institutional medium that (1) assigns roles to various "players"; (2) facilitates exchanges of goods, information, and other resources; (3) defines the protocols and processes that rule exchanges; and (4) even creates a common language. Thus, marketplaces, as related to the party plan economy, become a medium for consciousness raising among women from all parts of the globe while also providing the language and tools for spurring meaning into action.

Grieger also refers to the distinction between marketplaces and market-spaces. He defines a marketplace as the physical meeting ground for products and resources, whereas "marketspaces" refers to a virtual world where information is the point of exchange. At Michelle's party, for example, several attendees asked about a website, wondering if they could buy something later without actually picking up a phone. I laughed to (and at) myself, because I had thought the same thing. The digital world may reduce certain kinds of interactions, but it expands others. The virtual exchange of ideas and information remains an ever-growing segment of our marketplaces.

Global marketplaces of meaning. Connell contends that global theories, paradoxically, are overly narrow; she refers to the dominant form as Northern theory. Northern theory, Connell suggests, is also standpoint theory, one that is limiting, not all-inclusive. Dominated by an economic twist and a bias toward so-called industrialized societies, much of Northern theory has seen globalization as an ever-enveloping process. Instead, an inclusive global theory must recognize the stops, starts, contradictions, and conflicts within and between its margins.[22]

Although a comprehensive treatment of globalization is beyond the scope of this discussion, marketplaces of meaning incorporate just such a possibility. That is, we acknowledge that gender parties and gender markets are incomplete metaphors for a much more complex and layered social world. This book represents a modest start by scrutinizing the party plan economy for underlying global gender linkages.

Women in Informal Employment: Globalizing and Organizing (WIEGO), for example, assists women's movements across the globe. One of their publications, by Renana Jhabvala and Jane Tate, reports on a study by the Self-Employed Women's Association (SEWA), "Out of the Shadows." This pivotal 1996 study records examples of women's home-based work and exposes exploitative conditions, underscoring the point that work for many informal workers is more than a "party."[23] Another example is the Revolutionary Association of the Women of Afghanistan (RAWA), now supporting millions of women around the world.[24] Meena (many people in Afghanistan go by one name) started the organization in her home with just a few women. Gradually expanding in size, RAWA fought for gender equality in Afghan laws, continuing with a multitude of projects to assist women and their families, even after Meena's murder. A third example, the Deccan Development Society, is an organization of women volunteers who assist the poorest women in India, creating a better living environment by educating them and helping them regain land rights. One of their primary projects is a marketplace for women to sell their goods and support their families.

A New Party Line

In stark contrast to marketplaces of meaning, with its deeply political and humanitarian issues, lies a late-modern thread running through the world of gender parties: fun. Part of the focus on fun is generational. Generation X and the Millennials (or Y-Gens), defined largely by MTV, digital entertainment, and gaming, place a premium on amusement. Cultural theories suggest that Xers and Y-Gens may participate in fun and entertainment as a kind of subcultural resistance to their parents' commitment to work and hyper-economic accomplishment.[25]

In our work with gender parties, we noted a high premium on fun. In particular, young women valued fun above products, food, or prizes. College-age women reported that the promise of fun and alcohol assured good attendance. When I questioned Michelle about her motivation for holding the Pampered Chef party, she said, "I just always wanted my house to be where people came to have fun." Over and over, I heard the exclamation about fun.

Certainly, there is nothing wrong with having fun. A subculture of resistance has emerged called "fun feminism," including "sassy sexy young urban consumers of femininity," supposedly embodied by *Sex and the City*'s character Carrie Bradshaw.[26] Other women push back, claiming that a focus on such superficial issues detracts from the seriousness of gender inequality. Often, women who identify as feminists are touted as un-fun, as serious to a fault, and unable to appreciate humor. The problem arises when the *idea* of fun (not fun itself) masks what some call the politics of fun.[27] The politics of fun plays upon the allure of gender parties, feeding the fallacy that women's value lies in being the "good wife," the "good host," and the pleaser of all people.

It is our hope that this book brings about a woman-centered consciousness that resolves competing notions of our party lives and our true selves—a new party line that is collective, inclusive.

The perfect storm. Several contemporary factors line up to suggest the gathering of a perfect storm for change—politically, economically, socially. A gathering storm need not be interpreted as doom and gloom. Indeed, some claim that change mounts only through conflict and that the collection of issues constituting the current milieu in the United States is spectacular. The times are reminiscent of the unrest of the 1960s and 1970s in the United States, when pockets of grassroots organizations prepared for opportunities for change. Those of us interested in changing the gender power structure should take note. Just as the Black church structure provided scaffolding for the advancement of the civil rights movement, the party plan economy sits waiting for a gender revolution.

A revolution requires dissent, and recent years have seen plenty. Denial of global climate change has only fueled an environmentalist backlash. The housing bubble and financial crisis on Wall Street instigated a major economic recession. Political dissent has fomented thanks to the "War on Terror," bailouts of Wall Street, and the failure of government to respond to Gulf Coast hurricanes and the environmental ravages of oil spills. Change has come as Nancy Pelosi became the first woman speaker of the House and Hilary Clinton became the first woman to run for president on a major ticket.[28] Clinton lost the nomination to Barack Obama, who became the country's first African American president.

Despite notable advances made by a few women, the United States lags embarrassingly behind other countries in terms of women's rights. Today women still account for only 2 percent of top corporate officers[29] and 17 percent of Congress,[30] and they outnumber men by seven-to-one as single parents.[31] Overall, women earn about 77 percent of what equally qualified men earn.[32] In the 2008 Global Gender Gap Report by the World Economic Forum, the United States placed only twenty-seventh. In the meantime, hate crimes are on the rise, and many define the term to include gender crimes.[33] All these factors—political, social, economic, cultural, religious, military, sexual— provide overwhelming evidence that the perfect storm looms large, and gender issues are squarely in its path.

Fourth-wave challenges. We may be at the emergence of a fourth wave of feminism that is even more inclusive than the last. Evidence emerges in our classrooms and boardrooms, as young women and men work to resolve tensions and contradictions between their personal and professional lives. We see it in the political world as women edge into positions of power and as men campaign for equal rights legislation. We see it as young people turned out in record numbers to vote in 2008 and became invested in global issues.

Evidence gathers that gender movements will include men this time around. There is greater awareness that some men are also disadvantaged by the gender power structure, and studies of masculinities are on the rise.[34] Just as women's public and economic activities are eclipsed, men's access to private realms and intimacy is curtailed. Further, the public/private divide is not equally salient to all classes of women and men. Homeless women and men alike, for example, must contend with a lack of private space. And although violence against women has not subsided, marginalized men are also vulnerable to violence when they fail to exhibit the normative, hegemonic version of masculinity.

There is also evidence of gender blurring. Barrie Thorne, in *Gender Play*, pointed out that even in the face of heightened gender inequality among children, some situations were identified (and thus could be potentially manipulated) to hold gender less salient.[35] New generations of professional women seem less concerned with the "missing feminist revolution" and more concerned with practical issues of getting fair pay and promotions, of equal labor in the home, and an increasing awareness of a global gender gap.[36] Younger generations of women are increasingly willing, even insistent, that men join the quest for gender equality. Crawford, in blogging to young lawyers, asserts, "Today's consciousness raising does and must involve men."[37]

Pop culture follows suit with the idea of gender blurring. The 2009 season of *American Idol* saw two very different versions of masculinity embodied by the finalists, both relatively equal in acceptance and popularity. When runner-up Adam Lambert came out as gay, the news was hardly remarkable. Thousands (if not millions) of bloggers talked of "guyliner" and "gayliner," not in derogatory terms, but with curiosity and imitation of Lambert's makeup prowess. Other cultural trends, like the emergence of the "metrosexual" to describe heterosexual as well as homosexual men who have an eye for fashion and personal appearance, demonstrate a distinct muting of gender lines in the twenty-first-century world.[38]

These social winds, though not fully revolutionary, suggest that we as a society may be moving toward a more fluid interpretation of gender. This may be an overly optimistic reading, but gender scholarship also moves in that direction. There is greater recognition that transsexual strategies are more about gender practices (as a collective project) than individual negotiating or "passing."[39] In other words, the strategies of accountability for transgender and transsexual individuals are also available and applicable to all gendered people, not simply those previously seen as unusual or deviant. Finding common ground across boundaries opens up the possibility of seeing and reaching beyond sex categories.

Theoretical challenges. Just as Connell critiqued the North/South divide in theories of globalization, Nader writes of challenges that come from studies conducted by Western and so-called Third World scholars about development.[40] Western world scholars tend to perpetuate a "myth of the incremental model," assuming that movement is always linear and progressive. They urge other nations and cultures to emulate their own. Western-world advocates assume everyone needs to be like them.

Nader points out the fallacy of assuming such positions of superiority, but not for the reason one might think. She asserts:

This paper is not about scaling societies to prove who is better or worse, nor is it geared toward answering questions of improved status for women. In fact, it steers away from such simplistic notions of "progress" and "improvement" so prevalent among Westerners and Eastern elites, and which are worthless tools in comparative research.[41]

Nader goes on to explain that the issue is not simply one of value, morality, civilization/progress, or even humanity. It's much more complicated. In a convincing argument, she demonstrates that such critiques of "the other," especially for women, are tools of patriarchy. Anthropologist Ruth Benedict was one of the first to suggest that distinctions between "us" and "them" actually reinforce in-group moral authority.[42] Nader argues that images of the Muslim world are constructed in Western society to reinforce Western hegemonic ideals—that is, ruling ideals that uphold the relative position of superiority. As "good" Western women, we are conditioned to be grateful for our relative freedom of movement and other rights. Similarly, the Muslim world pushes up against Western gender liberalism (e.g., open sexuality, prostitution, divorce, scant clothing, so-called loose morals, single motherhood, and so forth) to justify the control of Arab women.

Nancy C. M. Hartsock spoke of multiple systems of female subordination, reminding us that we must be prepared to address new forms of resistance.[43] Similarly, Nader emphasizes that cultural variation actually assists in the maintenance of different patriarchal systems. "Misleading cultural comparisons support contentions of positional superiority, which divert attention from the processes which are controlling women in both worlds."[44] In other words, both Eastern and Western mores play into the hands of patriarchy.

Global variation in patriarchy is why marketplaces of meaning remain crucial to studying the party plan economy. Images of women in Guatemala, working in hot fields, may seem oppressive to Western women. But recognizing common goals of fair trade, equal rights, and providing for families places us on equal ground. Stories of Brazilian street women working long hours at home and in the market may make our Passion Parties seem fun, until we recognize that both settings hold the same possibilities for fellowship and for tyranny. All of us operate under conditions of fun and fear, pressure and celebration, hopes and dreams. Individual situations vary, but women everywhere live with gender constraints; the objective is to identify them. If we think that women are being disadvantaged because of their own system of exploitation, we fail to see our own.

The party plan economy, like all facets of the gender system, is rife with contradictions. It holds the seeds of both oppression and revolution. The four cases that follow triangulate our study and take parties beyond simply product-based activities, showing the promise for what is possible.

From the Field

The following field study represents an important bridging device, clarifying both common and distinct characteristics between the conventional party-based economic structure, most common in the United States, and other forms of economic enrichment strategies for women, here illustrated through "kitty parties" in India. Weaving a story never before recognized, Mangala Subramaniam, Gregory Gibson, and Beth Williford skillfully identify several underlying dimensions of empowerment for women that, although set in contexts thought to hold almost no similarities, are tied by common threads to a global party plan economy. The identification of such universal mechanisms—sometimes affixed to patriarchy and other times used to empower—demonstrate the malleability (and thus potential) of social systems. Intersections of gender, culture, and class paint a three-dimensional portrayal of parties.

Case Study 6.1
Indian Kitty Parties as Models of Women's Empowerment
Mangala Subramaniam, Gregory Gibson, and Beth Williford

You have already read much about US corporate parties such as Mary Kay and Pampered Chef. This case study aims to compare that model to a type of party popular in India that you have likely never heard of: kitty parties.

A kitty party does not have any formal name, but all potential members are well aware of what it means. Kitty parties last for two to three hours and take place in the afternoon. A group of women specify an amount of money to be collected from each member every month. The pooled amount for the month is referred to as the "kitty." Who will receive the money is decided by lots. Each month's kitty party is organized at the home of the previous month's winner.

The two models—corporate-based parties in the West and kitty parties in India—demonstrate how such gatherings provide potential empowerment for women within quite different organizational styles. Kitty parties lack the rationalized tradition of US-based corporate structures, but both models capture a dimension of economic power and make use of the home, which traditionally has been a woman's or feminine space. Also in both models, empowerment reaches beyond simple products or economic benefit.

The two models can produce change for women through relational mechanisms; the sharing and bonding with others in groups creates a sense of sisterhood in solidarity. Group-related activity involving the creation of feminine spaces may emerge through economic activities not necessarily connected to the formal production or sale of goods. We propose to examine such activities through a gendered lens; that is, we analyze how gender is central to the formulation and organization of these activities.

Intersections of gender and class have received much attention,[45] yet sociological conceptualizations of class primarily revolve around men and overlook the complex actualities of women's labor.[46] This is mainly due to the close proximity of patriarchy and capitalism in the class systems of both cultures. To formulate and work with a conceptualization of class inclusive of women (the other half of the world!), one must embrace a new version of class that includes gender processes, as Joan Acker writes: "The total social organization of labor is highly differentiated by gender and includes productive and reproductive work, paid and unpaid, wherever it is carried out, in different places and settings, in changing networks and connections."[47] This view of class as a set of active social relations expands previous notions of class predicated solely on economic labor and productive work.

Focusing on two types of house parties that are differentially empowering for women, we propose to address three questions: (1) What practices shape the use of the home space to combine domesticity and commerce in the cultural context of India and the United States? (2) How do these practices reflect gender-class intersections? (3) What are the implications of these practices for the economic empowerment of women? We are particularly interested in how different dimensions of economic power—earning income and controlling (spending) money—play out in the two models.

We will weave together personal experiences and convergent life histories to unveil the features of gender at work in the house parties attended by women in India and the United States. Our use of the case study method helps to address Shulamit Reinharz's concern about generalizations based upon a lack of sociologically informed case studies conducted on women.[48] We address this concern by examining two women-only sites and by disseminating our findings in this book focused on women's lives. An important aim of our work is to document both female and feminine space within empowerment parties, continuing to make women's lives visible for social scientists.

Evelyn Glenn states, "Social relations outside the realm of formal politics—art, literature, ritual, custom, and everyday interaction—establish and reinforce power; for this reason, oppositional struggle also takes place outside the realm of formal politics, in forms such as artistic and cultural production."[49] Her statement underscores how class and race, across time and space, help constitute gender relations. The private domain of the family and the public domain of the market collide, influencing women's access to information, services, and resources. These resources may differ dramatically, dividing women by social class. Yet this study demonstrates how women—regardless of social class—challenge established structural systems of the market as a public domain often dominated by men.

Whether at a kitty party in India or a Pampered Chef party in Indiana, women use gender parties as a source of personal and sometimes collective empowerment. Using home spaces for parties rooted in cultural and class-based elements empowers women, although imperfectly. Our analysis underscores the importance of class in the gendering process as middle- and upper-class women are particularly keen on relational connections rather than financial resources.

An important implication of this new conceptualization of class is the phenomenon of the "feminization of labor," a term used to describe the decline in jobs that are full-time and provide valued benefits such as health care and retirement plans. This term also signifies the increasing number of women among the world's paid laborers. Hence, the feminization of labor denotes a subordinate condition of employment in today's global workforce.

A gender analysis of labor also must account for positioning women as primary caregivers. The need for both men and women to participate in today's global labor force, balancing productive work, reproductive work, and caregiving duties with the need to raise money, has led women to consider innovative mechanisms that integrate the fulfillment of economic needs with caretaking and housekeeping activities.[50] The feminization of labor further encompasses the corporate model of home-based work that we discuss below. In addition, we shall see women combine domesticity, homemaker activities, and commerce through processes and practices that are empowering.

Although the outcome of economic power is often emphasized, the process dimension also has been recognized, particularly in feminist literature.[51] This dimension includes the significance of intangible resources in the cultural and political spheres: internal strength and confidence, collective organization, reflection and analytical skills, information, autonomy, and knowledge.[52] Women's sharing of everyday life experiences in what can be described as a feminine space is empowering. In sum, we argue that in a class-oriented capitalist economy, the focus of the rational, formal model is individual achievement. But this model is adapted to home-based retail parties that combine domesticity and commerce, enabling women to gain a sense of economic independence, even though they are earning an income without traditional benefits.

Although such parties provide a space for interacting and sharing experiences that have empowering effects for women, they differ from other forms of parties that do not entail retailing but still contribute to economic empowerment. This form of economic empowerment differs from the corporate model and lacks capitalist characteristics; women do not sell products at kitty parties, and the contributions are the earnings/savings of their husbands. In both models, we argue that gender-class intersections are visible in the practices and processes. Both models use home space for sharing and building bonds in a feminist tradition that emphasizes empowerment through consciousness raising. Such processes are embedded in friendship networks—"solidarity in sisterhood."[53] Both have implications for the ways in which gender is constructed and maintained: there is an emphasis on individual women's goals and profits in product parties (earning as economic power), but more broad family interests in kitty parties (control of money as economic power).

Data and Methods

Our personal and familial biographies, combined with information from several secondary sources, serve as data for this study. The first author's mother (henceforth referred to as Ms. S) attended kitty parties in multiple towns and cities across India. She is an insider who participated in and hosted kitty parties. This familial relation provides a unique platform for gaining insight into the preparation for hosting a kitty party as well as participating in it. As an upper-middle-class woman, Ms. S was welcomed into a group that was often less educated than she was and belonged to the middle or lower-middle class. Her experiences with kitty parties therefore span the more "elitist" and middle-class groups. Most recently, Ms. S was a kitty party group member in a middle-class neighborhood in a western Indian city.

The experiences of the second and third authors, in contrast to that of the first author, pertain to home-based retailing activities and what we refer to as the corporate model. The second author, Greg, has been an independent contractor with a large and very well-known personal coaching and self-improvement company. Greg witnessed thousands of people on the hunt for empowerment via structured self-improvement programs—seminars—that spanned entry-level to advanced and in some cases lasted well over ten days. In addition, Greg has been involved in numerous corporate models of financial empowerment, including Body Wise, Arbonne, and Fox Telecommunications.

The third author, Beth, attended her first Mary Kay party around the age of twelve with her mother. It was an experience she remembers well: women sitting around the table, pink personal mirrors, tips from the Mary Kay representative about how best to apply the colorful makeup sitting in front of each woman, and chatty conversations among all the invitees. In the past several years Beth has attended several retail parties hosted by friends. Beth's mother continues to regularly and actively participate in parties (particularly Pampered Chef) hosted by friends and neighbors. Beth's personal experiences at the parties, her discussions with participants and hosting friends, and the reflections of her mother provide insight for this case study.

Kitty Parties

In this section, we focus on the practices and processes underlying kitty parties. We begin by providing a broad overview about kitty parties in India.

Generally, about twenty women from the same neighborhood comprise a kitty group. Families are socially networked such that a new family moving in to a neighborhood is soon approached by those living close by. Groups are formed as women informally contact each other; there are no formal means for starting a group or inviting new women to join, but such groups almost never include single women. Members range in age from mid-twenties to late sixties.

The kitty collection ranges from 1,000 rupees (about $25) to 100,000 rupees (about $2,500) or even more, depending on the members' class status. Because members are expected to contribute equal amounts, kitty party groups generally include members from the same income group, although there may be exceptions, as in the case of Ms. S. Party attendance is generally 100 percent.

Class status dictates the conversation at kitty parties. In an upper-class kitty group, the discussion may center on a member's exotic holiday or the purchase of a new car. But most kitty group discussions cover topics pertaining to the family, particularly household chores, recipes of new delicacies (particularly the items prepared by the host), and children's achievements. Kitty parties of the elite are often organized in three-star hotels, but most middle-class kitty groups gather in the homes of members.[54] There women talk, listen, empathize with each other, and provide advice. Thus, kitty parties serve as a forum for exchanging information and details about household activities often perceived as mundane. Differences among members are ignored or kept low key.

Preparation and practices. Preparing for a kitty party is an elaborate and time-consuming process. The first piece of work involves writing up the names of members and putting the names on chits. These chits are then put into a large pot to draw a winner for that month. Housework is central to the organizing of the party—presenting the physical and subjective dimension of the home space to others who have similar life experiences. As a result, displaying new and brightly colored upholstery or art adds to women's regular cleaning chores.

An important aspect of preparation for the party is deciding on the cuisine. Indian cuisine varies across India as well as across caste and class groups. A special delicacy of the region from which the host hails is often the main course for the party. The entrée is supplemented with a side dish and dessert, followed by tea or coffee. For instance, Ms. S is from southern India, and people in other regions often crave what they refer to as "authentic" southern Indian food. Ms. S often prepared traditional southern Indian dishes, such as *idlis* (rice pancakes) with two side dishes and coffee. She had to plan because of the intricate preparation required and the fact that kitty party meals are much larger than regular family meals. Ms. S notes that serving a variety of delicacies at kitty parties is a matter of status and prestige.

The day of the party is exciting and somewhat stressful for the host. Hiring a part-time domestic servant for chores such as cleaning the house and washing dishes is not unusual in middle-class households. Upper-middle-class households are more likely to have additional help in the form of a cook or a car driver, but the host organizes and leads the work. She feels a sense of power in harnessing her skills and directing the domestic servant, and often draws on the help of her grown children too. As a point of pride, catered or purchased food is never served at kitty parties.

Afternoon is the most convenient time for the party because husbands are away at work and children are at school. In addition, the major chores of cleaning and preparing can be completed in the morning. Toddlers and infants accompany their mothers if the mother has no help at home. Unlike parties for teenagers, music is not a part of these parties.

Figure 6.1 Indian women in traditional sari dress. *(Mangala Subramaniam)*

Arrival and initial interaction. Guests begin to arrive soon after two in the afternoon. Dressed in fine saris (the Indian dress) and calling out to neighbors as they make their way to the home of the host, members come in chatting about the weather and their day's activities. These initial chats flow into long conversations at the party. There is a strong sense of camaraderie among the women as they listen to one another's woes, celebrate the successes and achievements of their children, or discuss newly acquired gadgets or pots and pans. Each member gives her month's rupees to the host, who stores the money safely for the next few hours. Ms. S says that very often conversational noise grows loud enough that the host must ring a bell to get the women's attention and invite them to continue dining.

Dining and games, interaction and exchange. Conversation and discussion continues as eating and drinking commence. Ms. S recalls that members generally appreciate the tasty food, but snide remarks about inadequate salt in the food or excessive sugar in the tea do occur.

The parties provide a unique space for the women to learn about groceries available at particularly low prices. Although groceries are available in retail outlets in some major cities, a large proportion of the population prefers vendors and local markets. Oftentimes, information about an unreliable domestic servant or her poor quality of work is passed on to other party attendees so that they may avoid hiring the same servant. As mothers, they often share concerns about the performance of their children in school and whether those in high school will be able to secure admission to the best engineering colleges. Women also share light moments in conversations about weddings of siblings or new movies. On one occasion, a kitty party included the demonstration of a new model of vacuum cleaner. So the parties are a comfortable space where married women share the concerns and excitement of everyday happenings. These spaces are personally oriented because members are very familiar with each other, but they are neither entirely private nor public.

Dining is followed by a short period of games. At most middle-class and upper-middle-class kitty parties, the women play *tambola*, a form of gambling similar to bingo. Various prizes are announced, but prizes come from ticket purchases; the kitty is not used for the games. Ms. S says that one can hear laughter and squeals of delight as members win prizes and refer to their good or bad luck. The shared game experience and excitement facilitate solidarity rather than competition among the women.

The kitty and empowerment. After food and games comes the drawing of lots to decide the winner of the month's kitty. The host has written the name of each member on a chit. These chits are then put into a large pot to draw a winner for the month. Sometimes an announcement is made that a specific member has requested the kitty to meet household needs. Members often accede to such requests, but most of the time lots are drawn to decide the winner.

To the clapping of hands and some yelling, everyone asks the winner what she plans to do with the kitty. Most women plan on buying a consumer durable good that will help with household chores, such as a vacuum cleaner, washing machine, or microwave. There are also instances of middle-class women using the kitty to buy basic necessities, such as six month's supply of rice for the family. (Families often purchase rice and/or lentils in bulk when these items are available at wholesale during specific months of the year.)

Kitty parties provide a vital space for women to meet, bond, and enrich each others' lives. These parties use the home for sharing and building bonds in a feminist tradition that emphasizes consciousness-raising processes that facilitate women's empowerment. The friendship networks of women involve noneconomic exchanges, mainly information about daily needs pertaining to the family and home, processes that build solidarity.

But these processes vary by class. Gender-class patterns are visible in the practices adopted for kitty parties and reflect the class status of the members, such as whether the party is held in a member's home or a hotel. In the case of middle- and upper-middle-class women, the winning of the kitty provides access to and control over money. That could be partially true even for women from among the elite and upper classes who are not earning money but rely on the income of their spouses.

For most upper-class women, the kitty is less significant because they probably have access to and control money, but they may find empowerment through the sharing and bonding with other, similar women. Network exchanges and relational exchanges are made most visible through this group, in which women participate in the marketplace of interaction even though they do not need the economic/material products. So even though the variations in practices are class-based, participation in kitty parties is economically empowering for these women who do not work outside the home.

Corporate Model Parties

Now we turn our attention to the United States, a class-oriented, capitalist economy where again the home serves as a marketspace for exchanges. We identify a corporate model of economic relations that predominates in the house parties that women host in the United States, such as Mary Kay and Pampered Chef. Direct sellers are typically "younger than the age of 45, married, middle class, and have another paying job."[55] According to J. Denalli, about 90 percent of direct sellers are women who do not rely solely on direct sales as their income.[56] The products sold in house parties are "those which need demonstration or trying-on and those which are not generally available in the shops."[57] An organization or company that uses direct selling has three roles critical to its success: the consumer (party guests), the retailer (the consultant presenting the products), and the recruiter—the consultant inviting guests to become consultants.[58] All three roles depend upon the use of the home and women's networks.

Host and invitees. Parties typically occur in the home of a working-class or middle-class woman who is responsible for inviting a group of women to her home. The parties may last anywhere from one and a half to two hours and are scheduled to capture the most convenient time of day for the women attending. For example, the host may plan to invite women from work and therefore be inclined to host the party in the evening during the week or on the weekend to best suit her invitees. The host may contact her planned guests first by phone or face-to-face and follow up with either a phone call or a postcard in the mail to remind them of the scheduled party. The dress for home party attendees is typically casual to dressy-casual.

The number of invitees is determined, in part, by the type of product that will be demonstrated and sold. Hosts of Mary Kay parties would rarely invite more than a dozen women because each will be applying makeup based upon step-by-step tips offered by the Mary Kay consultant. The number of guests at a Pampered Chef party can range from one to two dozen.

The interactions among guests are influenced by cultural factors such as race, ethnicity, and residential location and how well the guests know one another.[59] The mood at parties where all in attendance already know each other is typically much more open and conversational as the women catch up on details of each other's lives. At parties where an invitee may only know a few other women, the party is usually shorter, with less time devoted to casual conversation. In all cases, however, the guests know in advance what kinds of products will be showcased (makeup, kitchen supplies, etc.). Repeat customers who are invited but cannot attend the party may tell a friend who plans to attend to bring back information on a new product or to ask for an extra catalogue of the products, or she may ask the friend to place an order for her while at the party.

Entertainment and interaction. After all guests have arrived, festivities often begin with a round of introductions or an icebreaker so that all attendees get to know each other. At Mary Kay parties, light refreshments are passed around before women put on makeup or have it applied for them. At Pampered Chef parties, heavy hors d'oeuvres prepared using the line of products on display or found in the catalogue are distributed to each attendee. At both kinds of parties, the dealer or consultant constantly moves around the room, talking about the products and describing their use as well as the advantages each offers. These activities make it possible to forge relationships among invitees and provide a space for sharing experiences.

Parties wind down when an order form is distributed and guests are asked to sign up for the products they wish to purchase. The cheapest products at both Mary Kay and Pampered Chef are typically just under $10. At parties attended by the authors, guests usually purchased about $20 worth of products at a Mary Kay party and upward of $40 to $50 at a Pampered Chef party. Guests are not required to purchase products, but some pressure does exist when in the company of friends. As a reward for organizing the party, the host receives a gift from the company and a gift certificate or some company products, based upon the volume of sales produced by her party. When the products arrive a week to ten days later, the host is responsible for getting the purchased goods to the buyers from her party.

Exchange and empowerment. The dealer/consultant is invariably a former guest and host of house parties. She may choose to become a consultant while at a party by discussing it with the dealer in attendance or by making a note on the order form asking to receive more information directly by mail. The idea of direct sales appeals to many women because it requires very little start-up funding or formal business training.[60] Moreover, each woman is thought to be in a position to influence how far and how fast she advances in the company.[61] Company training programs and literature advise consultants on how to organize a party and how to encourage other women to host parties; consultants learn to ask, "When are you going to have a party?" rather than "Will you host a party?"[62] The training gives women the feeling that they can be successful even as they continue their familial responsibilities.

One of the most important reasons that women decide to become consultants is self-employment, as it "offer[s] ways of accommodating women's dual roles as mothers and professionals. . . . The total amount of their time devoted to selling can fluctuate and they can fit direct sales into their day. . . . Therefore, restructuring their work as a Mary Kay consultant is one way of coping with juggling paid and unpaid labor."[63] Women can stay at home with their families but also have paid work. Pampered Chef markets itself as an opportunity for women to start home-based careers, most notably in its magazine *Empowering Women*.[64] However, most consultants do not view home-based work as "real" work.[65] Furthermore, adding paid work to the list of domestic work defined as feminine extends the workday for many women. As Sheila Allen and Carol Wolkowitz noted, "the work is always before one's eyes."[66]

A woman's success in the corporate model that we identify here is determined by individual economic earnings on products she is able to sell and the commission she receives from recruiting new consultants. "It is the dealer who mobilizes ascription and in so doing achieves gain for herself and success for the enterprise."[67] Sales are largely due to the social bonding that occurs between the consultant and the host and how the parties are organized as a sales strategy that combines sociability and commerce.[68] To continue to increase her income, a consultant relies on social networks among women in order to expand her business. Operations generally begin with friends, neighbors, and relatives.[69] As she recruits more people to host parties for her, a consultant increases her earnings but also increases the chance that she will be relying on more distant networks and thus coming into increasing contact with strangers.[70] Former consultants have commented that this is a difficult aspect of growing one's business, as it requires putting more and more time into making new contacts.

In spite of the hardships in expanding one's networks as a direct seller, women note that selling and earning commissions is empowering.[71] Monetary gains as well as the skills learned in the process help increase women's feelings of independence. Women cite other nonmaterial gains, one of which is praise they receive through excitement and applause in regional and national meetings: "many dealers [admit] that it was the only real recognition they had received since leaving school."[72] Incentives such as impressive public ceremonies are used by direct sales organizations to keep women from quitting when personal networks are saturated, often stressing other kinds of achievement such as maintaining goals.[73] Mary Kay is known for using much more than psychological incentives—including clothing—to indicate rank.[74] Women with high earnings (higher rank) in the Mary Kay company are rewarded with diamond rings, fur coats, and pink Cadillacs.[75] Pampered Chef boasts material incentives such as vacations, jewelry, and free products for sales and recruiting.[76]

The US form of the economic empowerment party involves earning money by selling products. While earning, women learn about managing a business and typically juggle these responsibilities with those of domestic life. But the structure of the work—organizing parties in the home to sell products to friends and neighbors—provides a unique feminine space for women to talk about everyday life issues and earn an income. This restructuring of work offers women a chance to avoid the low wages typical of pink-collar jobs, thus playing into women's desire to enhance their earnings, but it leaves them with no health care or retirement benefits. These corporate-style home parties, like the kitty parties, are nevertheless important distinct spaces for sharing information, daily life events, and providing advice.

Conclusion
This comparative case study of kitty parties and corporate parties highlights the use of the home for exchanges of information as well as eco-

nomic activities that are not necessarily connected to the formal production of goods. Both models can produce change for women through relational mechanisms; the sharing and bonding with similar women in groups create a sense of solidarity. Although the parties have two different cultural contexts and used different means of economic exchange, both types facilitate bonding and sharing daily life experiences that are empowering for women.

Gender scholars will benefit from our discussion of the party models of empowerment, which exemplify different types of social solidarity and yet insert gender relations into the empowerment process. The goals of both models of parties have implications for the ways in which gender is constructed and maintained: the emphasis on individual women's goals and profits in the product parties (earning as economic power) and the more broad "family interests" in the kitty parties (control of money as economic power). The form of economic empowerment that women in kitty parties may experience differs from the corporate model of the United States and lacks capitalist characteristics; women do not sell products at these parties, and the contributions are earnings/savings of their husbands. Women's sense of economic power is not connected to learning about business or earning an income. Thus, each model captures one dimension of economic power: earning and controlling earnings versus controlling money.

The use of the home for market-based exchanges is significant in both models of parties, and domestic chores are central to hosting friends and neighbors. Our analysis emphasizes a strong notion of family that affects several important aspects of the home space, in particular, how family serves to focus the rewards of group-facilitated empowerment. The practices associated with organizing parties in both models entail gender-class effects. Although serving food or having a variety of dishes prepared is not important in the US-based corporate model parties (except at Pampered Chef parties), they are central to the kitty parties in India because they signal class status and privilege. Hosting kitty parties and serving delicacies testifies to the host's culinary skills, one measure of a woman's ability to manage a home.

Outcomes differ in the two models of parties. In the corporate model, the host's earnings depend on orders placed by invitees who may not choose to return. The host can expect other rewards from the company itself. In contrast, women at the kitty parties do not rely on such earnings. In fact, kitty parties almost never involve sale of products. In India, retail selling at home is perceived as an activity engaged in by those from the lower classes. The practices involved in organizing and hosting parties in the United States and India represent markers of cultural distinctions of status. Gender parties are also *class* parties.

The case study of US-based gender parties and kitty parties reinforced the reality that the party plan economy, as a structural entity, reaches far beyond a simplistic view of gatherings to sell and consume products; the party plan economy incorporates global marketplaces of interaction, which hold the promise of empowerment for women. In the following field study, BeEtta Stoney takes a bold step further: the party plan model, as a conceptual vision of connections among women, preserves culture and produces ideas. Women gather in reading circles and friendship circles, all the while renegotiating and redesigning communities. The party plan scope is revealed as broader and deeper when products are removed from immediate consideration.

Case Study 6.2
Lasting Legacies and Sister Friends: Literacy in African American Communities
BeEtta Stoney

The National Endowment for the Arts (NEA) 1982 study "A Nation at Risk" warned that young people, in particular, were vulnerable to the loss of an understanding of literature as a cultural legacy. Twenty years later, a follow-up study, "Reading at Risk," informed us that, indeed, a "'rising tide of mediocrity' had overtaken the school system and threatened a generation of students."[77] Reading books, it seemed, was quickly becoming a lost art.

From a young age, I often heard the joke, "If you want to keep information from Blacks, just put it in a book." As a young reader, I did not understand the impact of this "joke," but now I fully understand its gravity and have worked to discover if it holds any truth. According to the 2002 NEA report, reading has increased among African Americans by 15 percent but only by 8 percent among whites. Less than half of the adult US population now reads literature; more women (55.1 percent) read literature than men (31.6 percent), but reading by both groups is declining at significant rates.[78]

When first invited to write on this subject, I pondered several questions: How often do African Americans read and what works are they reading? If reading has increased for African American adults, then the aforementioned joke holds no truth. As an educated African American woman, reading has always been an important concern for me. I learned a great deal about the history of African American literary writers and the impact they have had on Black readers. For African American women, "storytelling," "talking books," and "clubs" connect to the thirst for knowledge and importance of literacy. Literacy is a luxury product in today's society, unequivocally so for African American women.

Elizabeth McHenry contends that literacy is "the ability to read" but disassociates the spectrum of communication (both oral and written) from a dissemination of knowledge that is a form of resistance.[79] Before the late-nineteenth and early-twentieth centuries, literacy was a closed-door society that excluded Blacks, particularly African American women, from participating. At the same time, African American women's book clubs, before the turn of the century, were meeting in churches, living rooms, basements, or any other quiet and inconspicuous place. This form of resistance was key to the pursuit of literacy for disenfranchised Black people. D. T. Max asserts that book clubs blur boundaries between cultural and economic capital, art and business, essentially serving as a homogenizing agent, but historically Black women have sustained a unique interest through book clubs.[80]

African American women have always found ways to connect to other African American women both individually and through community connections as readers. J. J. Royster discusses how literacy and knowledge were crucial for African American communities' success.[81] She further profiles a number of prominent Black women educators and discusses the Black women's club movement, providing a unique forum for public discourse.

In the form of book groups, African American women also preserve, maintain, and produce ideas and culture. In this discussion, I focus on preserving Black culture through these women's gatherings. Virtually no literature addresses this particular niche, yet this study will be guided by African Americans' writings and literary societies.

Further, this case study uses feminist epistemology and "women's ways of knowing," which are based on common, everyday experiences that provide the basis for resistance to mainstream power structures. In particular, I seek to understand the motivations, challenges, and benefits that African American women, individually and collectively, garner through book clubs. African American women use book clubs as a way to connect with other women as "keepers of the culture," as it relates to African American history in the United States.

Literary Societies Among African American Book Clubs

> Your crown has already been bought and paid for, so go ahead and wear it. —*Toni Morrison*

Although much has been written about the Great Book clubs and other literary groups, there is limited information regarding how book clubs function among African Americans and their communities. The achievement of literacy, especially the publication of poetry and autobiographies, demonstrated that Blacks have the ability to create works of literary merit and achieve the same accomplishments as whites—a creative and cultural dimension that provided opportunities for Blacks to write, publish, and create a legacy of literacy. Before Carter G. Woodson instituted Negro Week (today known as Black History Month), a small group of women in Atlanta were making history of their own, meeting monthly to discuss books, as well as social, political, and other issues relevant to the Black community.[82]

US slave owners institutionalized illiteracy to prevent slaves from challenging their authority, assuming that illiterates could not participate in legal or public discourses. Nevertheless, thousands of slave narratives were published between 1820 and 1860.[83] Slave women used their narratives to convey both their sense of identity and familial relationships. Despite laws regulating slave literacy, African Americans learned many English language elements out of necessity.

African American readers became vocal and eager learners. Elizabeth McHenry and Shirley Heath chronicled this in *The Literature and the Literacy: African Americans as Writers and Readers, 1830–1940*.[84] They note that from the 1830s onward, African American literacy societies supported reading and writing, which led to a nationwide community of authors, editors, and publishers. Today, African American book clubs still follow the same format, with many inviting authors to be special guests at their meetings to share their works and thoughts with the groups.

Although most book clubs were generally comprised of women participants, there were a few book clubs that crossed the gender barrier. Book clubs of African American men and women date back to the literary societies, which demonstrates their determination to support books written by African American authors and exchange ideas regarding events occurring in their communities and around the world. To further discussion about events within their communities, African Americans began forming their own societies, debating social, economic, and political issues.[85]

In the late 1990s, a new generation of readers came to light, known as the Oprah Book Club (OBC). Rooney describes how Winfrey singlehandedly changed how Americans, namely African Americans, came to the forefront in establishing book clubs and literacy.[86] There are many critics who would describe her as the "gatekeeper" of tradition, the canon, and high culture, and OBC has had an indisputably significant impact upon the nation's culture and economy. Moreover, the "club" provided an opportunity to promote literacy and examine how sociocultural attitudes were shaped through literature.

In McHenry's *Forgotten Readers,* the author's discussion of the club movement of the late-nineteenth and early-twentieth centuries demonstrates how Black women's reading and "talk" (essays, literary discussions, lectures, and reading circles) became instruments of social change in African

American communities.[87] *Forgotten Readers* also highlights the influence reading communities had on Black women's lived and publicly presented lives and reveals how, through their commitment to middle-class codes of decorum and to training in writing, literary analysis, and oral presentation, clubwomen instructed Black women on everything from household management to sharing responsibility for the social advancement of the race.[88] Club activities prepared Black women to use literacy to create and connect the social and literary worlds.

Feminist Epistemology

From participants in my study, I learned that their book selections for the month were chosen from past and present African American feminist authors, and I was empowered by that fact because African American women are typically excluded from the dialogue when feminist epistemologies discuss women's issues. These conversations discuss women's issues from a white woman's perspective, but race is almost never part of the dialogue. Patricia Hill Collins notes that in a historically created system, white women are privileged by their gender and their race.[89] African American women's book clubs select African American feminist texts to connect them with someone's "story" that is "real," preferring to read literary works about *our* culture and connect the readings to *our* experiences. African American women's book clubs allow members to learn about the experiences and challenges of Black women. Through these discussions, I also learned why it is important that African American women maintain the title "keepers of the culture."

Anne J. Cooper, a feminist ahead of her time, argued for women's rights, particularly roles for Black women.[90] Fighting through sexism, desegregation, and civil rights, she found herself in the emergence of the Black women's club movement, which grew among women dissatisfied with being cast aside as "colored" units of white clubs and angered by racial intolerance, even among religious groups. Cooper believed that "the struggle for human rights might be waged more effectively with the perspective and balance of intelligent Black women."[91]

During the 1960s and 1970s, African American women were making inroads through their unique contributions to the struggle for women's rights. They demonstrated inextricable connections between their concerns as African Americans and as women.[92] I support Elsa Barkley Brown's words that "all women do not have the same gender." Feminist epistemologies do not have the same experiences.[93] My experiences as an African American woman are different, and I understand that historically and through the years, although I personally experience gender and race issues on a daily basis, my white female counterparts have the privilege of focusing on their gender issues, often ignoring race.

Writings of African Americans

African American writers have contributed greatly by writing about lynchings, the impact of the Great Depression during the Harlem Renaissance, civil rights movements during the turbulent moments of equality, and personal and observational experiences that occurred in Blacks' lives and communities. This section will depict those great writers who contributed to the African American literary canons and provide brief summaries of the complex history of this literary tradition. The term "literary canon" refers to literature that is considered to be the most important from a particular time or place.[94] The works in the African American literary canons provided a historical context for authentic descriptions of African American life.[95] Today, many writings from various literary canons have been read, discussed, and analyzed at great length in African American book clubs.

The Harlem Renaissance, which began in the Roaring Twenties, was an exciting time for African American writers, bringing their culture and experiences to light and reaching back to their African roots and African American communities in the United States. In his poem, "Mother to Son," Langston Hughes confronts struggle and survival in Harlem.[96] Hughes tells the story of a mother encouraging her son to keep going despite any obstacle. During the Great Depression, Hughes wrote about the real experience of African Americans, and the poem parallels the struggles of African Americans during that era. African American readers related to Hughes's messages, as many Black communities were living these experiences and overcoming impossible obstacles.

The African American literary tradition also contained another theme that further defined Blacks' worldview, the color line of light-skinned versus dark-skinned Negroes. *The Blacker the Berry: A Novel of Negro Life* depicts Emma Lou Morgan as a dark-skinned woman who grew up as a mulatto.[97] Her family despised her because of her skin color. These attitudes and mistreatments caused her to despise herself and all dark-skinned people—a topic still relevant today.

The 1930s witnessed many events that posed new challenges and obstacles to African Americans. Black authors voiced frustrations and rage in their writings. Although the writing retained the intensity it had at the beginning of the Harlem Renaissance, the themes and motivations began to change; authors addressed modern day racism, poverty, self-assertion, and race relations.

From the 1950s through the 1970s, multiple changes affected African American communities and the literary themes reflected in authors' writings. In the 1950s, African Americans took a stand on blatant racism and homosexuality. James Baldwin's *Giovanni's Room* (1958) was about a white American student who had an affair with an Italian bartender, ultimately confronting sexuality—a topic not discussed in most African American communities during that era. The 1960s, known as the "Second Black Renaissance," were significant for Blacks as controversial social issues came to the forefront, and they became participants in and conscious about their lives in the United States. Authors wrote about justice, Black pride, self-actualization, Black sexuality, and race relations.

In the 1970s, writers focused on relationships among African American men and women, but not many authors stayed on topic, returning instead to the general literary themes of the 1960s. However, female authors such as Maya Angelou, Shirley Chisholm, and Toni Morrison changed how African American women were viewed, portraying them as productive women and active role models. These literary writers wrote practical stories for African Americans, relating to their real-life experiences.

The Legacy of Resistance: Sister Friends

Why do African American women establish book clubs? Some do so for the sake of sisterhood with a small group of women friends. Others form clubs for intellectual stimulus, spiritual connections, or simply to gather and discuss classic and contemporary fiction (usually African American), along with the occasional nonfiction book. Most African American women would agree that the purpose of establishing a book club is to join together a group of book lovers who enjoy thought-provoking, in-depth discussions about literature. Whatever their reasons, one of the common goals is to find strong, like-minded African American women who enjoy reading.

Sister friend is a term used often in the African American community of women and can be seen in many organizations. African American women play important roles in their communities, churches, and extended networks, but no relationship is more important than a sister friend. A sister friend is a caring, loving, and supporting "sistah." She is considered as close to family as you can get without actually being one. When I asked one woman why a sister friend is important, she replied, "You can be yourself when you are with your sister friends. We do not hide anything. We can be silly, cry, laugh, and we do not judge." She continued, "As sister friends, we have intellectual conversations regarding politics, literature, and social environments. I believe this is why our book club has been successful over the years. Our club meetings are also based on this exactness. We actually select our books based on our interests of our sister friends' experiences, both personally and professionally."

When I asked why they thought the legacy of sister friends has been maintained over the generations in African American women's book clubs, the women said they believe that it helped establish communal relationships and defined the importance of building bridges with other African American women. One participant stated,

Sister friends is a supportive network of women whom I dearly treasure. I mean it has been my experience in the past that when most women groups get together, progress was not productive. Yet, with this group of sister friends I can be myself and share personal and professional information that will remain with the group. For me, this was a welcomed relief. They truly are my sisters.

African American Book Clubs

> With one Black sistah plus another we are united to widen literacy among our own, to eliminate negative stereotypes against us and to place a positive impact on the society as a whole.
>
> —*"Black Sistahs United Book Club*
> *South Carolina," Mosaic Books*

Being a member of a book club has brought meaning to the lives of many African American women. The participants that I spoke with had a range of ages, interests, employment, social gatherings, and education and were pleasantly excited "that someone has taken an interest in their book club and the lives of African American women gatherings." The participants were from the Midwest, Northwest, and South. The women were dynamic and personable, and I learned that from the youngest to the oldest, as "keepers of the culture," they unanimously agreed that there is a cultural loss in storytelling today. For example, one club, before every meeting, would pray and share a story.

Storytelling is powerful. When sharing stories, their conversations were rich, inviting, experiential dialogues. It felt as though I was living the stories, and I missed storytelling from people who have lived the real African American experience. One of the senior members commented, "The young women in our club have not lived the life we have lived. We have to *prepare* them and *teach* them how to be storytellers so that our culture, ancestry and life experiences are not lost in translation." Initially, I did not give this comment much thought, but she is right. I do not hear the stories that were once shared by my mother and grandmother about our culture and ancestry. It is as though young African American women, including me, are missing out on our rite of passage as Black women.

During the question-and-answer sessions, I was enthralled with the elder women's ability to answer questions with a story. Yes, they could tell stories, reminding me of my grandparents and parents who shared their personal histories with us as children, and, even as adults, we felt as though we were living in their moment, their lives. For me, this was powerful, and I was mesmerized.

I selected three particular African American women's book clubs to discuss, based on my personal connection with their members during the face-to-face interview process. The women were asked to respond to a series of questions that were e-mailed, respond to the questions via phone interview, or participate in a face-to-face interview. I have selected anonymous "club names" based on their group mantra and the name of their clubs. The groups shared how they came together as a club. One club, the Spiritual Women Book Club, came together per a request from their pastor. Their ages ranged from eighteen to sixty and beyond. The second book group, Sister Friends, was established because they felt a need to support each other based on their common life experiences. They ranged from thirty-five to fifty-five years of age. Members of the Librarians Women Book Club were ages fifty-five and up—a "mature group." The members of each group had a variety of jobs, hobbies, and education levels, but in each case members understood one another despite differences. At a typical meeting, a discussant (usually assigned previously) briefly explained the book topic to the group and then led the discussion.

Selection of books. The selected books covered a variety of different genres and subjects, including women, self-esteem, political or social issues, spirituality, poetry, and self-help. The themes that emerged during group discussions were the process for selecting books, how to find books relating to their personal and professional experiences/lives, the importance of connecting to the African American culture/communities, self-empowerment, and the importance of having a safe environment for discussion.

When asked how books were selected, one reader responded, "First, we should broaden our learning curve. We read books from all genres to educate ourselves, but we prefer African American authors." They select their books based on what is happening in their own personal communities but may venture beyond African American authors because they believed that from a political standpoint, "we must educate ourselves on issues that impact Black folks, directly and indirectly." The young readers in this particular book group did not find some books as interesting as the seniors, but it was the storytelling of the elders that taught the young women how they would take their place in life to protect and secure their culture politically and socially.

All members encouraged lead readers to seek out titles that they were unfamiliar with, and that led to uncomfortable discussions about sex, sexual orientations, interracial relationships, spirituality, and self-help. In addition, women used reviews from local Black radio stations or *Jet, Ebony,* and *Essence* magazines to make their choices.

One member from a mixed-gender book club suggested reading about LGBT issues in the African American community. Most members did not want to read that "mess" because they felt it did not concern them as readers. In response, this group member said, "Reading about these issues [affects] our community on many levels. If we as a group want to learn about 'us' as a group, then we must stretch our way of thinking and quit hiding our heads in the sand." She went on to explain that the group did not want to read about "S-E-X" or anything with that word in the book. I asked her why the group opposed certain topics. She explained, "When we lost our 'lead reader,' the dynamics of the group changed. We changed how our book sessions were ran [*sic*] or what was selected to read. I wished she had not passed away. When we lost her, we lost our group." It was obvious that the lost leader had made an incredible impact on the group.

An interesting book mentioned by a younger African American book club is *Letters to a Young Sister: DeFine Your Destiny,* in which the author shares the importance of focusing on becoming your best self. In other words, "focusing on individual accomplishments and doing the things that help you become a whole person."[98] Many readers noted that they did not have African American women as role models when they read this book, but since what the author discussed was so relevant to their lives, most wished they had read the book sooner.

Relating books to personal and professional experiences. I asked the participants how the book club had affected them personally and professionally. One member responded, "You learn so much from helping that you manage to find your own self-worth. We read books that discuss self and how to build self-esteem." Another member mentioned that she "finds herself talking to more African American women, whereas before she did not trust or would not give women the time of day." A member from the spiritual club said:

> God gave me the strength not to let things affect me the way it used to. For example, if someone is mad with me or we have a disagreement, before the book club and the type of spiritual books we read, I would not have made any attempts to talk the problem through. After joining the book club, I have learned to broaden my relationships with others by talking the situation through instead of allowing the problem to pass me by.

Books connected these women to their personal and professional worlds.

Connecting books to African American culture and communities. The Secret Lives of Bees is a good example. Although written by a white author, the story focuses on four African American women in the South during the turbulent civil rights era; the love and support of African American women demonstrates the power of women coming together to heal those wounds, to mother each other and themselves, and to create a sanctuary of true family and home.[99] There were interesting discussions as older women shared their insights about the era and how African Americans "knew their place" in dealing with racism, whereas younger women in the same group thought the women "took too much from the Man."

Expanding on this statement, the young African American women felt that the characters should have not held back and should have spoken their minds about the injustice and mistreatment they received from the white man. The senior members thought the younger women missed the irony and parallelism of race relations between the Black and white characters. The senior women began to connect the book's past and present events that had taken place between the two groups and shared how the author's storytelling connects the reader to the cultures and the communities of African Americans. The young women became learners and listeners during this book discussion, sought clarification through storytelling, and connected the discussions to their communities and African American culture.

Safe environments for conversations. The book club readings had many agreements and disagreements, but despite their differences, all members felt safe to speak their opinions. Relationships established in the clubs prompted safe environments for healthy conversations. One participant stated:

> It was a mutual respect of trust. Trusting the women in the group was difficult at first. I have had negative experiences with African American women and knowing that I was free to express my feelings, or "speak the truth," I knew that I did not have to worry about gossiping. This was my "safe haven," a place where I could go in feeling low and end the meeting as a strong courageous woman.

Another member expressed appreciation of the club as a positive environment and said it provided a good "attitude adjustment" for her. "I have been a member for five years and I have never heard anything I shared, personal or professional, be repeated. In previous organizations I have been a member of, I had to deal with the bickering, back-biting, and gossiping. This book club of intelligent women has been a welcome relief."

Self-empowerment. The book that stands out for me and other women participating in African American book clubs is the book *Act Like a Lady, Think Like a Man.*[100] The no-nonsense guide says women should learn the principles and rules men follow to beat them at their own game. While I was visiting the Northwest, to meet with Sister Friends, the conversations surrounding this book were quite interesting. Many women agreed with the author's appeal to women to understand men from a Black male perspective, yet a select few did not find the book as useful. One reader noted she thought the book made African American men appear shallow and as constant "playas."

Personally, this book gave me insight on how to respond to men and not allow myself to be set up with certain expectations. I enjoyed reading the book and discussing it with the women. I must agree with one of the members who said, "Harvey just let the cat out of the bag! Now . . . we know and African American men cannot get away with his [*sic*] antics." One reader felt empowered, particularly since she was going through some difficult events in her life. She thought the book brought her peace and a sense of "getting back to her old self."

Conclusion
African American women's book clubs provide a wealth of knowledge. In the words of one member, "As African Americans we must negotiate or redesign community culture as women. Even though we are everywhere, we must look at our behaviors, contributions to our communities, but we must not forget to be mentors to young women." Another member commented, "For us to maintain as keepers of the culture, we must share our experiences and teach the next generations how to be storytellers or lead by example. If we do not continue, then our stories will be lost. At this rate, our cultural legacy is missing. We stopped teaching the truth. Our younger generations do not want to learn about the past."

The great-grandmothers and grandmothers who were expert storytellers have passed away, and the next generation's young mothers are not telling the stories because they have not mastered the skills. Children, especially young girls, are missing out on their histories, their rites of passage. I understand the women's motivations, challenges, and benefits in reading and recognize my role as a future storyteller, understanding, participating in, and passing this legacy forward.

BeEtta Stoney's piece delved into the connections between motivation and cultural legacy among book club participants. The following field study by Dena Wallerson speaks to echoes of political activism in the African American community, but also the heterogeneity of Black women's book groups. Expanding on the idea of knowledge-as-product, Wallerson explores the roots of literacy and the goals of two groups of African American women from different parts of the United States. Wallerson discusses the daily rules and practices of these social groups, issues regarding reading selections, regional differences that affect interactions, and the potential for collective activism. A measure of "quiet activism" runs as a thread through women's everyday recitals.

Case Study 6.3
The Politics and Power of African American Women's Book Groups
Dena Wallerson

Ain't I a woman? —*Sojourner Truth, 1851*

These four words spoken by Sojourner Truth represent, arguably, one of the most poignant passages in US history, documenting African American women's struggle toward equality in the United States. As part of her speech in Akron, Ohio, at the 1851 Women's Rights Convention, Sojourner Truth spoke to the effort of Black women to gain power wherever it could be gleaned: "I can't read, but I can hear."[101]

Like Truth, Black women have always been at the forefront of resistance in the Black community, often leading political movements. A few examples are instructive. Maria Stewart, between 1829 and 1833, became the first Black woman to lecture and publish declarations about women's rights.[102] During the same era, slave women often led their communities in resistance, sometimes through song and other times through more public defiance. An account of one woman, Milla Granson, speaks to the significance of literacy to the Black community:[103]

> The historical sources that tell her story vary as to whether Granson's home was in Natchez, Louisiana, or Natchez, Mississippi. However the storyline remains the same: Granson taught slaves to read in her cabin in class sessions that began at eleven p.m. and ended at two a.m. She taught hundreds of slaves to read over the years, each in a group of twelve classmates. Some of the slaves learned how to write their own passes and set out from Natchez to Canada. When her activities were discovered, enough discussion was generated to affect the Legislature; a law [eventually] was passed making it legal for a slave to teach a slave to read.[104]

Also exploring the history of African American literacy, Kalenda Eaton further demonstrates the power of political activism during the post–civil rights era.[105] Activities and activism often began and were sustained through women's readings and writings. Women participated in a wide variety of activities, such as voter registration drives, demonstrations, education, fundraisers, religious studies, choirs, prison reform, health care delivery, and politics.

Bridging History and Now
When I first agreed to interview African American women about their participation in book groups, I expected that their involvement in these groups was rooted in the history of slaves being prohibited from learning to read and the underground networks that resulted from taking literacy into their own hands. Given the resultant empowerment of slaves and freed Africans in the United States, together with their collective conquest for human and civil rights, I expected this tradition and history of literacy through book group engagement might persist.

Given the historical prohibition on literacy, I discovered there was little documentation of Black literacy history and engagement in literary groups. One recently published book and a small body of articles describe how slaves and freed Africans in America learned to read, but few publications exist regarding African American engagement in book groups as a vehicle for collective action and sharing of resources.[106] Much documentation of literary societies and present-day book groups are about white women's participation and how the meetings and collective actions liberated them.[107] Oprah Winfrey did reinvigorate the US interest in book groups in 1995, and sales of books by African American authors began to increase around the same time, but I was convinced that these groups experienced a revitalization because the history of literacy and empowerment of the Black community had been passed down through the generations.[108]

Reading remains a strong tradition in the African American community. Although a 2007 Associated Press poll found that one in four Americans hadn't read a book in the past year, 80 percent of Blacks reported reading at least one book, a higher proportion than whites or Hispanics.[109] This field study explores the experiences of African American women's participation in contemporary book groups, speaking to the promise of continued empowerment when women gather together.

Interviews

I traveled to Aspen, Colorado, in January 2008 to join other Black women at a meeting of the National Brotherhood of Skiers (NBS), a historically Black organization. The NBS is the world's largest ski club with over 6,000 members. Originated by African Americans, the NBS is open to everyone regardless of race or ethnicity. They have annual events at ski resorts around the world, where families and singles network and socialize. The NBS attempts to make their ski trips affordable, and a percentage of their membership and trip fees help subsidize youth who seek to join the Olympic ski team. Meetings last a week or more, with 3,000 to 5,000 members present.[110]

At the NBS event, I was confident that I would encounter African American women who participate in book groups from around the country, and I was ultimately led to a group of four women who were recent transplants to the Atlanta area (originally from Chicago and Detroit).[111] They work, have families, and feel they don't have as much time for themselves as they'd like. Some stated that the relocation of their families to the South reduced their free time because they had to establish their new home (find housing, schools, work) and then develop a network of friends. These women participated in different book groups in Georgia.

During the summer of 2008, I interviewed four additional women who belonged to a book group in Martha's Vineyard, an island off the coast of Massachusetts with a year-round population of 12,000. The island comes to life during the summer, when over 100,000 people come to enjoy the beaches, seafood, and networking with others. There is a long history of African American families vacationing on Martha's Vineyard.

I spoke with a total of eight women, four from each location. The women ranged in age from thirty-five to sixty. All of the women I spoke with have attended college and some have post-baccalaureate degrees.

Involvement

Members of the Massachusetts book group had participated in their current book group for two to five years, and most had participated in a prior group. One participant had belonged to a group that kept records of the books read for the past five years, and the list was extensive. Their prior moves to new groups were due to members relocating to other towns or because of a general inability to keep the group intact and meet regularly. When asked why they participate in book groups, the women stated that they enjoy talking about books with other women with whom they are friendly. Their plan was to decide on books to read, meet monthly over dinner and drinks, and talk about the book and other topics in general. Their book groups came together to be sociable, to share time with friends, and to talk about books.

The Atlanta women had participated in book groups for less time than those from Massachusetts but had joined for the same reasons: personal entertainment, enlightenment, and socializing with friends. The Atlanta women specifically mentioned talking about books and general issues at their workplaces, in their children's schools, and in their families and communities as reasons to participate. They had joined these groups since relocating to the South within the past three years, and most had not been involved in book groups prior to moving.

Women in both groups reported that their female elders had read when they were young, especially those who had gone to college. Having grown older, the women again have time to read for pleasure; the middle of their lives having been consumed with family, parenting, and work. So, the women I interviewed did not join as a result of a legacy of family members and friends who were also in book groups, as I had expected. For various reasons, though, they found the time to participate in book groups during their midlife and more advanced years. Women in both groups reported that young people in their families are not reading as much as the women would like, with the Atlanta women adding that reading beyond what is required for school is minimal.

Literature Selection

The women found that their book groups got off to a good start, but some challenges emerged. The first involved choosing the literary genre of books. The women all reported having had lengthy discussions in their groups about whether they should exclusively read books about African American life or written by African American authors. There were women in each of the book groups who did not want this limitation. Others felt

Figure 6.2 A display of children's books by African American authors. Reading and book groups are a strong tradition in many African American communities. *(Flickr Creative Commons)*

strongly that they should read race-specific writings as a way of under-standing their own lived experiences, and here the issue of Afrocentrism and allegiance to one's cultural heritage entered the dialogue. Some partici-pants reported feeling pressured to read "Black-only" books and yearned for a wider range of writings.

The Martha's Vineyard group eventually agreed to read primarily African American literature, with exceptions made when other books were deemed worthy of selection. However, very few of the books they had se-lected were not by or about African American life. Some reported that they would read books on their own that did not fit within the parameters of the group. It seemed that although they supported the idea of reading one genre, they felt the limitations of their decision as well. I wondered if the women who exited the group had done so because of a desire to read a broader range of literature. Even with these few points of contention, the Massachusetts women were fairly avid readers, reading at least two books a month (more when traveling or on vacation); all read before bedtime as time permitted. Although the Atlanta women reported some of the same tensions regarding Black-only literature, they were more willing to agree since their moves to the city were in part due to their wish to connect with the larger Black community there.

Another sore point involved the decision to read classics versus new authors—particularly popular and Internet-press authors. Older group participants preferred reading the more notable writings by James Baldwin, Dorothy West, and Zora Neale Hurston; slave narratives; plays by Pearl Cleage; and the like. Younger participants were inclined to read a broader range of African American authors, including those publishing with independent or Internet presses. Much of this writing is less complex and addresses stereotyped conflicts in the Black community, including fighting over boyfriends, dating outside one's race, participating in crime and gangs, dropping out of school, keeping a job, and determining who "really" is the father of a child.

These writings have been popularized by many traveling theater groups, and Tyler Perry, the producer/actor/writer of the Madea films, has further popularized the "drama" of life in the African American community on film and television. The plots of these books and films are simple and revolve around the same themes. Characters make wrong decisions, suffer consequences for their actions, and then realize what they must do to make better decisions. This genre of pop literature is laden with morals and guidance on how to live one's life while still being entertaining.

This literature is often confined to African American book sections in major bookstores and rarely makes it to short lists of distinguished book award committees. Yet, according to Ken Smikle, publisher of *Black Issues Book Review*, this genre of books generated $300 million in sales in 2006, more than twice as much as in the early 1990s.[112]

Of the genre of work written by and about African Americans, I learned that none of the books read by the Martha's Vineyard women included writings by African American feminists or academics, with the exception of popular English professors such as Jamaica Kincaid and Toni Morrison. The work of bell hooks and Angela Davis, for example, were not on their list of proposed readings. I anticipated that because these women had gone to college (and some earned terminal degrees) that they would be interested in discussing critical commentary or nonfiction books that addressed current events affecting the African American community. However, they were more inclined to read writings by African American male academics and activists, including Cornel West and Tavis Smiley, when they ventured beyond works of fiction.

The Atlantans were more willing to read newer writers from independent presses, some of whom are also in the South. Although they enjoyed the classic African American literature, they sought new authors who write about contemporary issues. They also reported going to book talks to meet authors they have read. They were quite familiar with the traveling theater groups that perform plays about Black culture and have watched many of the television shows and movies about Black life in the United States. The Atlanta women also were familiar with Cleage's plays and had seen those that traveled to the Atlanta area but were less familiar with writings of Black female academics and activists. Due to time constraints, the Atlanta women didn't read as many books outside the group. They were not the avid readers they would like to be, but their participation in the groups helped keep them moderately versed in African American fiction. On average, they read one book a month, sometimes struggling to squeeze it in.

Sociality
All enjoyed the combination of food, drink, and friendship. The group gatherings were viewed as "their time," and they looked forward to having this time away from family and work. Meetings typically rotated between members' homes. They began with cocktails and beverages and engaged in general conversation until everyone arrived.

On Martha's Vineyard, food was provided by potluck or the host, but the varying levels of service were an issue for some members, who believed that each host should provide a good range of quality foods and drinks. In Massachusetts, women reported that their group needed someone to serve as a timekeeper to ensure that social conversations would transition more quickly into book discussion, which had been a problem from time to time. The book groups were described as valuable (if not sacred) time, and some of the women I interviewed were disturbed that others in their group did not appear to take it as seriously as they did.

In the South, food preparation and hosting the book group was viewed as a big deal; each host invested time and money into her event to make it as pleasurable as possible. If an Atlanta host didn't have time to cook (which both groups deemed to be most desirable), then she hired African American caterers to cook for the event. During the social portion of the meetings, members took time to catch up on each others' lives while drinking and dining. Children, spouses, love, and work issues were the main themes discussed. The women were careful to talk selectively about these issues so as to prevent gossip about private matters. As a result, clusters of women would talk during this social time, and as the book group discussion was about to begin, clusters would join together in a circle for a common discussion. These were enjoyable times but also opportunities for them to speak freely, offer and receive advice, and share common interests. Bonds were strengthened among these women, and, as a result, they stayed in communication more often.

The Atlanta groups also frequently ran later than the agreed-upon end time, and women who had to depart to put children to bed did so, while others continued the discussion and had a final beverage before departing. There seemed to be less tension about the start and end of these groups; they didn't require a timekeeper to ensure the shift would occur. There seemed to be a collective energy and enthusiasm for talking about their lives as well as the books they'd read at the meetings. The Atlanta women may not have had as much time to read as the Massachusetts group, but they reported fewer instances of lateness and absences at their meetings. The Atlanta women seemed to value this time for their own relaxation and to enjoy a night out with "the girls." They often discussed how they would have responded to incidents that occurred in the stories they'd read; sometimes debates and even more heated discussions ensued when participants believed that others in their own book groups did not always make the best decisions. The constant interplay between what was occurring in the story and their own lives created a feeling of anticipation yet uncertainty about how each session would transpire.

I learned that friendships were so deep among some of the Atlanta members that they offered extensive advice and assistance to one another. These book groups were patronized by women who had become very close personal friends, and if the need arose for activism or support on a larger scale, these women were willing to offer support. I wondered if these new transplants may have taken longer to make friends as they sought to be established in their new communities but developed strong bonds with other women in the group as a result.

From the Martha's Vineyard book club, I learned that the solidarity that developed as a result of participating in the group did not translate into activism or collective action in their communities. Members of the group would use resources they might have to help another member or a relative of a member, but this did not lead to a mobilization of efforts to address community projects or concerns. In some ways, the extended kinship network once used by Blacks to help others during and after slavery through the civil rights era is not needed by this group of resourceful, middle- to upper-middle-class Blacks today. For these women, the book group served as interactive entertainment. I believe that if an issue arose, however, these women could call upon one another for more organized support.

Commitment

The Massachusetts women reported that their group always struggled with members' commitment to doing what is necessary for the group to thrive. Being consistently late to the meetings, leaving early, or being unprepared to discuss the book was viewed by some as not taking the book group seriously enough. They were unsuccessful in enforcing rules about asking members to step down if they were chronically late or could not attend a number of successive meetings.

Lateness and absenteeism were less of an issue for the Atlantans. Because they had limited time to devote to reading and were expanding their network of friends, they made the effort to be ready for their meetings, whether as hosts or regular participants. Chronic lateness and absenteeism was minimal, and members made every effort to be present or to be excused from the meetings.

With these particular findings arises the unanswerable question of what makes for the "best" book club: one with strict rules where all members are completely dedicated to the club, or a more casual arrangement.

Final Reflections

For all the women I interviewed, their book group serves as a respite away from their daily lives. The group meetings are restorative: they allow the women to bounce ideas off one another. Although the Massachusetts women noted that they do not share every personal matter with the group, I suspect that some women have developed relationships that are very close. For the Atlanta women, cooking and presenting a generous spread of food and drink was part of a southern hospitality tradition that they enjoy and take seriously.

After interviewing the Atlanta women, I immediately wished that I had the opportunity to visit with some of them during their book group sessions. I sensed that I would have gotten a much richer sense of group dynamics and could have had more opportunities to discover whether the groups merely provide a social network, as the women from Massachusetts emphatically stated, or more of an extended kinship network, as has been documented among earlier generations of formal and informal reading groups of African American women.

Most of the women I interviewed are of middle-class status or higher. It may be that these groups of women have a lower level of need than other women. It is important to recognize that a multitude of experiences coexist within African American communities. At the same time, the mechanisms that have been historically available to African American women through extended kinship networks have been negated by higher mobility and movement. If this is true, such groups hold even greater potential to bring women together in a sense of community.

With the recent decline in book sales, the availability of free reading materials on the Internet, and the rise in e-book sales, I wonder if book groups will become obsolete or be replaced by other forms of entertainment and social networking that can be shared by African American women.[113] My hope is that, regardless of the future of book groups, African American women will continue to use the power of social gatherings as a resource for sharing ideas, bartering services, and organizing the community.

Case Study 6.4 further illustrates the power of the party plan model to reach beyond product-centered events. Much of the book thus far has been devoted to recognizing and analyzing material forms of the party plan economy, from

Tupperware and its Western world contemporaries, to ways in which gender parties have been exported to other regions, to other forms of woman-centered economic activities around the globe. Various discoveries emerged, such as how the party plan economy shores up an artificial bifurcation of women's lives into private/public and personal/political arenas, and even as nonwork (or parties). This chapter extends the boundaries of the party plan economy, first through the comparison of kitty parties in India with US corporate models, then through African American book clubs. All of these models use ideas as product and share certain characteristics such as networking tactics, information sharing, resource gathering, and survival strategies.

Once material constraints are removed, a world of possibilities emerges—thoughts, ideas, creations, dreams, linkages—a virtual collage of imaginings. The following case study, which extends even beyond women's gatherings, provides just such an instance. Dusty Garner challenges the reader to take yet another step: into a world where gender is muted, fluid, blended, changing, daring. At first perhaps startling and disconcerting, Garner's essay may appear to be addressing nonnormative gender performance or even deviance. Given the book's goal to raise our consciousness as gendered individuals, this study affords a rare but critical view of our deepest self, one beyond sex groupings. Exploring the world of drag, the author guides us into a place where gender is, indeed, not a category but an imagined world of home and promise. It crosses personal and political, melds public and private, mocks categories of male and female. A living-color marketplace of interaction, it reveals a deeply human dimension.

Case Study 6.4
Instant Family—Just Add Eyeliner
Dusty Garner

> We all came into this world naked. The rest is all drag. —*RuPaul*

It is impossible to discuss the world of drag queens without first having a discussion of gendered pronouns. Unfortunately, as human beings we have been indoctrinated into the practice of placing individuals into categories. This becomes a problem when you place someone into a box that doesn't fit, and is especially acute when it comes to the gay community—a group in which the spectrum of gender expression is as varied as the people included. Just as much of the heterosexual community subconsciously ties itself to gendered stereotypes, the homosexual community segregates itself along similar gender expression stereotypes.

I am personally a unique study of gender expression. In day-to-day life I present a very masculine image and refer to myself in masculine terms. However, in my life as a drag queen, it is my job to present a hyperfeminine image. Things get really interesting when those two parts of my life intersect.

As I share with you part of my story, I will intermingle pronouns; know that all of the daughters, mothers, and sisters I mention are what society would identify as biological males, but in various ways they surpass the categorical box that society has put them in. You will see that our gendered worlds often collide with and contradict what we are "supposed" to be; however, I hope you will also see how, if our biological sexes matched our performance genders, we would fall right into the mainstream, heterosexist, misogynistic stereotypes.

Drag Mothers, Drag Daughters

When Williams and Bemiller first sat down and talked with me about the topic of *gender parties*, I had no idea what they were talking about. After further conversations and reading some early sections of the book, I started to identify. My mother has used various party plans to make extra money my entire life. One of my earliest memories of my mother is her preparing for a Home Interiors party and being so excited to spend her bonus and incentives on things for the house. As I continued to mull over the concept and the gender roles that go with these parties, I started thinking about my own life and how this fits. It was glaringly obvious. I was my mother, but without the commissions, bonuses, and incentives.

Figure 6.3 The many dimensions of Dusty Garner/Monica Moree. *(Dusty Garner)*

You see, I have been a drag queen since I was about fifteen years old. I started because I thought that was what gay men did (it just so happened that all the gay men I knew at that time were also drag queens). Not every new drag queen has a similar experience; in fact I think that, unfortunately, it is safe to say that the model I started under is not as common now. With that caveat, I will share with you my early experiences and how they translate to my current life in the female impersonation community.

I started out like a lot of young entertainers: when I expressed my desire to try drag to my circle of friends, I knew that word would make its way around the local drag scene, and I would eventually be adopted by a seasoned professional. In the drag world that person becomes my "drag mother" and I their "drag daughter." Other entertainers become my "sisters." Some families have elaborate setups, which include aunts and uncles, grandparents, you name it. The key is to notice that all the titles are based on family roles.

For drag queens, as in everyday life, these roles are very important and come with a lot of responsibility. As a drag mother, it is your responsibility to teach your daughter everything she needs to know, both onstage and in life. You teach her the importance of good foundation garments, how to find (or make) clothes that are flattering to her figure, how to style hair, how to do makeup (or "paint your face," as we call it), and how to create her character. You even name her. If she is new to the gay community, you introduce her to friends and peers; if she has recently come out as being gay or transgender, you help her find inner confidence. Sound familiar? For the vast majority of people, especially women, there is someone in their lives who plays that same role.

My drag mother was Tasha Foxx. Eighteen years ago, she and her drag mother (my grandmother) put me in drag the first time on my fifteenth birthday. We spent weeks shopping for the right outfit and shoes, styling a wig, and learning to walk in high heels. Every time we got together for practice, there were at least five or six other "family members" there to throw in their two cents' worth. On the night of my first show, I was named. My drag mother and her mother both thought I looked a lot like Marilyn Monroe, so they wanted to keep the "M" initials. That night, Monica Moree was born.

As time went on, my mother and grandmother taught me everything I needed to know. Over the next several years, I would sit in on countless practice sessions for my new sisters as they also learned what they needed. When there wasn't a new person learning the ropes, we would spend time together watching movies or eating dinner—things a family would do together. There was always hair being styled or costumes being rhinestoned, but that was always second to the socializing. If a sister had trouble with her boyfriend, we were there to help pick up the pieces of her broken heart or at least drown her sorrows in a pint of ice cream. When I graduated from a very small, rural Kansas high school with only thirty classmates, my entire drag family was in attendance. They were as much a part of my family as my blood relatives. They have supported me along my journey through life as I experienced various amounts of success in this business and outside it.

Today I am living in Manhattan, Kansas, a small, conservative town that is home to Kansas State University, a school especially known for its agricultural program. With that comes a community that is largely from very rural areas. Many students have not met a person of color, much less an openly gay person. When I arrived three years ago, there wasn't an established place for gay people to hang out. The gay community was largely built around raucous house parties highlighted by massive amounts of binge drinking and poor decisionmaking. There certainly weren't drag queens, and they certainly weren't prepared for me to take over.

That drag queens have an immense amount of power within a gay community is one of the greatest lessons I ever learned from my "sister" Penny. They have the ability to bring the community together and build on that foundation, or they have the ability to keep it very separated and clique-ish. I immediately set out to bring the gay community of this small town together, to give them something to rally around. I worked with a student organization to bring to campus the first (of what has become an annual) campus drag show. We brought in some of my sisters from all over the country and showed this town a really exciting show. We garnered about 250 people for our first show and 500 the following year, and last year we sold out with over 700 people.[114] Each year the line is longer for audience members wanting their picture with the entertainers or a signed program.

I soon found that Manhattan had no public space in the bar district (always vital in a college town!) where people in the gay community could feel welcome and safe. One of my original goals was to provide a safe party space, where they were less likely to partake in risky behaviors. I approached a local bar owner to inquire about letting us hold a gay dance night in his bar. I created a proposal that outlined his nightly income on a weeknight (approximately $120) and compared it to his potential income when hosting a gay dance night. I pointed out that with 25,000 students at the university, if even 5 percent of them were gay or supportive, there would be the potential for hundreds of customers on any given night. He instantly saw dollar signs but also pointed out that he never realized there was a need for such a night. Our partnership was born, and I started "Heat!— Aggieville's ONLY Alternative Dance Night."[115]

Before long, the community started coming together. Soon people began asking if I would put them in drag, meaning paint their face for a night. I found my most recent daughter from this exact situation. She asked

---

PJ's Pub Events *Before* "Heat"
Live local band or no entertainment

Average Nightly Register: $100
Average Total Cover Charge Revenue: $20

PJ's Pub Events *With* "Heat"

Dance Night	Food Drive
Bitchy Bingo	HIV Fundraiser
Theme Party	Drag Show

Average Nightly Register: $1,200
Average Total Cover Charge Revenue: $425

---

me to do her makeup for Halloween. I gladly said yes and could immediately tell that she was going to be very good. A few months later, she approached me and said, "Would you be willing to teach me everything I need to know about drag? Would you kind of be my Momma?" I told her that I would gladly help out when I could, but I couldn't promise to be her mother, as I am very busy. This man had had a very tortured coming-out process, and I wasn't sure I was prepared to take on that kind of stress. One day, as we were getting ready for a show, I started asking him about why he wanted to do drag so badly. He said, "I had an awful coming-out experience. I wanted to die. I think that I can use drag to make coming out easier for other people. I don't ever want someone to go through what I did."

I was stunned. Finally, someone else who wanted to use this art form to create a better place! From that moment on, Mitzy was my daughter. She even took my last name, Moree. Since then, we have added to our small Manhattan family. I have three other drag queens who are taking their art very seriously and working at perfecting it and creating a better community. We also have a group of about five other men who are interested in trying out drag. They are fun to watch as they come into their own and develop their own personas.

The Sweat Shop
Earlier in the book, Williams mentioned the women's group that her mother joined. This got me thinking about the gatherings that we have every week

or so, when our "family" comes together. We call it the "Sweat Shop" because our focus is on creating as many new costumes, music mixes, or props as we possibly can in one evening. Everyone who attends is working maybe not on something for herself, but working nonetheless. We are a modern, slightly offbeat version of those mothers from the 1950s, sitting around the living room exchanging casserole recipes.

As I sit at my desk, which doubles as a makeup table, I see my supplies. I am struck by the fact that every single thing in my makeup kit is something that my drag mother or sisters encouraged me to purchase or that I have purchased and passed on as a tool to my daughters and sisters. When I look at the clothing rack next to me, there isn't a single garment that I created entirely by myself. Every single one of them was created with the help of the family. We want nothing more than for each other to succeed because we understand that the success of one is our collective success.

A Mother's Love: Both Sides of the Coin
Of course, along with the makeup tips, sewing sessions, and dance rehearsals comes the real role of a mother: love and protection. I am no different than my mother, who still waits up for me to come home from going out, pretending that she was up doing things anyway, when, in reality, she couldn't sleep until she knew that I was safe.

Once, while I was performing in Las Vegas, the family had gathered for one of our sweatshop evenings, because one of my daughters was preparing to compete in a national drag pageant. While we were attaching rhinestones to her evening gown, the conversation turned to some recent incidents in the gay bars. Some young men unknowingly had their drinks drugged, waking up the next day to find that they had been raped and robbed. Although people may think of rape as a crime against women, with males making up 9 percent of rape and sexual assault victims, I wasn't going to take any chances with my kids.[116]

I had been performing at a comedy club in the downtown area, so I didn't go out to the gay bars very often. Their bar stories terrified me and led me to talk with them about what they were doing to keep themselves safe. We talked about not leaving drinks unattended, making sure they always went out in pairs, and having my phone number on speed dial with "In Case of Emergency" (ICE) listed next to my name. I made them show me that they had taken these precautions, just as my mother had chastised me for various indiscretions. They knew I was serious, and even though they might have thought I'd lost my mind, they understood and appreciated my concern.

My fretting over them would turn back on me. A few weeks later, I landed my first contract as a headline performer at a hotel on the Strip. My daughters were all in Dallas, Texas, watching their sister compete for the

Miss Gay USA pageant, so, having no one to celebrate with, I decided to go to the little bar where I got my first show in Las Vegas. Once I was there, I decided to stay for the show, looking for up-and-coming talent. I sat alone at the bar; when I am not in drag, I am not very social. At one point, I went to the restroom and asked the bartender to keep an eye on my drink.

When I returned to my station, there was a guy sitting next to my stool. I asked the bartender if the drink in front of me was mine, subtly asking if she had watched it. That is the last thing I remember from the bar.

When I woke up the next day, it was very clear that I had been a victim of exactly what I had tried to prevent for my family. When I found my way back to my car, I called Ginger, one of my older daughters, and told her what had happened. A few hours later, as I was retelling the story to the third detective, my phone rang; it was Ginger. She could tell I was very frustrated and asked where I was. I told her that I was at my house talking with a detective. Less than ten minutes later, the doorbell rang, and there stood Ginger, madder than hell and scared as could be.

Ginger had gotten on the first plane back to Las Vegas. He never asked me what happened, although I am sure he overheard most of it as I retold the story to investigators. He accompanied me to every doctor visit and every police lineup and never said a word to the other girls until I told them what happened. He was my hero and is one of my closest friends.

The Family Tree
When Williams asked me to write for the book, I spent some time looking back at my life, reflecting on the wonderful people who have made up "The House of Moree." We truly have been the stuff of daytime television. There have been fights and rivalries, stunning successes and amazing failures, weddings (as close as we can get) and separations, even adoptions (the cutest baby girl on the planet, but as her godfather, I'm a little biased). We have had additions, and, unfortunately, death has come earlier than it should for some of my sisters and my children. However, through it all, the one thing that got me through was the small group of men who dress like women who I call family.

Today I have sisters or daughters in just about every major city in the United States and a couple around the globe. I have twenty-three daughters, several of whom have their own daughters and granddaughters now. Among us there are doctors, nurses, scientists, cosmetologists, construction workers, actors, singers, and even an attorney. Some of my family have never met face-to-face, but they all know where their family members are located. If we ever end up in the same area, we are guaranteed to have a friendly face available to join us for dinner. We are family.

Together, as a family, we have raised millions of dollars for charity. Each of us has committed to improving the communities we live in, and we have strived to make coming out a little easier for every LGBT person going through that process. Individually, each one of my daughters has made this mother as proud as can be.

Beyond the Party

Chapter 6 moves beyond parties centered on material consumption. Demonstrating the promise of alternative forms of gender parties, this chapter highlighted four field studies that focused on gatherings and exchanges of ideas, knowledge, and friendship. A common thread throughout all these studies is the weight given to gender awareness, group consciousness, and personal relationships. Unlike corporate-based parties, women's book clubs, Indian kitty parties, and drag queen get-togethers offer the possibility of empowerment without exploiting relationships within the groups.

The level of group consciousness, as well as individual wakefulness, is influenced by intersecting standpoints. Common structural locations create opportunities to bond, often resulting in a sense of empowerment well beyond the mundane. In fact, economics—the front-runner in corporate party plan recruitment—fades far into the background, mostly disappearing for the field studies in this section. The relational structure of a marketplace of interaction, so instrumental for the party plan economy, becomes a critical resource for other woman-centered (and race/class/gender/sexuality-conscious) gatherings.

The African American women in Stoney's study, for example, used the power of social gatherings to share ideas, exchange services, and organize. Readings were centered on African American authors and African American issues, demonstrating a need to support others who share a common racial location. Although white women participate in book clubs, the level of kinship among the African American women seems unrivaled and provides an opportunity for collective action that relates to these women's experiences of marginalization throughout history. Yet, as Wallerson clearly demonstrates, the gathering of Black women, in itself, should not be romanticized and cannot ensure activism. It is a powerful reminder that the designation of Black or African American or woman-centered is a category constructed within a hegemonic social system and should not be assumed to take on a homogeneous quality. Yet, taken together, the book club studies demonstrate the potential to model empowerment for all women.

Indian women's participation in kitty parties is also much more about enrichment and relationships with like-minded women. Regardless of their social class location—remember that some were upper class while others were middle class—the kitty party provided an opportunity for interaction. The kitty itself did not matter as much as the concentrated time with friends, and the Indian women in Subramaniam and her colleagues' study understood this fact.

Drag queen gatherings allow explorations deep into intersectionality. Garner discusses his everyday life as a white male, but when he performs in drag, he and his drag family transcend sex categories, and the audience is swept along. This transformation is partly for entertainment and partly to dramatize a political statement about gender bifurcation and its consequences in Western society.

These field studies are awe-inspiring. At the same time, we cannot address intersectionality, gender consciousness, and activism without also addressing the oppressiveness of a gender system that can dangerously divide, alienate, and harm. As Lorber reminds us:

> Political power, control of scarce resources, and, if necessary, violence uphold the gendered social order in the face of resistance and rebellion. Most people, however, voluntarily go along with their society's prescriptions for those of their gender status because the norms and experiences get built into their sense of worth and identity as a certain kind of human being and because they believe their society's way is the natural way.[117]

We have, for the most part, skirted the issue of gender violence. This is where one would typically state that the topic is "beyond the scope of this project," though that now seems like a copout: gendered violence is undeniable and must be addressed. In particular, sexual violence is on the rise. In 2008, 2,424 LGBT victims reported violence to the National Coalition of Anti-Violence Programs, representing a 26 percent increase over a two-year period. Reports of sexual assault rose 48 percent, continuing a trend spanning three years of marked increases in hate-motivated sexual violence.[118] These are but a few reminders of the really ugly side of gender hegemony.

Lest our silence on gender violence be taken for denial, we want to emphasize the menace of a system that excludes, injures, and sometimes destroys those who do not fall into lockstep with its ambition (to maintain the current power structure). Garner's important work is a stark reminder that gender is not always pretty, parties are not always fun, and gender violence exacts a horrible cost on individuals and, ultimately, on society.

The take-away message from this chapter is that women and men can and should come together in an effort to create positive change related to the larger gender order. Coming together does not have to happen at product-based parties centered on production and consumption but can and should find alternative structures where ideas, support, and friendship can be shared.

Notes

1. Raewyn Connell, *Gender and Power: Society, the Person, and Sexual Politics* (Palo Alto, CA: Stanford University Press, 1987), 61.

2. L. Susan Williams, "Trying on Gender, Gender Regimes, and the Process of Becoming Women," *Gender & Society* 16, no. 1 (February 2002): 29–52.

3. Anne Kingston, *The Meaning of Wife* (New York: Farrar, Straus and Giroux, 2005).

4. Ibid., xii.

5. *The Princess Bride*, directed by Rob Reiner, MGM, 1987, DVD (July 18, 2000).

6. For a more comprehensive critique of role theory, see Helen Z. Lopata and Barrie Thorne, "On the Term 'Sex Roles,'" *Signs* 3, no. 3 (Spring 1978): 718–721.

7. Laurids Hedaa and Jan-Åke Törnroos, "Understanding Event-Based Business Networks," *Time and Society* 17 (2008): 324.

8. Ibid., 325.

9. Ibid., 323.

10. Malcolm Gladwell, *The Tipping Point: How Little Things Can Make a Big Difference* (Boston: Little, Brown, 2000), 38.

11. Ibid.

12. Hakan Håkansson, *Industrial Technological Development: A Network Approach* (London: Croom Helm, 1987); Hakan Håkansson and Ivan Snehota, *Developing Relationships in Business Networks* (London: Routledge, 1995).

13. Connell, *Gender and Power*.

14. Judy Anne Breneman, "Gathering Around the Frame—The Quilting Bee," Women Folk: The Art of Quilting, 2001, http://www.womenfolk.com (June 14, 2009).

15. Betty Friedan, *The Feminine Mystique* (1963; reprint, New York: W. W. Norton, 2001).

16. Marge Piercy and Jane Freeman, "Getting Together: How to Start a Consciousness-Raising Group," University of Maryland–Baltimore County, 1972, http://userpages.umbc.edu (June 14, 2009).

17. R. Claire Snyder, "What Is Third-Wave Feminism? A New Directions Essay," *Signs* 34, no. 1 (2008): 175–196.

18. For a short discussion of consciousness-raising groups, which were designed for the explicit purpose of raising women's awareness about their common issues, see Janis L. Edwards, "Womanhouse: Making the Personal Story Political in Visual Form," *Women and Language* 19 (1996): 42–46.

19. Bridget Crawford, "Consciousness Raising and Contemporary Feminist Method," Feminist Law Professors, January 31, 2008, http://feministlawprofs.law.sc.edu (June 14, 2009).

20. Melinda Gallagher and Emily Kramer, *A Piece of Cake: Recipes for Female Sexual Pleasure* (New York: Atria, 2005).

21. Martin Grieger, "Electronic Marketplaces: A Literature Review and a Call for Supply Chain Management Research," *European Journal of Operational Research* 144, no. 2 (2003): 280–294.

22. Raewyn Connell, "The *Northern Theory* of Globalization," *Sociological Theory* 25, no. 4 (December 2007): 368–385.

23. Renana Jhabvala and Jane Tate, "Out of the Shadows: Homebased Workers Organize for International Recognition," SEEDS, no. 18 (New York, Population Council, 1996).

24. Melody Ermachild Chavis, *Meena, Heroine of Afghanistan: The Martyr Who Founded RAWA, the Revolutionary Association of the Women of Afghanistan* (New York: St. Martin's, 2003).

25. Ken Gelder, *Subcultures: Cultural Histories and Social Practice* (New York: Routledge, 2007).

26. Page Rockwell, "Feminists Just Want to Have Fun," *Salon*, September 29, 2006, http://www.salon.com (June 14, 2009).

27. Mark A. Blythe et al., *Funology: From Usability to Enjoyment* (Norwell, MA: Klewer Academic Publishers, 2003); Asef Bayat, "Islamism and the Politics of Fun," *Public Culture* 19, no. 3 (October 2007): 433–459.

28. Clinton was not, however, the first woman to ever run for president. In fact, there have been a number of women who have done so, the earliest being Victoria Claflin Woodhull in 1872. She was the nominee for the Equal Rights Party at a time when many women still could not vote. Her running mate was Frederick Douglass. For more information, see Joe Richman and Samara Freemark, "The First Woman to Run for President—in 1872," *All Things Considered*, NPR, October 13, 2008, http://www.npr.org (June 17, 2009).

29. Del Jones, "Women CEOs Slowly Gain on Corporate America," *USA Today*, January 2, 2009, http://www.usatoday.com (June 17, 2009).

30. Gloria Penner, "The Pitiful Progress of Women in Politics," KPBS, February 27, 2009, http://www.kpbs.org (June 13, 2009).

31. Geoffrey D. Paulin and Yoon G. Lee, "Expenditures of Single Parents: How Does Gender Figure In?" *Monthly Labor Review*, July 2002, http://www.bls.gov (June 16, 2009).

32. Institute for Women's Policy Research, "The Gender Wage Gap: 2008," April 2009, http://www.iwpr.org (June 16, 2009).

33. Leadership Conference on Civil Rights Education Fund, "Confronting the New Faces of Hate: Hate Crimes in America," June 2009, http://www.civilrights.org (June 17, 2009); Ricardo Hausmann, Laura D. Tyson, and Saadia Zahidi, *The Global Gender Gap Report* (Geneva: World Economic Forum, 2008), 8.

34. For example, see Raewyn Connell, *Masculinities* (Berkeley: University of California Press, 1995); James W. Messerschmidt, *Nine Lives: Adolescent Masculinities, the Body, and Violence* (Boulder, CO: Westview, 2000); Michael Kimmel and Michael Messner, *Men's Lives*, 8th ed. (Boston: Pearson/Allyn and Bacon, 2010).

35. Barrie Thorne, *Gender Play: Girls and Boys in School* (Piscataway, NJ: Rutgers University Press, 2004).

36. For examples of such professional women, see Nancy Pelosi, "Equal Pay Day," US House of Representatives, Office of the Speaker, 2009, http://www.speaker.gov (June 10, 2009); American Federation of Labor–Congress of Industrial Organizations (AFL-CIO), "Women in a Global Economy," 2009, http://www.aflcio.org (June 10, 2009); Cristen Conger, "Is There a Gender Gap in the Workplace?" February 17, 2009, http://money.howstuffworks.com (June 12, 2009).

37. Crawford, "Consciousness Raising."

38. Global Oneness, "Metrosexual—Evolution of Usage," http://www.experience festival.com (June 17, 2009); and Global Oneness, "Metrosexual—Narcissism and Changing Masculinity: The Metrosexual," http://www.experiencefestival.com (June 17, 2009).

39. Connell, *Gender and Power.*

40. Laura Nader, "Orientalism, Occidentalism, and the Control of Women," *Cultural Dynamics* 2, no. 3 (1989): 137–169.

41. Ibid., 137.

42. Ruth Benedict, *Patterns of Culture* (New York: Houghton Mifflin, 1934).

43. Nancy C. M. Hartsock, *Money, Sex, and Power: Toward a Feminist Historical Materialism* (Boston: Northeastern University Press, 1985).

44. Nader, "Orientalism," 137–169.

45. See Joan Acker, "The Future of Women and Work: Ending the Twentieth Century," *Sociological Perspectives* 35 (1992): 53–68; Joan Acker, "Rewriting Class, Race, and Gender: Problems in Feminist Rethinking," in *Revisioning Gender,* ed. Myra Marx

Ferree, Judith Lorber, and Beth H. Hess (Lanham, MD: Rowman and Littlefield, 2000), 69; Joan Acker, *Class Questions: Feminist Answers* (Lanham, MD: Rowman and Littlefield, 2006); Margaret L. Andersen and Patricia Hill Collins, *Race, Class, and Gender* (Belmont, CA: Wadsworth, 2002); Joey Sprague, "Holy Men and Big Guns: The Ca(n)on in Social Theory," *Gender & Society* 11, no. 1 (1997): 88–107.

46. Acker, "Rewriting Class," 44–69; Acker, *Class Questions.*

47. Acker, *Class Questions*, 31.

48. Shulamit Reinharz, *Feminist Methods in Social Research* (New York: Oxford University Press, 1992), 166.

49. Evelyn Nakano Glenn, *Unequal Freedom: How Race and Gender Shaped American Citizenship and Labor* (Cambridge, MA: Harvard University Press, 2002), 16.

50. Debra L. Berke, "Coming Home Again: The Challenges and Rewards of Home-Based Self-Employment," *Journal of Family Issues* 24 (2003): 513–546.

51. Anne Marie Goetzé and Rina Sen Gupta, "Who Takes the Credit? Gender, Power, and Control over Loan Use in Rural Credit Programs in Bangladesh," *World Development* 24, no. 1 (1996): 45–63; Syed M. Hashmi, Sidney Ruth Schuler, and Ann P. Riley, "Rural Credit Programs and Women's Empowerment in Bangladesh," *World Development* 24, no. 4 (1996): 635–653; Amartya Sen, "Economics and the Family," *Asian Development Review* 1, no. 2 (1983): 14–21.

52. Naila Kabeer, "Resources, Agency, Achievements: Reflections on the Measurement of Women's Empowerment," *Development and Change* 30 (1999): 435–464; Gita Sen and Harriet Presser, eds., *Women's Empowerment and Demographic Processes: Moving Beyond Cairo* (Oxford, UK: Oxford University Press, 2000); Ann Bookman and Sandra Morgen, *Women and the Politics of Empowerment* (Philadelphia: Temple University Press, 1988); Marilee Karl, *Women and Empowerment: Participation and Decision-Making* (London: Zed Books, 1995).

53. Goetzé and Gupta, "Who Takes the Credit?"

54. Aruna Randhir, "Three Cheers to Kitty Parties," *Deccan Herald*, January 30, 2004, http://deccanherald.com (June 9, 2009).

55. Berke, "Coming Home Again," 513.

56. J. Denalli, "Opportunities in Direct Selling," *Nation's Business* 81 (1993): 69–70.

57. Rex Taylor, "Marilyn's Friends and Rita's Customers: A Study of Party-Selling as Play and as Work," *Sociological Review* 3, no. 26 (1978): 573–594.

58. Pei-Chia Lan, "Networking Capitalism: Network Construction and Control Effects in Direct Selling," *Sociological Quarterly* 43, no. 2 (2002): 165–184.

59. Susan Vincent, "Preserving Domesticity: Reading Tupperware in Women's Changing Domestic, Social, and Economic Roles," *Canadian Review of Sociology and Anthropology/La Revue Canadienne de Sociologie et d'Anthropologie* 40, no. 2 (2003): 171–196.

60. Berke, "Coming Home Again," 513; Nicole Woolsey Biggart, *Charismatic Capitalism: Direct-Selling Organizations in America.* Chicago: University of Chicago Press, 1989.

61. Berke, "Coming Home Again," 513.

62. Taylor, "Marilyn's Friends," 573–594.

63. Berke, "Coming Home Again," 519.

64. Pampered Chef, "Our Company," August 7, 2007, http://www.pamperedchef.com (June 9, 2009).

65. Annie Phizacklea and Carol Wolkowitz, *Homeworking Women: Gender, Racism, and Class at Work* (Thousand Oaks, CA: Sage, 1995).

66. Quoted in Berke, "Coming Home Again," 537.

67. Taylor, "Marilyn's Friends," 574.

68. Vincent, "Preserving Domesticity," 171–196.

69. Taylor, "Marilyn's Friends," 573–594.

70. Ibid.

71. Martha McCaughey and Christina French, "Women's Sex-Toy Parties: Technology, Orgasm, and Commodification," *Sexuality and Culture* 5, no. 3 (2001): 77–96.

72. Taylor, "Marilyn's Friends," 575.

73. Ibid., 573–594.

74. Berke, "Coming Home Again," 513.

75. Catherine Egley Waggoner, "The Emancipatory Potential of Feminine Masquerade in Mary Kay Cosmetics," *Text and Performance Quarterly* 17 (1997): 256–272.

76. Pampered Chef, "Come Join Us!" August 7, 2007, http://www.pamperedchef .com (June 9, 2009).

77. National Endowment for the Arts, "Reading at Risk: A Survey of Literary Reading in America, Executive Summary," 2002, xiii, http://www.arts.gov (May 28, 2009).

78. Ibid.

79. Elizabeth McHenry, *Forgotten Readers: Recovering the Lost History of African American Literary Societies* (Durham, NC: Duke University Press, 2002), 5.

80. D. T. Max, "The Oprah Effect," *New York Times Magazine* (December, 26, 1999): 37–41.

81. J. J. Royster, *Trace of a Stream: Literacy and Social Change Among African American Women* (Pittsburgh: University of Pittsburgh Press, 2000).

82. Karen Hunter, "Atlanta Literacy Club Makes History with 100th Anniversary," Black Voices Bookshelf, 2009, http://www.bvonbooks.com (May 3, 2009).

83. "Speak Sister, Speak: Oral Empowerment in *Louisa Picquet: The Octoroon,*" *Legacy: A Journal of American Women Writers* 15 (1998): 98–103.

84. Elizabeth McHenry and S. Heath, "The Literature and the Literary: African Americans as Writers and Readers, 1830–1940," *Written Communication* 11, no. 4 (1994): 419–444.

85. Norman Crockett, *The Black Towns* (Lawrence, KS: Regents, 1979).

86. Kathleen Rooney, *Reading with Oprah: The Book Club That Changed America,* 2nd ed. (Fayetteville: University of Arkansas Press, 2005), 8.

87. McHenry, *Forgotten Readers.*

88. A. Abdur-Rahman, "Review of *Forgotten Readers: Recovering the Lost History of African American Literary Societies,*" *Black Renaissance* 5, no. 1 (Spring 2003): 154.

89. Patricia Hill Collins, *Black Feminist Thought: Knowledge, Consciousness, and the Politics of Empowerment* (Boston: Unwin Hyman, 1990), 221–238.

90. Anne J. Cooper, *A Piece of Mind* (New York: Double Daily, 1984).

91. J. Douthis, "A Former Slave Made Great Strides in Education," *Miami Times,* January 28–February 3, 2004, 4A.

92. S. M. Hartman, "Pauli Murray and the Juncture of Women's Liberation and Black Liberation," *Journal of Women's History* 14, no. 2 (Summer 2002): 74.

93. Elsa Barkley Brown, "What Has Happened Here? The Politics of Difference in Women's History and Feminist Politics," *Feminist Studies* 18 (Summer 1992): 300.

94. Devon Pryor, "What Is a Literary Canon?" Wise Geek, n.d., http://www .wisegeek.com (June 16, 2009).

95. Barbara Christian, "Trajectories of Self-Definition: Placing Contemporary Afro-American Women's Fiction," in *Conjuring: Black Women, Fiction, and the Literary Tradition,* ed. Marjorie Pryse and Hortense Spillers (Bloomington: Indiana University Press, 1985).

96. Langston Hughes, "Mother to Son," in *The Collected Poems of Langston Hughes,* ed. Arnold Rampersand. NewYork: Vintage Books, 1995.

97. Wallace Thurman, *The Blacker the Berry: A Novel of Negro Life* (1929; reprint, Austin, TX: Touchstone, 1996).

98. Hill Harper, *Letters to a Young Sister: DeFine Your Destiny* (New York: Gotham Books, 2008), 18.

99. Sue Monk Kidd, *The Secret Life of Bees* (New York: Penguin, 2002).

100. Steve Harvey, *Act Like a Lady, Think Like a Man: What Men Really Think About Love Relationships, Intimacy, and Commitment* (New York: HarperCollins, 2009).

101. Mary J. Butler, "The Words of Truth," *Heritage Battle Creek: A Local Journal* 8 (Fall 1997), http://www.sojournertruth.org (May 10, 2009).

102. Marilyn Richardson, *Maria W. Stewart, American's First Black Woman Political Writer: Essays and Speeches,* Blacks in the Diaspora (Bloomington: Indiana University Press, 1982).

103. Some current researchers have re-identified Milla Granson as Lilly Ann Granderson. See Elizabeth A. Sackler Center for Feminist Art, *The Dinner Party: Heritage Floor: Milla Granson,* Brooklyn Museum, 2009, http://www.brooklynmuseum.org (June 19, 2009).

104. Jan Doherty, "Louisiana Black Women: An Ignored History," *Loyola University Student Historical Journal* 17 (Spring–Fall 1986).

105. Kalenda Eaton, *Womanism, Literature, and the Transformation of the Black Community, 1965–1980,* Studies in African American History and Culture (New York: Routledge, 2007).

106. McHenry, *Forgotten Readers.*

107. Elizabeth Long, *Book Clubs: Women and the Uses of Reading in Everyday Life* (Chicago: University of Chicago Press, 2003).

108. Rooney, *Reading with Oprah.*

109. Marti Parham, "Blacks Read More Than Whites, Hispanics: Poll," *Jet,* September 10, 2007, http://findarticles.com (June 19, 2009).

110. For more information on this organization, see http://www.nbs.org.

111. Attendance, however, was down 80 percent, as many club members chose to spend their travel money on attending the inauguration of the United States's first African American president.

112. Jeffrey A. Trachtenberg, "Why Book Industry Sees the World Still Split by Race," *Wall Street Journal,* December 6, 2006.

113. Book sales in the United States for the month of January 2009: Adult hardcovers, down 33.9 percent from the previous year to sales of $60.5 million; adult paperbacks, down 24.7 percent to sales of $102 million; adult mass market, down 12 percent to sales of $56.4 million; audiobooks, down 45.9 percent to $7.7 million; e-books, up 174.6 percent to $8.8 million. Association of American Publishers, "AAP Reports Publishing Sales for Month of January," press release, April 3, 2009, http://publishers.org (June 19, 2009).

114. In 2010, Forum Hall, in the K-State Student Union, had a standing-room-only crowd of more than 700 and turned away at least 100. In 2011, the show will be held in McCain Auditorium, with a capacity of 1,750.

115. Aggieville is Manhattan's historic bar district. It has over forty bars and restaurants in just a two-block radius. See Yale Daily News Staff, *The Insider's Guide to the Colleges, 2006* (New York: St. Martin's, 2005), 363.

116. Callie Marie Rennison, "Rape and Sexual Assault: Reporting to Police and Medical Attention, 1992–2000," US Department of Justice, August 2002, http://ojp.usdoj.gov (June 20, 2009).

117. Judith Lorber, "Believing Is Seeing: Biology as Ideology," *Gender & Society* 7, no. 4 (1993): 568–581.

118. Avy Skolnick, Crystal Middlestadt, Edward Cervantes, Jake Finney, Jarad Ringer, Joseph Barretto, Julio Gonzalez, Kelly Costello, Lindsey Moore, Melissa Pope, Michelle Kaufman, Patricia Duffett, Rebecca Kloek, Tina D'Elia, and Victoria Cruz, "Hate Violence Against LGBT People in US Report," National Coalition of Anti-Violence Programs, 2008, http://www.avp.org (June 30, 2009).

7

Taking Back, Talking Back

> Comfort zones are most often expanded through discomfort.
> —*Peter McWilliams, www.debrarussell.com*

As coauthors, we could have closed the book with Chapter 6. Instead, we choose to scrutinize the party plan economy up close and personal, even if it means baring our own vulnerabilities. This book presents an emerging framework of study for an alternative work structure, the party plan economy. But it is marketplaces of interaction that render the party plan economy viable from one situation to another. Again and again, gender scholarship insists that we all are accomplices in the gender order; this final chapter looks at that participatory role. The concept of gender practice links individual involvement to collective action and clarifies how underlying markers of gender parties transfer to other forms of interactions such as those illustrated through book clubs and a drag community. This idea of transference implies agency and change and is reminiscent of other instances in which groups, even relatively small groups, have invoked words and vision in one venue to inspire a larger project of collective action.

Gender as Practice

In this chapter, we use Michelle's Pampered Chef party to make sense of our own gender practices. We (we personally, and the collective *we* of women and men) continue to prop up gender parties—hosting, attending, inviting, buying, smiling, performing, pretending—thus perpetuating the very challenges this book exposes. These brief annotations reveal gender parties as a collective and ongoing project, one that encompasses many facets of gender construction, including the enticement, fellowship, and fun, as well as the oppressive face of a system that buttresses inequality for half its members.

233

The concept of gender-as-practice brings a specific meaning to the study of gender. Just as gender is conceived as a "doing," not a "thing," practice is also de-categorized and ongoing; that is, understanding gender as practice, as Patricia Yancey Martin claims, is "to view it as a 'system of action' that is institutionalized."[1] As gendered actions become institutionalized (that is, take on specific meaning, with scope and permanence), they grow to be gendered practices. Recall, however, that structures (i.e., institutions) are constructed and maintained through human interaction; thus it is individuals who practice gender. The two meanings of practice—gendered practice and practicing gender—remain distinct but tightly intertwined. As Martin astutely notes, "Over time, the saying and doing become what is said and done."[2] This linking of practice and structure is critical in understanding the connection between "partying" on the one hand, and gender parties on the other, as an instrument of the larger gender order.

Raewyn Connell points out that injecting practice into theory rescues the study of gender from an abyss of extremism on either side; "free will" perspectives overestimate voluntarism and individualism, whereas fully structural frameworks are overly deterministic and fail to account for human agency and responsibility. Practicing gender (as a concept) and, in this instance, practicing partying, refocuses on "what people do by way of constituting the social relations they live in."[3] In other words, gender, we are reminded, is not what we are or even the roles we learn; it is encased in what we do, or practice.[4]

At some point, practicing becomes the outcome and vice versa. Just as the Olympian's sport becomes near-perfect and mechanical, we practice gender over and over, without stopping and, eventually, without thinking. At Michelle's party, we fell right into the practice of upholding conventional gender lines. That is, we played the part of the "good woman," who is neither radical nor political but who fits comfortably into the prescribed role, without question. Either or both of us could have stood up and said, "Wait a minute . . . what is going on here? Why are we letting this woman cook for us while we observe? Why are we purchasing overpriced products that none of us needs? Why are we here?" But we didn't.

Gender-as-practice is either invisible (as in home-based work) or seen as blatant caricature (as in drag queen performances), neither of which is taken seriously as work. Certainly, the fun need not be sacrificed at the altar of gender politics; everyone wants to have fun. A broader critique asks how parties and rituals of fun, left unchallenged, may undermine women's ability to enjoy meaningful and equally gratifying social experiences with other women. Within a gender framework, the instances just referred to—product parties, home-based work, drag performances, and other social rituals—may be seen as substantially reinforcing masculinist power. Still, when under a critical reading, each situation *may* be transformed into resistance. The distinction is one that comes only with collective awareness.

From the gender-as-practice vantage point, it comes as somewhat less surprising that we (as authors) continued to support the party plan, even as we were writing this book. We bought, consumed, pretended, and promoted the party plan economy, all the while proclaiming to be agents of change. We looked at each other afterward, sharing emotions ranging from ribald humor (We're such bitches!), to bewilderment (What were we thinking?), to anger and self-blame. The words of Audre Lorde mirror our own reflections: "How often have I demanded from another Black woman what I had not dared to give myself—acceptance, faith, enough space to consider change."[5]

We came to realize that we asked the contributors, our friends and colleagues, our staff, and readers of this book to do something we had not fully done ourselves—accept our discomfort, allow ourselves not simply to acknowledge participation but to *feel* it.

Prior to that moment, neither of us had experienced this degree of discomfort with our practice of gender. It took actually being there and using what we had written in *Women at Work* to critically evaluate and understand the gendering of such a gathering. The paradox is that participating in the party is what led to discomfort, but only after great effort to examine our own performance. Becoming aware of our own contributions to the gender order familiarizes us with how the system remains intact. Recognizing our own complicity was a very uncomfortable moment but also an exceptional learning tool.

Awareness can be a beautiful thing, even in small ways. When turning into the final laps of this project, we hired several student workers, consciously choosing people with diverse backgrounds and perspectives. Brett, the general project manager, is a graduate student in economics. Truthfully? I think he struggled with the concept of fluid gender boundaries and flinched ever so slightly the day we pointed out his feminine qualities. But, to his credit, he now speaks fluently about "unnecessarily gendered pronouns" and compulsory heterosexuality, and he now understands that Fendi is, indeed, a purse label and is not misspelled. In his reflections, he wrote, "The first day that I read the piece on workers in the Czech Republic and how little their husbands help around the house, I made sure to do more than my fair share of the housework when I went home that night." Practicing awareness is a beautiful thing.

We often watch with eyes half shut as the party plan economy seduces and then divides, ignoring critical gender problems. Studying gender as practice helps unpack the conundrum of both enticements and pitfalls related to gender construction.

Gender as Identity Politics

Awareness is seldom isolated; more often, it becomes attached to a recognition of patterns outside our individual experiences. Recall that we started this book by looking at parties, tiny little entities, seemingly isolated, but now illuminated as occupying a niche situated between two other institutional structures, formal and informal markets. Due to this structural position, the party plan has heretofore remained unexamined and its gendered positions largely invisible. However, once characteristics of the party structure became evident, patterns emerged, and connections became visible. Street vendors in Brazil use personal networks in much the same way as do Tupperware "ladies" in the United States; Indian women share resources in ways similar to quilting or scrapbook parties in the West; and mothers in the Czech Republic look to combine work and child care through an ideology shared by women around the world. Such linkages give rise to gender identity politics and, in particular, a group consciousness of women as women.

As noted, history has failed to recognize women's labor generally, and specifically the hierarchical gender arrangement of the party plan economy. This lack of recognition, especially since the 1960s, is due in part to a lack of awareness of women's common issues, and in part to our singular understanding of economic markets as rational, bureaucratized organizations. Trapped within such a structured world—what Max Weber refers to as an "iron cage" of rationality[6]—we fail to recognize seemingly irrational, loosely structured markets; in such a milieu normative gender conventions operate freely, virtually unfettered . . . until a gender consciousness is brought to bear. Just as our experience with the Pampered Chef party created an acute sensitivity to our own participation in gender party exploitation, other contributors expressed similar awareness, none either purely positive or singularly negative but always insightful, about how gender parties work as a part of the larger system. Mangala Subramaniam expressed awareness of the empowering nature of Indian kitty parties through conversations with her mother:

> It was quite revealing to hear my mother describe the party and what it meant to her and her friends. As my mother explained, there was a sense of excitement recalling the many activities involved in preparing and organizing a kitty party. She repeatedly insisted that it was not really winning the "kitty" that mattered; there was a feeling of fun and joy trying to steer away from the daily routine chores . . . that the camaraderie was central to the parties.

The sense of women's communities as empowering spilled over into the studies of women's book clubs, another venue in which personal networks invoke the sharing of ideas and gender consciousness. While working on this project, both BeEtta Stoney and Dena Wallerson learned about their African American heritage and recognized the importance of African American women coming together through book clubs. Stoney said of her participants:

> I want to thank the African American book club members for allowing me to relearn about myself as a Black woman. I want to thank the Sister Friends group

for reminding me that you can actually depend on [a woman who is] not your biological sister and that she is there for you, even when you do not need her shoulder. I want to thank the Spiritual Book Club for reminding me that God is everywhere providing strength, comfort, and camaraderie in women.

Similar to Stoney's reflection, and reminiscent of the sociability tradition that Sue Zschoche mentioned in the first case study in this book, Wallerson spoke of a longing "for social relationships with women as the women in the book groups have. They are friends for life." Her study ends with hopes and plans for collective activism, readily available in just such settings.

As we read the field studies of women's gatherings around the world, underlying expressions of gender and celebrations of womanhood emerged. Adryanna Siqueira, a native Brazilian, understood all too well the work that went into street vending as she completed her study of Brazilian women street vendors. She saw their work regularly while growing up in Brazil, but now she observed their labor through the lens of a researcher and as a woman newly conscious of her connection to them. She wondered about women's emotional attachment to their work and their strident motivation to be successful:

I feel an intense energy every time I am in a market . . . of the feirantes, eager to sell, despite the heat or the fact that everyone else is having barbecue and beer. Sometimes I think they are just a special group of people who came to the markets because they are natural salespeople and love being in contact with the public. Other times I feel that this vibe comes from the intense need to make ends meet, and that enthusiasm is just emotion work.

Siqueira's reflections highlight the performance of gender through work and emotion management within this regime.

Whether in a Brazilian street market or at a Mary Kay party, women participated in gendered activities culturally connected to femininity. They spoke of fun, friendship, family, and domestic work. They cooked, cleaned, and enjoyed many aspects of party plan work. Whether or not the participants enjoyed the work and found satisfaction in their fellowship, their participation (and ours) tracked straight into a party plan regime that reinforces a gender culture of disadvantage for women as a group. How often do we think about this?

Hopefully, it is impossible now for all of us to attend a gender party and not see gender as an artificial and repressive system. With recognition, we can better understand how larger institutions infiltrate microlevel systems, and vice versa. Women's book club participation, for example, illustrates how women's choice of literature may support a culture of romance or one of quiet activism. Numerous field studies reveal everyday connections between gender construction and market consumption—Kimber Williams's study on brand obsession and Akiko Yoshida's research on Mary Kay consultants' motivation to sell cosmetics serve as two material illustrations, while Summer Lewis's fair-trade research and Leigh Fine's exploration of sex toy parties demonstrate how women sometimes resist such power structures. All such gatherings hold the promise of melding products, people, and influence to better understand the inner workings of parties as part of a gender regime.

Doing Gender: Taking Back, Talking Back

Although practice is based on "a compromise between past experience and an imagined future,"[7] implying a *system* of action,[8] *doing* centers on individual action (though Candace West and Don Zimmerman point out that it is a "situated doing").[9] Certainly, doing and practice are interrelated, but doing illuminates the link between individual action and collective projects. We see "doing" as the potentially activist component of gender.

This chapter draws attention to doing gender as resistance and activism—the specific reference to what we call "taking back and talking back." In fact, West and Zimmerman underscore the political implications of doing: "If the gender attributes deployed as a basis of maintaining men's hegemony are social products, they are subject to social change (however challenging such change may be)."[10] In the words of Joan Baez, singer/songwriter/social critic: "Action is the antidote to despair."[11]

First, several very brief historical examples prove instructive to understanding what individual actions and political "doings" by women look like: In 1857, women garment workers in New York led the first organized protest for women's work rights;[12] Mary Jackson, armed with a Bowie knife and six-gun, led bread riots in 1863 to protest high food prices;[13] and Clara Zetkin led a proposal for equal pay before the International Socialist Congress in 1889.[14] The twentieth century saw Emmeline Pankhurst and her daughters chain themselves to the British Parliament in 1905, leading hunger strikes to promote suffrage;[15] in 1908, women needleworkers led a major trades strike in New York;[16] and in 1933, Frances Perkins headed a New York workers' protest after the Triangle Shirtwaist fire (she eventually became the first woman to serve in a presidential cabinet).[17]

These brief but impressive examples may overwhelm the rest of us. Where do we start, and how can we measure up? The words of an influential mentor came back to me: "We cannot live without our lives."[18] This phrase, taken from an article by Russo, reminds us that guilt is a waste of time and that we must start where we are.[19] What matters, she explains, is what we do with our newfound awareness. Gender parties provide just such an instrument to reawaken and renew our collective selves.

Though deeply social, the "doings" of activism begin with individuals. Research by social psychologists demonstrates what Malcolm Gladwell calls a "mental valet" effect, referring to the idea that we take in cues very quickly (like rapid-fire practice) and, for the most part, unconsciously perform daily tasks.[20] (This is not so surprising, considering we often go through traffic unaware of turns and signage!) Similarly, the psychologist John Bargh and his colleagues at New York University discovered a process they call "priming," which actually guides our unconscious thoughts.[21] In testing the priming hypothesis, Joshua Aronson and Claude Steele found that they could manipulate what takes place in the unconsciousness of subjects through cues, which included subtle references to age or race.[22]

In much the same way, we, as individuals deeply engaged in doing gender, become subject to the mental valet effect. At Michelle's party, we took priming cues from the party. It seemed like fun (and genuinely was), it took place in the home (where business does not happen), friends and acquaintances were there (without their business hats, so to speak), and we were being presented products that affirmed our femaleness[23] (lots of sophisticated kitchen tools, which assumed we were accomplished cooks and "housewives"). It would have been ludicrous if we (as authors) did the scholarly work of gender (pointing out ideology and inequality and citing literature) in such a setting. And thus we fell right into the work of doing a very emphasized femininity, despite the fact that professionally we deny such as our "true" identity.

The point is this: If we consciously condition ourselves to develop an awareness of our position and our participation, we gain power over it. If we raise our gender consciousness in the presence (real or imagined) of other women, we develop group consciousness. A step toward promoting group consciousness is to see ourselves as part of the larger whole—how we can come together in everyday ways to effect change.

As we pay it forward, it is important to remember that while trails are blazed, others are waiting. This chapter is about reclaiming, resisting, and repurposing the party plan economy. As Audre Lorde reminds us, "We do not live single-issue lives"; gender parties offer an instrument for group change.[24]

Not Just Words

Parties are collective and coactive, multifaceted and multipurpose: again, instruments. To illustrate, please indulge us one more party reference.

I (Sue) recently attended another women-only party for a friend who was just diagnosed with cancer. Several facets of the party paralleled Michelle's Pampered Chef party. Most of the women (again, about twelve or so in attendance) were affiliated with the university in one way or another. All were bright, aware, energetic women with careers. We met at a nice house in the suburbs, with lots of good fun and good food. This time, no wine flowed; alcohol doesn't mix well with cancer medication. At a pivotal point in the party (we called it Chris's Chemo Kickoff Party), the guest of honor, Chris, announced loudly, "OK, girls, gather around, 'cause I'm just going to say this once." Again, in a surreal moment, I watched. Chris was perched on a kitchen bar stool, which held her about a foot above the rest of us. Every woman gathered around, forming a tight little circle of friendship and mindfulness. No one spoke as Chris told, with perfect commentary and clarity, the details of her illness, the diagnosis, the upcoming treatment, and the prognosis. The story lasted twenty minutes, and a lifetime. There were a few questions, lots of hugs, but no tears (not then); there were offers and plans and optimism but no speculation. We all posed for a group photo. The circle could not have been more complete.

Consider the contrast with Michelle's party. At first blush, one seemed inappropriately jocular and shallow, the other inadequately somber and too mundane. But, in the end, perhaps they were, interchangeably, just right. Both told stories of women's lives.

There is a nice line in a song that says, "Are you brave enough to see?"[25] It testifies to the importance of vision. What we see is a Lipstick Summit. Bear with us on this one. We envision a time when the party plan economy becomes a medium for bringing together people across the globe, united around a movement toward greater gender awareness and equality. The scaffolding is there; we just need to use it in a way that connects not only ideas and concepts, but real people in an actual setting.

We see our Lipstick Summit as a world conference held in, oh, Vienna, Austria, the second week of September 2015.[26] The weather is predicted to be sunny, the temperature moderate. The Women's World Oversight of PPE (party plan economy) will organize and host the event; its symbol, a giant sculpture of women with outstretched arms, designed by architectural guru Maya Lin, welcomes all as they enter the epic event.[27] (We selected Lin because of her magnificent design of Yale University's *The Women's Table,* which bears 268 zeroes, one for each year there was no room for women at that citadel of higher learning.) What better way to celebrate the twentieth anniversary of the last world conference sponsored by the United Nations Commission on the Status of Women?[28] It's about time.

It's about time that the world fully understands that women constitute half the world's population, perform nearly two-thirds of its work, receive one-tenth of the world's income, and own less than one-one-hundredth of the world's property.[29]

It's about time that we understand that inequality is embedded in everyday practices of gender. One example, as told by Irene Stuber, comes from Kenya, where "men sit in groups under the shade trees so they can protect their women working in the fields from lions. That there are no lions in that part of Kenya is unimportant."[30] The lessons of history are hard to learn and even harder to keep.

Though readers may have perceived that this book is about only women, it is about humanity and dignity. Feminist ideals of the past century and a half

Figure 7.1 Maya Lin's *The Women's Table* at Yale University.
(Flickr Creative Commons)

necessarily focused on experiences, concerns, and lives of women. This was essential because the world, and especially science, concerned itself with the other one-half of the population—men and men's lives. Even now, many believe the great effort is over: Men and women? The same. Equality? Done.

We have ample evidence that this is not the case, but far too often, young women hesitate to identify with the category *women*, undermining collective efforts. We, as feminists, as womanists, and as humanists struggle with the balance between learning from the past and leaning on the past.[31] But we are also heartened by the awareness of young women all around us, exemplified by Lewis as she reflected on women's station in her own field study: "Not only is the personal political, but the personal is global; we are all connected."

That aside, the fact remains that this is a humanist issue, one that should concern men and women equally.[32] Exposing the party plan economy, with all its inner workings, convincingly demonstrates that systems of gender exploitation are connected globally and that patriarchy has continued to reconstitute itself, in part, through the party plan economy.

As we close, we are reminded of the deep conviction that we eagerly consume from our feminist friends. As but one example, Zschoche compels us to think deeply about our scholarship and its place in the world. When I asked for her final thoughts on the project, here is what she wrote:

> Feminism, it seems to me, demands that we see our situation as a woman as somehow connected to the fate of all other women. Consumerism asks us to reach for the personal fulfillment hawked on every corner of our lives. How, I find myself wondering, do we break through that personal fantasy bubble so we can better confront the very real demons that threaten the lives of so many women? Trust me, this is not what I thought I would be thinking about when I started this project. All of which is to say that this project has been remarkably provocative of odd thoughts. And for the record, that is the highest compliment I can offer.

And just like that, we are reminded: Words are never just words.

We hope to see you all in Vienna in 2015. We will be wearing red.

Notes

1. Patricia Yancey Martin, "'Said and Done' Versus 'Saying and Doing': Gendering Practices, Practicing Gender at Work," *Gender & Society* 17, no. 3 (2003): 342–366.

2. Ibid., 352.

3. Raewyn Connell, *Gender and Power: Society, the Person, and Sexual Politics* (Palo Alto, CA: Stanford University Press, 1987), 62.

4. Candace West and Don H. Zimmerman, "Doing Gender," *Gender & Society* 1, no. 2 (1987): 125–151.

5. "Audre Lorde," ZAMI, 2004, http://www.zami.org (June 28, 2009).

6. Max Weber, *The Protestant Ethic and the Spirit of Capitalism*, translated by Talcott Parsons (New York: Charles Scribner's Sons, 1958), 181.

7. Martin, "Saying and Doing," p. 351.

8. Raewyn Connell, *Masculinities* (Berkeley: University of California Press, 1995).

9. That is, all individual action is located within the constraints of, and guided by, institutional arrangements and local practices. West and Zimmerman, "Doing Gender."

10. Candace West and Don H. Zimmerman, "Accounting for Doing Gender," *Gender & Society* 23 (2009): 114.

11. Jone Johnson Lewis, "Joan Baez Quotes," About.com: Women's History, 2005, http://womenshistory.about.com (June 28, 2009).

12. Kathy Durkin, "A Rich Tradition: International Women's Day," Worker's World, March 7, 2008, http://www.workers.org (June 25, 2009).

13. Sara Margaret Evans, *Born for Liberty* (New York: Free Press, 1997), 116.

14. Gerd Callesen, "The International Socialist Women's Conference," Sources on the Development of the Socialist International (1907–1919), Friedrich-Ebert-Stiftung, http://library.fes.de (June 25, 2009).

15. Marina Warner, "Emmeline Pankhurst," *Time*, June 14, 1999, http://www.time.com (June 25, 2009).

16. Women and the Economy, United Nations Platform for Action Committee Manitoba, "Globalization and Clothes," 2006, www.unpac.ca (July 2, 2010).

17. American Federation of Labor–Congress of Industrial Organizations (AFL-CIO), "Frances Perkins," http://www.aflcio.org (June 28, 2009).

18. Myra Marx Ferree, esteemed gender scholar, colleague, and friend, has selflessly mentored hundreds of young women throughout her career. Though she has not been at my side physically, virtually every page of this book is marked by her influence. In particular, this passage is from the reading list in a gender seminar that she led in 1992.

19. Ann Russo, "We Cannot Live Without Our Lives," in *Third World Women and the Politics of Feminism*, ed. Chandra Talpade Mohanty, Ann Russo, and Lourdes Torres (Bloomington: Indiana University Press, 1991).

20. Malcolm Gladwell, *Blink: The Power of Thinking Without Thinking* (New York: Back Bay Books, 2005).

21. It is important to note that Bargh's "priming" does not equate to brainwashing. For more information about psychologist Bargh's "priming," see Gladwell's *Blink*, 53–56.

22. For additional information about psychologists Claude Steele and Joshua Aronson, see Gladwell's *Blink*, 56–59.

23. West and Zimmerman, "Accounting for Doing Gender," 115.

24. Audre Lorde, *Sister Outsider* (Berkeley, CA: Crossing Press Feminist Series, 1984), 138.

25. Nine Inch Nails, "The Hand That Feeds," *With Teeth*, Island Records, CD, 2005.

26. "Vienna Second Most-Livable City in World, Claims *Economist*," *Austrian Times*, 2009, http://www.austriantimes.at (June 28, 2009).

27. Born in Ohio to Chinese Americans who immigrated to the United States, Lin developed an early interest in design, going on to the prestigious programs at Yale University and eventually receiving three degrees there as well as honorary degrees from three other prominent universities. After her design for the proposed Vietnam Veterans Memorial won first place in a blind-review contest (Lin was an undergraduate at the time), the fact that she was a woman of Chinese descent emerged. Her background, coupled with the unconventional design of the memorial, stirred heated controversy. After much debate and testimony before Congress, the memorial was built but is joined by two other memorials. The memorial wall has become one of the most visited sites in Washington, D.C., today. Lin's story, documented in the film *A Strong Clear Vision*, illustrates courage and tenacity. But more important, it demonstrates the importance of acting on one's vision. Freida Lee Mock, "Maya Lin: A Strong Clear Vision," American Documentary, 2007, http://amdoc.org (July 7, 2010).

28. There have been only four UN World Conferences on Women, the last held in 1995 in Beijing, China. Secretary-General Boutros Boutros-Ghali delivered a statement that included: "There is a deplorable trend towards the organized humiliation of women." Unfortunately, Boutrous-Ghali, as well as the large majority of world leaders, has not followed through with repeated declarations to improve upon gender equality around the globe. It also takes women in high places. After Boutrous-Ghali's failure to deliver, Madeleine Albright (then US secretary of state) was instrumental in getting Kofi Annan appointed as the new Secretary-General of the UN, and he appointed Mary Robinson as UN High Commissioner for Human Rights. Irene Stuber, "The UN's Role of Advancing the Rights of Women," The Liz Library, Women's History Month Collection, 2000, http://www.thelizlibrary.org (July 7, 2010).

29. Irene Stuber, "Women's History Month Collection," The Liz Library, 2006, http://www.thelizlibrary.org (June 28, 2009).

30. Ibid.

31. The problem is that the beast (patriarchy and its corollaries) keeps finding fire to breathe. Eleanor Roosevelt proclaimed in 1958: "Where, after all, do universal human rights begin? In small places, close to home, so close and so small that they cannot be seen on any map of the world. Yet they are the world of the individual person: the neighborhood he lives in; the school or college he attends; the factory, farm or office where he works. Such are the places where every man, woman and child seeks equal justice, equal opportunity, equal dignity without discrimination. Unless these rights have meaning there, they have little meaning anywhere. Without concerted citizen action to uphold them close to home, we shall look in vain for progress in the larger world." Eleanor Roosevelt, remarks on universal human rights at presentation of booklet on human rights, *In Your Hands,* to the United Nations Commission on Human Rights, United Nations, New York, March 27, 1958, http://quotationsbook.com (June 28, 2009).

32. Again, in 1997, Hillary Clinton said (or, as Clinton might claim, Roosevelt as channeled through her) in an address at the Vital Voices conference in Vienna, Austria: "We are here to advance the cause of women and to advance the cause of democracy and to make it absolutely clear that the two are inseparable. There cannot be true democracy unless women's voices are heard. There cannot be true democracy unless women are given the opportunity to take responsibility for their own lives." Of course, the examples from Roosevelt and Clinton are only two of the millions of times we are reminded that the principles of democracy and equality go hand in hand. But they are important ones, ones that should strike a chord of familiarity. Hillary Clinton, "'Women's Rights Are Human Rights': Famous Speech by Hillary Clinton, Beijing, China, 5 September 1995," Famous Quotes, http://www.famousquotes.me.uk (June 28, 2009).

References

Abdur-Rahman, A. "Review of *Forgotten Readers: Recovering the Lost History of African Literary Societies.*" *Black Renaissance* 5, no. 1 (Spring 2003): 154.

Acker, Joan. *Class Questions: Feminist Answers.* Lanham, MD: Rowman and Littlefield, 2006.

———. "The Future of Women and Work: Ending the Twentieth Century." *Sociological Perspectives* 35 (1992): 53–68.

———. "Hierarchies, Jobs, Bodies: A Theory of Gendered Organizations." *Gender & Society* 4 (1990): 139–158.

———. "Inequality Regimes." *Gender & Society* 20 (2006): 441–464.

———. "Rewriting Class, Race, and Gender: Problems in Feminist Rethinking." In *Revisioning Gender*, ed. Myra Marx Ferree, Judith Lorber, and Beth B. Hess, 44–69. Lanham, MD: Rowman and Littlefield, 2000.

Alexander, M. Jacqui. "Remembering *This Bridge*, Remembering Ourselves: Yearning, Memory, and Desire." In *Sing, Whisper, Shout, Pray! Feminist Visions for a Just World*, ed. M. Jacqui Alexander, Lisa Albrecht, Sharon Day, and Mab Segrest, 4. Fort Bragg, CA: EdgeWork Books, 2003.

Amendolara, Lauren D. "Knocking Out Knock-Offs: Effectuating the Criminalization of Trafficking in Counterfeit Goods." *Fordham Intellectual Property Media and Entertainment Law Journal* 15, no. 3 (2005): 789–819.

American Association of University Women. "Shortchanging Girls, Shortchanging America." Executive Report, 1991–1992. http://www.aauw.org (January 15, 2010).

American Federation of Labor–Congress of Industrial Organizations (AFL-CIO). "Frances Perkins." http://www.aflcio.org (June 28, 2009).

American Psychological Association. "Is Multitasking More Efficient? Shifting Mental Gears Costs Time, Especially When Shifting to Less Familiar Tasks." August 5, 2001. http://www.apa.org (June 30, 2009).

"Amway Sister Company, Quixtar Inc., Sued by Distributor Group Represented by Shughart, Thomson and Kilroy." Business Wire, 2007. http://www.businesswire.com (June 29, 2009).

Andersen, Margaret L., and Patricia Hill Collins. *Race, Class, and Gender.* Belmont, CA: Wadsworth, 2002.

Andersen, Margaret, and Dana Hysock. *Thinking About Women: Sociological Perspectives on Sex and Gender*, 8th ed. Columbus, OH: Allyn and Bacon, 2009.

Antonovics, Nick. "UPDATE 2: L'Oreal 2007 Sales Rise 8.1 Pct, Confident for 2008." Reuters, January 24, 2008. http://www.reuters.com (April 10, 2009).

AOL Small Business. "Home Party Sales." March 1, 2007. http://smallbusiness.aol.com (June 11, 2009).

Arbonne. "Arbonne International." http://www.arbonne.com (June 8, 2009).

———. "Arbonne International: Taking It to the Next Level." *Direct Selling News,* July 2006. http://www.arbonnemarketing.com (June 8, 2009).

———. "Global Office Executive Team." http://www.arbonne.com (June 8, 2009).

Association of American Publishers. "AAP Reports Publishing Sales for Month of January." Press release, April 3, 2009. http://publishers.org.

Atwood, Feona J. "Fashion and Passion: Marketing Sex to Women." *Sexualities* 8 (2005): 392–406.

"Audre Lorde." ZAMI, 2004. http://www.zami.org (June 28, 2009).

Auster, Carol J., and Susan C. Ohm. "Masculinity and Femininity in Contemporary American Society: A Reevaluation Using the Bem Sex-Role Inventory." *Sex Roles* 43 (2000): 499–528.

Avon. "Avon Around the World." http://www.avoncompany.com (June 20, 2009).

Babcock, Linda, and Sara Laschever. *Women Don't Ask.* New York: Bantam Books, 2007.

Banks, Jane, and Patricia R. Zimmerman. "The Mary Kay Way: The Feminization of a Corporate Discourse." *Journal of Communication Inquiry* 11 (1987): 85–99.

Bayat, Asef. "Islamism and the Politics of Fun." *Public Culture* 19, no. 3 (October 2007): 433–459.

Belenky, Mary F., Blythe McVicker Clinchy, Nancy Rule Goldberger, and Jill Mattuck Tarrule. *Women's Ways of Knowing: The Development of Self, Voice, and Mind,* 10th ed. New York: Basic Books, 1997.

Benedict, Ruth. *Patterns of Culture.* New York: Houghton Mifflin, 1934.

Benson, John. "Consumption and the Consumer Revolution." *ReFresh* 23 (Autumn 1996): 5–8.

Berke, Debra L. "Coming Home Again: The Challenges and Rewards of Home-Based Self-Employment." *Journal of Family Issues* 24 (2003): 513–546.

Biggart, Nicole Woolsey. *Charismatic Capitalism: Direct-Selling Organizations in America.* Chicago: University of Chicago Press, 1989.

Blau, Peter M. *Exchange and Power in Social Life.* Hoboken, NJ: John Wiley and Sons, 1964.

Blythe, Mark A., K. Overbeeke, and A. F. Monk. *Funology: From Usability to Enjoyment.* Norwell, MA: Klewer Academic Publishers, 2003.

Bookman, Ann, and Sandra Morgen. *Women and the Politics of Empowerment.* Philadelphia: Temple University Press, 1988.

Bourdieu, Pierre, and Loic Wacquant. *The State Nobility: Elite Schools in the Field of Power.* Palo Alto, CA: Stanford University Press, 1989.

Breneman, Judy Anne. "Gathering Around the Frame—The Quilting Bee." Womenfolk: The Art of Quilting, 2001. http://www.womenfolk.com (June 14, 2009).

Bromley, Dorothy Dunbar. "Feminist–New Style." *Harper's Magazine* (October 1927): 552–560.

Brown, Elsa Barkley. "What Has Happened Here? The Politics of Difference in Women's History and Feminist Politics." *Feminist Studies* 18 (Summer 1992): 295–312.

Butler, Judith. *Gender Trouble: Feminism and the Subversion of Identity.* New York: Routledge, 1990.

Butler, Mary J. "The Words of Truth." *Heritage Battle Creek: A Local Journal* 8 (Fall 1997). http://www.sojournertruth.org (May 10, 2009).

Callesen, Gerd. "The International Socialist Women's Conference." Sources on the Development of the Socialist International (1907–1919). Friedrich-Ebert-Stiftung. http://library.fes.de (June 25, 2009).

Carter, Ruth. *Amway Motivational Organizations: Behind the Smoke and Mirrors.* Winter Park, FL: Backstreet Publishing, 1999.

Chavis, Melody Ermachild. *Meena, Heroine of Afghanistan: The Martyr Who Founded RAWA, the Revolutionary Association of the Women of Afghanistan.* New York: St. Martin's, 2003.

Chen, Martha Alter. "Rethinking the Informal Economy: Linkages with the Formal Economy and the Formal Regulatory Environment." DESA Working Paper no. 46. New York: United Nations, Department of Economic and Social Affairs, July 2007. http://www.un.org (May 15, 2009).

Chen, Martha, Joann Vanek, Francie Lund, and James Heintz. *Progress of the World's Women 2005.* New York: United Nations Development Fund for Women, 2005.

Chicago Women's Liberation Union. "No More Miss America!" 2005. http://www.cwluherstory.org (June 15, 2009).

Child Care Providers Together. "National Women's Law Center Reports on Child Care and Early Education." 2007. http://ccptmn.org (February 12, 2010).

Christian, Barbara. "Trajectories of Self-Definition: Placing Contemporary Afro-American Women's Fiction." In *Conjuring: Black Women, Fiction, and the Literary Tradition,* ed. Marjorie Pryse and Hortense Spillers. Bloomington: Indiana University Press, 1985.

Christopher, Doris. *The Pampered Chef: The Story of One of America's Most Beloved Companies.* New York: Doubleday Business, 2005.

Clarke, Alison J. *Tupperware: The Promise of Plastic in 1950s America.* Washington, DC: Smithsonian Institution Press, 1999.

Clinton, Hillary. "'Women's Rights Are Human Rights': Famous Speech by Hillary Clinton, Beijing, China, 5 September 1995." Famous Quotes. http://www.famousquotes.me.uk (June 28, 2009).

Coltrane, Scott. "Elite Careers and Family Commitment: It's (Still) About Gender." *Annals of the American Academy of Political and Social Science* 596 (2004): 214–220.

"Company News: Avon to Lay Off 3,500 Workers, 8% of Work Force." *New York Times,* March 19, 2002. http://www.nytimes.com (June 8, 2009).

Conger, Cristen. "Is There a Gender Gap in the Workplace?" February 17, 2009. http://money.howstuffworks.com (June 12, 2009).

Connell, Raewyn. *Gender and Power: Society, the Person, and Sexual Politics.* Palo Alto, CA: Stanford University Press, 1987.

———. *Masculinities.* Berkeley: University of California Press, 1995.

———. "The *Northern Theory* of Globalization." *Sociological Theory* 25, no. 4 (December 2007): 368–385.

Connelly, Maureen, and Patricia Rhoton. "Women in Direct Sales: A Comparison of Mary Kay and Amway Sales Workers." In *The Worth of Women's Work: A Qualitative Synthesis,* ed. Anne Statham, Eleanor M. Miller, and Hans O. Mauksch, 245–264. Albany: State University of New York Press, 1988.

Coontz, Stephanie. *The Way We Never Were.* New York: Basic Books, 2000.

Cooper, Anne J. *A Piece of Mind.* New York: Double Daily, 1984.

Corrin, Chris, ed. *Superwomen and the Double Burden: Women's Experience of Change in Central and Eastern Europe and the Former Soviet Union.* London: Scarlet Press, 1992.

Cott, Nancy. *The Bonds of Womanhood: "Woman's Sphere" in New England, 1780–1835.* New Haven, CT: Yale University Press, 1977.

Crawford, Bridget. "Consciousness Raising and Contemporary Feminist Method." Feminist Law Professors, January 31, 2008. http://feministlawprofs.law.sc.edu (June 14, 2009).

Crawford, John C., and Barbara C. Garland. "A Profile of a Party Plan Sales Force." *Akron Business and Economic Review* 19 (1988): 28–37.

Crockett, Norman. *The Black Towns*. Lawrence, KS: Regents, 1979.

Curtis, Debra. "Commodities and Sexual Subjectivities: A Look at Capitalism and Its Desires." *Cultural Anthropology* 19 (2004): 95–121.

Denalli, J. "Opportunities in Direct Selling." *Nation's Business* 81 (1993): 69–70.

Derber, Charles. *The Wilding of America: Money, Mayhem, and the New American Dream*. New York: Worth, 2002.

De Soto, Hernando. *The Mystery of Capital: Why Capitalism Triumphs in the West and Fails Everywhere Else*. New York: Basic Books, 2000.

Direct Sales Association. "Estimated 2007 US Salespeople." http://www.dsa.org (June 5, 2009).

Doherty, Jan. "Louisiana Black Women: An Ignored History." *Loyola University Student Historical Journal* 17 (Spring–Fall 1986).

Dollar Times. "Inflation Calculator." http://www.dollartimes.com (May 19, 2009).

Douthis, J. "A Former Slave Made Great Strides in Education." *Miami Times*, January 28–February 3, 2004, 4A.

Durkin, Kathy. "A Rich Tradition: International Women's Day." Worker's World, March 7, 2008. http://www.workers.org (June 25, 2009).

Dyer, Susan K., ed. *Tenure Denied: Cases of Sex Discrimination in Academia*. Washington, DC: American Association of University Women, October 2004.

Eaton, Kalenda. *Womanism, Literature, and the Transformation of the Black Community, 1965–1980*. Studies in African American History and Culture. New York: Routledge, 2007.

Edwards, Janis L. "Womanhouse: Making the Personal Story Political in Visual Form." *Women and Language* 19 (1996): 42–46.

eHow. "How to Host a Mary Kay Party." http://www.ehow.com (May 28, 2009).

Equal Exchange. "Fair Trade." 2009. http://www.equalexchange.coop (April 25, 2009).

Evans, Sara Margaret. *Born for Liberty*. New York: Free Press, 1997.

Fairtrade Labelling Organizations International. "About Fair Trade." 2006. http://www.fairtrade.net (April 23, 2009).

FashionPhile blog. "Done to Death." Sept. 8, 2008. http://www.fashionphile.com (May 15, 2009).

Fernandes, Luis Felipe. "Comunidades: Hora de Crescer." *Tribuna do Planalto*, October 19, 2007. http://www.tribunadoplanalto.com (April 6, 2008).

Ferree, Myra Marx. "Beyond Separate Spheres." *Journal of Marriage and the Family* 52 (1990): 866–884.

Feree, Myra Marx, and Beth B. Hess. "Introduction." In *Analyzing Gender,* Beth B. Hess and Myra Marx Ferree. Newbury Park, CA: Sage, 1987.

Ferree, Myra Marx, and Aili Mari Tripp, eds. *Global Feminism: Transnational Women's Activism, Organizing, and Human Rights*. New York: New York University Press, 2006.

Ferree, Myra Marx, Judith Lorber, and Beth B. Hess. *Revisioning Gender*. Thousand Oaks, CA: Sage, 1999.

Findlay, Heather. "Freud's 'Fetishism' and the Lesbian Dildo Debates." *Feminist Studies* 18 (1992): 563–579.

Fisher, Claude S., and Stacey J. Oliker. "A Research Note on Friendship, Gender, and the Life Cycle." *Social Forces* 62 (1983): 124–133.

Fitzpatrick, Robert L. "The Myth of 'Income Opportunity' in Multi-Level Marketing." Pyramid Scheme Alert, 2004. http://www.pyramidschemealert.org (June 20, 2009).

Focus on Fair Trade: Scholarly Anthology Series in Fair Trade Studies. "Fair Trade Timeline." 2009. http://www.fairtradestudies.com (March 4, 2009).

Franklin, Ross D. "Forget Tupperware; It's Taser Party Time." Associated Press, MSNBC.com, http://www.msnbc.msn.com (January 4, 2008).

Freedom of Mind Center. "Criminal Charges Filed Against Amway in India." 2008. http://www.freedomofmind.com (June 29, 2009).

Friedan, Betty. *The Feminine Mystique*. 1963. Reprint, New York: W. W. Norton, 2001.

Friedman, Thomas L. *The World Is Flat: A Brief History of the Twenty-First Century*. Boston: Farrar, Straus and Giroux, 2005.

———. *The World Is Flat 3.0: A Brief History of the Twenty-First Century*. New York: Picador, 2007.

Frye, Marilyn. "Oppression." In *Politics of Reality: Essays in Feminist Theory*. Trumansburg, NY: Crossing Press, 1983.

Gallagher, Melinda, and Emily Kramer. *A Piece of Cake: Recipes for Female Sexual Pleasure*. New York: Atria, 2005.

Gallagher, Winifred. *Rapt: Attention and the Focused Life*. New York: Penguin, 2009.

Garey, Anita. *Weaving Work and Motherhood*. Philadelphia: Temple University Press, 1999.

Gelder, Ken. *Subcultures: Cultural Histories and Social Practice*. New York: Routledge, 2007.

Giroux, Henry A. *Theory and Resistance in Education: Towards a Pedagogy for the Opposition*. Santa Barbara, CA: Greenwood Publishing, 2001.

Gladwell, Malcolm. *Blink: The Power of Thinking Without Thinking*. New York: Back Bay Books, 2005.

———. *The Tipping Point: How Little Things Can Make a Big Difference*. Little, Brown, 2000.

Glazer-Raymo, Judith. "Gender Inequality." In *Women in Higher Education: An Encyclopedia*, ed. Ana M. Martinez Alemán and Kristen A. Renn, 226. Santa Barbara, CA: ABC-CLIO, 2002.

Glenn, Evelyn Nakano. *Unequal Freedom: How Race and Gender Shaped American Citizenship and Labor*. Cambridge, MA: Harvard University Press, 2002.

"Globalization and Clothes." Women and the Economy, United Nations Platform for Action Committee Manitoba. 2006. www.unpac.ca (July 2, 2010).

Global Oneness. "Metrosexual—Evolution of Usage." http://www.experience festival.com (June 17, 2009).

———. "Metrosexual—Narcissism and Changing Masculinity: The Metrosexual." http://www.experiencefestival.com (June 17, 2009).

Goetzé, Anne Marie, and Rina Sen Gupta. "Who Takes the Credit? Gender, Power, and Control over Loan Use in Rural Credit Programs in Bangladesh." *World Development* 24, no. 1 (1996): 45–63.

Goffman, Erving. *The Presentation of Self in Everyday Life*. New York: Doubleday, 1959.

"Good for Business: Making Full Use of the Nation's Human Capital." A Fact-Fing Report of the Federal Glass Ceiling Commission. March 1995. http://www.dol.gov (June 30, 2010).

Gordon, Liz, and Paul Willis. "Education, Cultural Production, and Social Reproduction." *British Journal of Sociology of Education* 5 (1984): 105–115.

Grieger, Martin. "Electronic Marketplaces: A Literature Review and a Call for Supply Chain Management Research." *European Journal of Operational Research* 144, no. 2 (2003): 280–294.

Guendouzi, Jackie. "'The Guilt Thing': Balancing Domestic and Professional Roles." *Journal of Marriage and Family* 58 (2006): 901–909.

Håkansson, Hakan. *Industrial Technological Development: A Network Approach.* London: Croom Helm, 1987.

Håkansson, Hakan, and Ivan Snehota. *Developing Relationships in Business Networks.* London: Routledge, 1995.

Hanisch, Carol. "The Personal Is Political." In *Notes from the Second Year: Women's Liberation: Major Writings of the Radical Feminists,* ed. Shulamith Firestone and Anne Koedt, 76–78. New York: Radical Feminists, 1970.

Harper, Hill. *Letters to a Young Sister: DeFine Your Destiny.* New York: Gotham Books, 2008.

Harris, Dena. *Lee Kirkman: Breaking In to a Woman's World.* Common Boundaries, 2004. http://www.commonboundaries.com (June 6, 2009).

Harris, Nonie. "Radical Activism and Accidental Philanthropy: The Impact of First-Wave Feminist Activism on the Later Construction of Child Care Policies in Australia and the United States of America." *Women's Studies International Forum* 31 (2008): 42–52.

Hartman, S. M. "Pauli Murray and the Juncture of Women's Liberation and Black Liberation." *Journal of Women's History* 14, no. 2 (Summer 2002): 74–79.

Hartmann, Heidi. "Capitalism, Patriarchy, and Job Segregation by Sex." *Signs* 1, no. 3 (Spring 1976): 137–169.

———. "The Unhappy Marriage of Marxism and Feminism: Towards a More Progressive Union." *Capital and Class* 8, no. 2 (1979): 1–33.

Hartsock, Nancy C. M. *Money, Sex, and Power: Toward a Feminist Historical Materialism.* Boston: Northeastern University Press, 1985.

Harvey, Steve. *Act Like a Lady, Think Like a Man: What Men Really Think About Love Relationships, Intimacy, and Commitment.* New York: HarperCollins, 2009.

Hashmi, Syed M., Sidney Ruth Schuler, and Ann P. Riley. "Rural Credit Programs and Women's Empowerment in Bangladesh." *World Development* 24, no. 4 (1996): 635–653.

Hattery, Angela. *Women, Work, and Family: Balancing and Weaving.* Thousand Oaks, CA: Sage, 2001.

Hattwick, Richard E. "Mary Kay Ash." *Journal of Behavioral Economics* 16 (1987): 61–69.

Hausmann, Ricardo, Laura D. Tyson, and Saadia Zahidi. *The Global Gender Gap Report.* Geneva: World Economic Forum, 2008.

Hays, Sharon. *The Cultural Contradictions of Motherhood.* New Haven, CT: Yale University Press, 1996.

Haywood, Leslie, and Jennifer Drake. *Third Wave Agenda: Being Feminist, Doing Feminism.* Minneapolis: University of Minnesota Press, 1997.

Hedaa, Laurids, and Jan-Åke Törnroos. "Understanding Event-Based Business Networks." *Time and Society* 17 (2008): 319–348.

Hess, Beth B., and Myra Marx Ferree. *Analyzing Gender: A Handbook of Social Science Research.* Newbury Park, CA: Sage, 1987.

Hesse-Biber, Sharlene Nagy. *The Cult of Thinness.* New York: Oxford University Press, 2007.

"Hillary Clinton Endorses Barack Obama." *New York Times,* June 27, 2008. http://www.nytimes.com (May 28, 2009).

Hill Collins, Patricia. *Black Feminist Thought: Knowledge, Consciousness, and the Politics of Empowerment.* New York: Routledge, 2000.

———. "The Meaning of Motherhood in Black Culture and Black Mother/Daughter Relationships." *Sage* 4 (1987): 3–10.

Hochschild, Arlie Russell. *The Managed Heart: Commercialization of Human Feeling.* Berkeley: University of California Press, 1983.

Hochschild, Arlie Russell, with Anne Machung. *The Second Shift.* New York: Avon Books, 1989.

Hoffman, Rose Marie, and L. DiAnne Borders. "Twenty-Five Years After the Bem Sex-Role Inventory: A Reassessment and New Issues Regarding Classification Variability." *Measurement and Evaluation in Counseling and Development* 34, no. 1 (2001): 39–55.

Home Party Millionaires. "The Ultimate Body Wrap by It Works!" 2008. http://www.wrapnlosefat.com (July 1, 2010).

Hondagneu-Sotelo, Pierrette. *Domestica.* Berkeley: University of California Press, 2001.

Hughes, Langston. "Mother to Son." In *The Collected Poems of Langston Hughes*, ed. Arnold Rampersand. NewYork: Vintage Books, 1995.

Hunter, Karen. "Atlanta Literacy Club Makes History with 100th Anniversary." Black Voices Bookshelf, 2009. http://www.bvonbooks.com (May 3, 2009).

Ingraham, Chrys. "The Heterosexual Imaginary: Feminist Sociology and Theories of Gender." In *Materialist Feminism*, ed. R. Hennessy and Chrys Ingraham, 275–290. New York: Routledge, 1997.

———. *White Weddings: Romancing Heterosexuality in Popular Culture.* New York: Routledge, 1999.

Institute for Women's Policy Research. "Fact Sheet: The Gender Wage Gap by Occupation." April 2009. http://www.iwpr.org (June 8, 2009).

———. "The Gender Wage Gap: 2008." April 2009. http://www.iwpr.org (June 14, 2009).

International Anticounterfeiting Coalition. "Get Real—The Truth About Counterfeiting." http://iacc.org (May 15, 2009).

International Confederation of Free Trade Unions. "The Informal Economy: Women on the Frontline." *Trade Union World: Briefing* 2 (2004): 1–16. http://www.icftu.org (June 8, 2009).

International Labor Office (ILO). "Global Employment Trends for Women, 2004." March 2004. http://kilm.ilo.org (June 15, 2009).

———. *Women and Men in the Informal Economy: A Statistical Picture.* Geneva, Switzerland: ILO, 2002.

Jhabvala, Renana, and Jane Tate. "Out of the Shadows: Homebased Workers Organize for International Recognition." *SEEDS*, no. 18 (1996). New York: Population Council.

Johnson, Allan G. *The Gender Knot: Unraveling Our Patriarchal Legacy.* Philadelphia: Temple University Press, 1997.

Jones, Del. "Women CEOs Slowly Gain on Corporate America." *USA Today*, January 2, 2009. http://www.usatoday.com (June 17, 2009).

Jost, John. "An Experimental Replication of the Depressed-Entitlement Effect Among Women." *Psychology of Women Quarterly* 21 (1997): 387–393.

———. "Negative Illusions: Conceptual Clarification and Conceptual Evidence Concerning False Consciousness." *Political Psychology* 16, no. 2 (June 1995): 397–424.

Kabeer, Naila. "Resources, Agency, Achievements: Reflections on the Measurement of Women's Empowerment." *Development and Change* 30 (1999): 435–464.

Kane, Emily W., and Mimi Schippers. "Men's and Women's Beliefs About Gender and Sexuality." *Gender & Society* 10, no. 5 (1996): 650–665.

Kanter, Rosabeth Moss. *Men and Women of the Corporation.* New York: Basic Books, 1977.

Karl, Marilee. *Women and Empowerment: Participation and Decision-Making.* London: Zed Books, 1995.

Kaufman, Sarah J. "Note: Trend Forcast: Imitation Is a Legal Form of Flattery—Louis Vuiton Malletier V. Dooney & Bourke, Inc." *Cardoza Arts and Entertainment* 23 (2005): 531–566.

Kealing, Bob. *Tupperware Unsealed: Brownie Wise, Earl Tupper, and the Home Party Pioneers.* Gainesville: University Press of Florida, 2008.

Kerber, Linda. *Women of the Republic: Intellect and Ideology in Revolutionary America.* New York: Norton, 1986.

Kidd, Sue Monk. *The Secret Life of Bees.* New York: Penguin, 2002.

Kimmel, Michael, and Michael Messner. *Men's Lives,* 8th ed. Boston: Pearson/Allyn and Bacon, 2010.

Kingston, Anne. *The Meaning of Wife: A Provocative Look at Women and Marriage in the Twenty-First Century.* New York: Farrar, Straus and Giroux, 2005.

Kirkham, Pat. *The Gendered Object.* Manchester, UK: Manchester University Press, 1990.

Klepacki, Laura. *Avon: Building the World's Premier Company for Women.* Hoboken, NJ: John Wiley and Sons, 2005.

Kocken, Marlike. "Fair Trade Organizations and Fair Trade Labelling." World Fair Trade Organization, February 9, 2009. http://www.wfto.com (Path: About Fair Trade; 60 Years of Fair Trade; Fair Trade Organizations and Fair Trade Labelling) (April 23, 2009).

———. "Where Did It All Begin?" World Fair Trade Organization, February 9, 2009. http://www.wfto.com (April 23, 2009).

Kwolek-Folland, Angel. "The Elegant Dugout: Domesticity and Moveable Culture in the United States, 1870–1900." *American Studies* 24 (Fall 1984): 21–37.

Lan, Pei-Chia. "Networking Capitalism: Network Construction and Control Effects in Direct Selling." *Sociological Quarterly* 43, no. 2 (2002): 165–184.

Landes, Joan B. "Further Thoughts on the Public/Private Distinction." *Journal of Women's History* 15, no. 2 (Summer 2003): 28–39.

Leach, William. "Transformation in a Culture of Consumption: Women and Department Stores, 1890–1925." *Journal of American History* 71 (September 1984): 319–342.

Leadership Conference on Civil Rights Education Fund. "Confronting the New Faces of Hate: Hate Crimes in America." June 2009. http://www.civilrights.org (June 17, 2009).

Lewin, Ellen. *Feminist Anthropology: A Reader.* Malden, MA: Wiley-Blackwell, 2006.

———. "Negotiating Lesbian Motherhood: The Dialectics of Resistance and Accommodation." In *Mothering: Ideology, Experience, and Agency,* ed. Evelyn Nanako Glenn, Grace Chang, and Linda Renney Forcey, 333–354. New York: Routledge, 1994.

Lewis, Jone Johnson. "Joan Baez Quotes." About.com: Women's History. http://womenshistory.about.com (June 28, 2009).

Lewis, Katrina, Torry Dickinson, and Summer Lewis. "Pedagogical Innovations in Sustainable Development: Fair Trade in the Classroom." Paper presented at the Leading Kansas in Sustainability Conference, Kansas State University, Manhattan, KS, January 23, 2009. http://krex.k-state.edu (April 25, 2009).

Little, Daniel. "False Consciousness." University of Michigan. http://www-personal.umd.umich.edu (June 19, 2009).

Littrell, Mary Ann, and Marsha Ann Dickson. *Social Responsibility in the Global Market: Fair Trade of Cultural Products.* Thousand Oaks, CA: Sage, 1999.

Long, Elizabeth. *Book Clubs: Women and the Uses of Reading in Everyday Life.* Chicago: University of Chicago Press, 2003.

Longaberger. "Become a Home Consultant." 2009. http://www.longaberger.com (May 15, 2009).

Lopata, Helena Z., and Barrie Thorne. "On the Term 'Sex Roles.'" *Signs* 3, no. 3 (Spring 1978): 718–721.

Lorber, Judith. "Believing Is Seeing: Biology as Idealogy" *Gender & Society* 7, no. 4 (1993): 568–581.

———. "Beyond the Binaries: Depolarizing the Categories of Sex, Sexuality, and Gender." *Sociological Inquiry* 66, no. 2 (1996): 143–159.

———. *Paradoxes of Gender.* New Haven, CT: Yale University Press, 1994.

Lorde, Audre. *Sister Outsider.* Berkeley, CA: Crossing Press Feminist Series, 1984.

Lucal, Betsy. "What It Means to Be Gendered Me: Life on the Boundaries of a Dichotomous Gender System." *Gender & Society* 13, no. 6 (1999): 781–797.

Magarey, Susan. *Passions of the First Wave Feminists.* Seattle: University of Washington Press, 2002.

Maines, Rachel P. *The Technology of Orgasm: "Hysteria," the Vibrator, and Women's Sexual Satisfaction.* Baltimore, MD: Johns Hopkins University Press, 1999.

Major, Brenda. "From Social Inequality to Personal Entitlement: The Role of Social Comparisons, Legitimacy Appraisals, and Group Membership." *Advances in Experimental Social Psychology* 26 (1994): 293–355.

Malina, Danusia, and Ruth A. Schmidt. "It's a Business Doing Pleasure with You: Sh! A Women's Sex Shop Case." *Marketing Intelligence and Planning* 15, no. 7 (1997): 352–360.

Markon, Jerry. "Va. Men Plead Guilty in Fake Purse Scam: Designer Knockoffs Were Sold at Parties." *Washington Post,* February 3, 2007, B03.

Martin, Patricia Yancey. "Rethinking Feminist Organizations." *Gender & Society* 4, no. 2 (1990): 182–206.

———. "'Said and Done' Versus 'Saying and Doing': Gendering Practices, Practicing Gender at Work." *Gender & Society* 17, no. 3 (2003): 342–366.

Mary Kay. "Global Growth Quick Facts." http://www.marykay.com (June 15, 2009).

———. "Mary Kay Around the World." http://www.marykay.com (June 2, 2009).

Mary Kay Canada. "Earnings Representation." 2000. http://web.archive.org (May 3, 2009).

"Mary Kay Earnings." Wikipedia, 2008. http://en.wikipedia.org (June 15, 2009).

Max, D. T. "The Oprah Effect." *New York Times Magazine.* December 26, 1999, 37–41.

McCaughey, Martha, and Christina French. "Women's Sex-Toy Parties: Technology, Orgasm, and Commodification." *Sexuality and Culture* 5, no. 3 (2001): 77–96.

McHenry, Elizabeth. *Forgotten Readers: Recovering the Lost History of African American Literary Societies.* Durham, NC: Duke University Press, 2002.

McHenry, Elizabeth, and S. Heath. "The Literature and the Literary: African Americans as Writers and Readers, 1830–1940." *Written Communication* 11, no. 4 (1994): 419–444.

McWilliams, Peter. Quoted in "Get Out of Your Comfort Zone." Debra Russell Coaching. http://www.debrarussell.com (June 25, 2009).

Messerschmidt, James W. *Masculinities and Crime: Critique and Reconceptualization of Theory.* Lanham, MD: Rowman and Littlefield, 1993.

———. *Nine Lives: Adolescent Masculinities, the Body, and Violence.* Boulder, CO: Westview, 2000.

Mies, Maria. *Patriarchy and Accumulation on a World Scale: Women in the International Division of Labour.* London: Zed Books, 1998.

Mies, Maria, and Veronika Bennholdt-Thomsen. *The Subsistence Perspective: Beyond the Globalised Economy.* London: Zed Books, 1999.

Mitter, Swasti. "On Organising Women in Casualised Work: A Global Overview." In *Dignity and Daily Bread: New Forms of Economic Organising Among Poor Women in the Third World and the First*, ed. Sheila Rowbotham and Swasti Mitter, 14–52. New York: Routledge, 1994.

Mock, Freida Lee. "Maya Lin: A Strong Clear Vision." American Documentary. 2007. http://amdoc.org (July 7, 2010).

Moghadam, Valentine. *Globalizing Women: Transnational Feminist Networks*. Baltimore, MD: Johns Hopkins University Press, 1995.

Mohanty, Chandra Talpade, Ann Russo, and Lourdes Torres. *Third World Women and the Politics of Feminism*. Bloomington: Indiana University Press, 1991.

Montemurro, Beth. "Sex Symbols: The Bachelorette Party as a Window to Change in Women's Sexual Expression." *Sexuality and Culture* 7, no. 3 (2003): 3–29.

———. *Something Old, Something Bold: Bridal Showers and Bachelorette Parties*. New Brunswick, NJ: Rutgers University Press, 2006.

Moore, Nathan P. "Re: Comments of Mary Kay Inc. to the Proposed Business Opportunity Rule, R511993." Federal Trade Commission, July 17, 2006. http://www.ftc.gov (April 7, 2009).

Morrell, Carolyn. *Unwomanly Conduct: The Challenges of Intentional Childlessness*. New York: Routledge, 1994.

Mosaic Books. "Black Sistahs United Book Clubs." 2002. http://www.mosaicbooks.com (April 28, 2009).

Mull, Amanda. "Can Counterfeit Bags Make You a Bad Person?" The Purse Blog, April 9, 2009. http://www.purseblog.com (June 5, 2009).

Nader, Laura. "Orientalism, Occidentalism, and the Control of Women." *Cultural Dynamics* 2, no. 3 (1989): 137–169.

Naples, Nancy, and Manisha Desai. *Women's Activism and Globalization: Linking Local Struggles and Transnational Politics*. New York: Routledge, 2002.

Nardi, Bonnie A., and Yrjö Engeström. "A Web on the Wind: The Structure of Invisible Work." A special issue of *Computer-Supported Cooperative Work*, May 17, 1998. http://www.darrouzet-nardi.net (June 4, 2009).

National Endowment for the Arts. "Reading at Risk: A Survey of Literary Reading in America, Executive Summary." Washington, DC: National Endowment for the Arts, 2002. http://ublib.buffalo.edu (May 28, 2009).

Nicholson, Linda. *The Second Wave: A Reader in Feminist Theory*. New York: Routledge, 1997.

Nine Inch Nails. "The Hand That Feeds." *With Teeth*. Island Records, CD. 2005.

Oberbeck, Steven. "Utah Woman a Star in Pink." *Salt Lake Tribune*, May 15, 2008, reproduced on Sequence, Inc.: Forensic Accounting Answers. http://www.sequenceinc.com (June 15, 2009).

Olson, Lynne. *Freedom's Daughters: The Unsung Heroines of the Civil Rights Movement from 1830 to 1970*. New York: Scribner, 2002.

Padavic, Irene, and Barbara Reskin. *Women and Men at Work,* 2nd ed. Thousand Oaks, CA: Pine Forge Press, 2002.

Page, Peter. "Fired Mary Kay Worker Wins Job Suit." Law.com, December 12, 2002. http://www.law.com (June 2, 2009).

Palmer, Bertha. "1893 Address." In *Modern American Women: A Documentary History*, ed. Susan Ware. Chicago: Dorsey Press, 1989.

Pampered Chef. "Come Join Us." http://www.pamperedchef.com (May 15, 2009).

———. "Company Facts." http://www.pamperedchef.com (June 2, 2009).

———. "Our Company." August 7, 2007. http://www.pamperedchef.com (June 9, 2009).

Parham, Marti. "Blacks Read More Than Whites, Hispanics: Poll." *Jet*, September 10, 2007. http://findarticles.com (June 19, 2009).

Partylite. "Become a Consultant." http://www.partylite.com (May 15, 2009).

Paulin, Geoffrey D., and Yoon G. Lee. "Expenditures of Single Parents: How Does Gender Figure In?" *Monthly Labor Review* (July 2002). http://www.bls.gov (June 16, 2009).

Pelosi, Nancy. "Equal Pay Day." US House of Representatives, Office of the Speaker. 2009. http://www.speaker.gov (June 1, 2009).

Penn, Serena. "Avon Calling for Layoffs." TheStreet.com, January 8, 2008. http://www .thestreet .com (June 8, 2009).

Penner, Gloria. "The Pitiful Progress of Women in Politics." KPBS, February 27, 2009. http://www.kpbs.org (June 16, 2009).

Perez, Marisol, and Thomas E. Joiner. "Body Image Dissatisfaction and Disordered Eating in Black and White Women." *International Journal of Eating Disorders* 33, no. 3 (2003).

Perry, William G. *Forms of Intellectual and Ethical Development in the College Years.* New York: Holt, Rinehart, and Winston, 1970.

Phizacklea, Annie, and Carol Wolkowitz. *Homeworking Women: Gender, Racism, and Class at Work.* Thousand Oaks, CA: Sage, 1995.

Piercy, Marge, and Jane Freeman. "Getting Together: How to Start a Consciousness-Raising Group." University of Maryland–Baltimore County, 1972. http://user pages.umbc.edu (June 14, 2009).

Pink Lighthouse. "Warm Chatter Training." April 2008. http://www.pinklighthouse.com (June 29, 2009).

———. "What Can We Learn from Mary Kay's Company Information?" April 10, 2008. http://www.pinklighthouse.com (June 15, 2009).

Platoni, Kara. "What a Steal! Counterfeiters Apply Tupperware Business Model to an Illicit New Enterprise: Purse Parties." *East Bay Express*, November 3, 2004. http:// www.eastbayexpress.com (June 5, 2009).

Presser, Harriet B., and Elizabeth Bamberger. "American Women Who Work at Home for Pay: Distinctions and Determinants." *Social Science Quarterly* 74 (1993): 815–837.

The Princess Bride. Directed by Rob Reiner. MGM, 1987. DVD, July 18, 2000.

Pryor, Devon. "What Is a Literary Canon?" Wise Geek. http://www.wisegeek.com (June 16, 2009).

Purkayastha, Bandana, and Mangala Subramaniam. *The Power of Women's Informal Networks: Lessons in Social Change from South Asia and West Africa.* Lanham, MD: Lexington Books, 2004.

"Purse Parties Funding Organized Crime?" WFTV (Omaha), July 2008. http://www .wftv.com (May 7, 2009).

Putnam, Robert D. *Bowling Alone: The Collapse and Revival of American Community.* New York: Simon and Schuster, 2000.

Rand, C. S. W., and J. M. Kaldau. "The Epidemiology of Obesity and Self-Defined Weight Problems in the General Population: Gender, Race, Age, and Social Class." *International Journal of Eating Disorders* 9, no. 3 (1990): 329–343.

Randhir, Aruna. "Three Cheers to Kitty Parties." *Deccan Herald*, January 30, 2004. http://www.deccanherald.com (March 25, 2007).

Reiman, Jeffrey. *The Rich Get Richer and the Poor Get Prison: Ideology, Class, and Criminal Justice,* 8th ed. Boston: Pearson/Allyn and Bacon, 2006.

Reinharz, Shulamit. *Feminist Methodologies in Social Research.* New York: Oxford University Press, 1992.

Rennison, Callie Marie. "Rape and Sexual Assault: Reporting to Police and Medical Attention, 1992–2000." US Department of Justice, August 2002. http://ojp.usdoj.gov (June 20, 2009).

Rich, Adrienne. "Compulsory Heterosexuality and Lesbian Existence." *Signs* 5 (1980): 631–660.

Richardson, Marilyn. *Maria W. Stewart, America's First Black Woman Political Writer: Essays and Speeches.* Blacks in the Diaspora. Bloomington: Indiana University Press, 1982.

Richman, Joe, and Samara Freemark. "The First Woman to Run for President—in 1872." *All Things Considered,* NPR, October 13, 2008. http://www.npr.org (June 17, 2009).

Rockwell, Page. "Feminists Just Want to Have Fun." *Salon,* September 29, 2006. http://www.salon.com (June 14, 2009).

Rooney, Kathleen. *Reading with Oprah: The Book Club That Changed America,* 2nd ed. Fayetteville: University of Arkansas Press, 2005.

Roosevelt, Eleanor. Remarks on universal human rights at presentation of booklet on human rights, *In Your Hands,* to the United Nations Commission on Human Rights, United Nations, New York, March 27, 1958. http://quotationsbook.com (June 28, 2009).

Rothbard, Murray N. "Free Market." In *The Concise Encyclopedia of Economics,* ed. David Henderson, 200–202. Indianapolis, IN: Liberty Fund, Inc., 2007.

Rothblum, Esther, and Sondra Solovay. *The Fat Studies Reader.* New York: New York University Press, 2009.

Royster, J. J. *Trace of a Stream: Literacy and Social Change Among African American Women.* Pittsburgh: University of Pittsburgh Press, 2000.

Rubin, Gayle. "The Traffic in Women: Notes on the 'Political Economy' of Sex." *Feminist Anthropology* (2006): 87–106.

Russo, Ann. "We Cannot Live Without Our Lives." In *Third World Women and the Politics of Feminism,* ed. Chandra Talpade Mohanty, Ann Russo, and Lourdes Torres. Bloomington: Indiana University Press, 1991.

Sackler, Elizabeth A., Center for Feminist Art. *The Dinner Party: Heritage Floor: Milla Granson.* Brooklyn Museum, 2009. http://www.brooklynmuseum.org (June 19, 2009).

Sawhill, Isabel, and John E. Morton. "Economic Mobility: Is the American Dream Alive and Well?" Economic Mobility Project, 2007. www.economicmobility.org (June 15, 2009).

Scheibeler, Eric. *Merchants of Deception.* Charleston, SC: Booksurge, 2009.

Schneider, Friedrich, and Dominik H. Enste. *The Shadow Economy: An International Survey.* Cambridge, UK: Cambridge Univeristy Press, 2002.

Schudson, Michael. "Delectable Materialism: Second Thoughts on Consumer Culture." In *Consumer Society in American History: A Reader,* ed. Lawrence B. Glickman. Ithaca, NY: Cornell University Press, 1999.

"Selling Tupperware Results in a Salad Bowl of Problems." Advocate, *Times Union,* Albany, NY, October 12, 2008. http://www.timesunion.com (June 2, 2009).

Sen, Amartya. "Economics and the Family." *Asian Development Review* 1, no. 2 (1983): 14–21.

Sen, Gita, and Harriet Presser, eds. *Women's Empowerment and Demographic Processes: Moving Beyond Cairo.* Oxford, UK: Oxford University Press, 2000.

Silpada Designs. "Polishing Off Juvenile Diabetes." http://www.silpada.com (June 2, 2009).

———. "The Silpada Story." http://www.silpada.com (May 15, 2009).

Šindlerová, Ivana. "Women and Home-Based Work in the Czech Republic: Home-Based Work: A Precarious and Underpaid Occupation Concealed Within the Walls of the Home, or a Flexible Option Ensuring Life-Work Balance?" 2002. http://www.ekscr.cz (June 17, 2009).

Skolnick, Avy, Crystal Middlestadt, Edward Cervantes, Jake Finney, Jarad Ringer, Joseph Barretto, Julio Gonzalez, Kelly Costello, Lindsey Moore, Melissa Pope, Michelle Kaufman, Patricia Duffett, Rebecca Kloek, Tina D'Elia, and Victoria Cruz. "Hate Violence Against LGBT People in US Report." National Coalition of Anti-Violence Programs. 2008. http://www.avp.org (June 30, 2009).

Smith, Adam. *An Inquiry into the Nature and Causes of the Wealth of Nations.* Middlesex, UK: Echo Library, 2006.

Smith, Dorothy. *The Conceptual Practices of Power: A Feminist Sociology of Knowledge.* Boston: Northeastern University Press, 1990.

———. *The Everyday World as Problematic: A Feminist Sociology.* Boston: Northeastern University Press, 1987.

Snyder, R. Claire. "What Is Third Wave Feminism? A New Directions Essay." *Signs* 34, no. 1 (2008): 175–196.

"Speak Sister, Speak: Oral Empowerment in *Louisa Picquet, The Octoroon.*" *Legacy: A Journal of American Women Writers* 15 (1998): 98–103.

Sprague, Joey. "Holy Men and Big Guns: The Ca(n)on in Social Theory." *Gender & Society* 11, no. 1 (1997): 88–107.

Stalp, Marybeth C. *Quilting: The Fabric of Everyday Life.* New York: Berg, 2007.

———. "We Do It Cuz It's Fun." *Sociological Perspectives* 51, no. 2 (2008): 325–348.

Stuber, Irene. "The UN's Role of Advancing the Rights of Women." The Liz Library, Women's History Month Collection. 2000. http://www.thelizlibrary.org (July 7, 2010).

———. "Women's History Month Collection." The Liz Library. 2006. http://www.thelizlibrary.org (June 28, 2009).

Taylor, John M. "Some Shocking Statistics: Comparing Recruiting MLM's with No-Product Pyramid Schemes, and with Gambling." Consumer Awareness Institute. http://www.mlm-thetruth.com (June 1, 2009)

Taylor, K., C. Marienau, and M. Fiddler. *Developing Adult Learners: Strategies for Teachers and Trainers.* San Francisco: Jossey-Bass, 2000.

Taylor, Rex. "Marilyn's Friends and Rita's Customers: A Study of Party-Selling as Play and as Work." *Sociological Review* 26, no. 3 (1978): 573–594.

Thomas, Pattie. *Taking Up Space.* Nashville, TN: Pearlsong Press, 2005.

Thorne, Barrie. *Gender Play: Girls and Boys in School.* Piscataway, NJ: Rutgers University Press, 2004.

Thur, Susan. "Alexander Hamilton Report on Manufacturers to Congress 1791." *Salon,* 2008. http://open.salon.com (July 7, 2010).

Thurman, Wallace. *The Blacker the Berry: A Novel of Negro Life.* 1929. Reprint, Austin, TX: Touchstone, 1996.

Tolman, Deborah L. "In a Different Position: Conceptualizing Female Adolescent Sexuality Within Compulsory Heterosexuality." *Rethinking Positive Adolescent Female Sexual Development: New Directions for Child and Adolescent Development* (2006): 71–89.

Trachtenberg, Jeffrey A. "Why Book Industry Sees the World Still Split by Race." *Wall Street Journal,* December 6, 2006.

Tupperware. "Opportunity." 2009. http://order.tupperware.com (May 15, 2009).

———. "Party Inspiration Center." http://www.tupperware.com (June 15, 2009).

———. "World Wide Presence." http://www.tupperwarebrands.com (June 2, 2009).

Tupperware! The Film and More. "Primary Sources: Brownie and Earl's Aphorisms." *The American Experience,* PBS, December 11, 2003. http://www.pbs.org (June 14, 2009).

———. "Timeline: Women, Work, and Plastics History." *The American Experience,* PBS, December 11, 2003. http://www.pbs.org (June 8, 2009).

Ulrich, Laurel Thatcher. *A Midwife's Tale: The Life of Martha Ballard, Based on Her Diary, 1785–1812*. New York: Vintage, 1991.

United Nations. "Guidelines to Women's Empowerment." http://www.un.org (June 5, 2009).

United Nations Department of Public Information. "Fourth World Conference on Women 1995." http://www.un.org (June 9, 2009).

United Students Against Sweatshops. "History and Formation of USAS." http://www .studentsagainstsweatshops.org (June 14, 2009).

US Department of Labor, Bureau of Labor Statistics. "Women in the Labor Force: A Databook." December 2008. http://www.bls.gov (June 1, 2009).

———. TED: The Editor's Desk. "Changes in Women's Labor Force Participation in the Twentieth Century." February 16, 2000. http://www.bls.gov (June 12, 2009).

US Department of State, Bureau of Democracy, Human Rights, and Labor. "Guatemala." March 8, 2006. http://www.state.gov (April 23, 2009).

"Vienna Second Most-Livable City in World, Claims *Economist*." *Austrian Times*, 2009. http://www.austriantimes.at (June 28, 2009).

Villemez, Wayne J., and John Beggs. "Culture, Opportunity, and Attainment: The Impact of the Local Area." Paper presented at the annual meeting of the International Sociological Association, Bielefeld, Germany, 1993.

Vincent, Susan. "Preserving Domesticity: Reading Tupperware in Women's Changing Domestic, Social, and Economic Roles." *Canadian Review of Sociology and Anthropology/La Revue Canadienne de Sociologie et d'Anthropologie* 40, no. 2 (2003): 171–196.

Viner, Katharine. "The Personal Is Still Political." In *On the Move: Feminism for a New Generation*, ed. Natasha Walter. London: Virago Books, 2000.

Voice Network. "Tell Avon to Support Workers Rights." 2004. http://www.union voice.org (June 5, 2009).

Waggoner, Catherine Egley. "The Emancipatory Potential of Feminine Masquerade in Mary Kay Cosmetics." *Text and Performance Quarterly* 17 (1997): 256–272.

Wald, Jenny. "Outlaw Mothers." *Hastings Women's Law Journal* 8 (1997): 169–193.

Walsh, Joan. "Feminism After Friedan." *Salon*, February 6, 2006. http://www.salon.com (June 6, 2009).

Walters, S. D. "Sex, Text, and Context: (In) Between Feminism and Cultural Studies." In *Revisioning Gender (The Gender Lens)*, ed. Myra Marx Ferree, Judith Lorber, and Beth B. Hess, 2nd ed. Thousand Oaks, CA: Sage, 2004.

Ware, Susan. *Modern American Women: A Documentary History*. Chicago: Dorsey Press, 1989.

Warner, Marina. "Emmeline Pankhurst." *Time*, June 14, 1999. http://www.time.com (June 25, 2009).

Weber, Max. *The Protestant Ethic and the Spirit of Capitalism*. Translated by Talcott Parsons. New York: Charles Scribner's Sons, 1958.

Webster, Murray, Jr., and Lisa Slattery Rashotte. "Fixed Roles and Situated Actions." *Sex Roles: A Journal of Research* 61 (2009): 325–337.

Weitz, Rose. "Women and Their Hair: Seeking Power Through Resistance and Accommodation." *Gender & Society* 15 (2001): 667–686.

Welter, Barbara. "The Cult of True Womanhood: 1820–1860." *American Quarterly* 18, no. 2 (Summer 1966): 151–174.

Werner International Management Consultants. "International Comparison of the Hourly Labor Cost in the Primary Textile Industry, Winter 2004/2005." *New Twist*, March 8, 2006. http://www.werner-newtwist.com (June 5, 2009).

West, Candace, and Don H. Zimmerman. "Accounting for Doing Gender." *Gender & Society* 23 (2009): 112–122.

———. "Doing Gender." *Gender & Society* 1, no. 2 (1987): 125–151.

West, M. S., and J. W. Curtis. "AAUP Faculty Gender Equity Indicators 2006." American Association of University Professors, 2008. http://www.aaup.org (May 25, 2009).

Wichroski, Michael. "The Secretary: Invisible Labor in the Workworld of Women." *Human Organization* 53 (1994): 33–41.

Williams, Christine L. "The Glass Escalator: Hidden Advantages for Men in Nontraditional Occupations." *Social Problems* 39 (1992): 253–267.

Williams, L. Susan. "Gender Regimes and the Prophecy of Place: Micro/Macro Dimensions of Stratification Processes for Young Women." PhD dissertation, University of Connecticut, 1997.

———. "Trying on Gender, Gender Regimes, and the Process of Becoming Women." *Gender & Society* 16, no. 1 (February 2002): 29–52.

Williams, L. Susan, Sandra D. Alvarez, and Kevin S. Andrade Hauck. "My Name Is Not María: Young Latinas Seeking Home in the Heartland." *Social Problems* 49, no. 4 (2002): 563–584.

Wilson, John, and Mark Musick. "Who Cares? Toward an Integrated Theory of Volunteer Work." *American Sociological Review* 62, no. 5 (1997): 694–713.

Women in Informal Employment: Globalizing and Organizing. "Main Findings." http://www.weigo.org (July 2, 2010).

———. "Programme Areas: Social Protection." http://www.wiego.org (May 20, 2009).

———. "Street Vendors." http://www.wiego.org (May 20, 2009).

———. "Sub-Group Case Studies: Home-Based Work." http://www.wiego.org (June 5, 2009).

World Fair Trade Organization. "What Is Fair Trade?" February 9, 2009. http://www.wfto.com (April 23, 2009).

Wyatt, Sarah. "Mary Kay Global Expansion Raises Hope, Concerns." *Women's International Perspective*, June 25, 2007. http://thewip.net (May 20, 2009).

Yale Daily News Staff. *The Insider's Guide to the Colleges, 2006*. New York: St. Martin's, 2005.

Young, Kathleen Z. "The Imperishable Virginity of Saint Maria Goretti." *Gender & Society* 3, no. 4 (1989): 474–482.

The Contributors

Michelle Bemiller, assistant professor of sociology and criminology, Kansas State University, specializes in gender, deviance, and family.

Leigh E. Fine is a PhD candidate in sociology at the Ohio State University, specializing in gender, sexuality, and education.

Dusty Garner has a long career in entertainment and activism. He is currently completing a degree in political science at Kansas State University, and will enter a graduate program in justice studies in 2011.

The Gender Parties Crew is a small but beautiful, dedicated, talented (and humble!) group of people who continuously demonstrated the true spirit of teamwork. They are better known as Dr. Sue the love doctor (Sue), Dr. B the cheerleader (Michelle), Machine Man (Brett), Babyface K (Kierston), That Guy (David), Mel-Mom (Melissa), Bionic Woman (Caitlin), Dirty Dusty (Dusty), and Leslie the Lips (Leslie).

Gregory Gibson, is an applied sociologist and director of research for the National Registry of Emergency Medical Technicians; his research interests include gender and heroism.

Karen Kapusta-Pofahl, PhD in anthropology, conducted dissertation research in the Czech Republic and currently teaches at Washburn University in Topeka, Kansas.

Eva Kavková, cofounder of the European Contact Group in the Czech Republic, currently trains migrants and service workers in nongovernmental organizations and the state sector.

Summer Lewis, formerly with Equal Exchange, the oldest US fair-trade co-operative, currently works in Bangladesh at the Asian University for Women, training women leaders.

Ivana Šindlerová, cofounder of the European Contact Group in the Czech Republic, designs training materials to combine work with family and child care.

Adryanna Siqueira, previously a clinical practitioner in her native Brazil, is currently in the PhD program in marriage and family therapy at Kansas State University.

Jana Smiggels-Kavková studied social movements in Leiden, the Netherlands, and is currently director of Fórum 50%, a nonprofit organization focusing on life-work balance.

BeEtta Stoney, associate professor of education at Kansas State University, specializes in multiculturalism and prepares future educators in diversity and cultural issues.

Mangala Subramaniam, associate professor of sociology at Purdue University, teaches, researches, and writes books about social movements and global gender issues.

Dena Wallerson is director of Citywide Initiatives at the After-School Corporation in New York City, where she designs programming for high school–age students.

L. Susan Williams, associate professor of sociology and criminology, Kansas State University, specializes in gender, crime, and inequality.

Kimber R. Williams received her juris doctorate from the Univeristy of San Diego, and is active in the California Innocence Project, the San Diego district attorney's office, and the San Diego Domestic Violence Council.

Beth Williford, assistant professor of sociology at Manhattanville College, New York, specializes in gender and globalization; she studied indigenous resistance in Ecuador.

Akiko Yoshida is assistant professor of sociology at the University of Wisconsin, Whitewater.

Sue Zschoche, associate professor of history at Kansas State University, has researched extensively on US home economics; she teaches feminist movements and women's history.

Index

Acker, Joan, 8, 187
Albright, Madeleine, 243*n28*
Alexander, M. Jacqui, 162
Allen, Sheila, 195
Amway, 8, 10, 30, 99
Androgyny, 27
Angelou, Maya, 203
Anthony, Susan B., 141
Arbonne Cosmetics, 7, 8, 30
Aronson, Joshua, 239
Ash, Mary Kay, 8
Avon Cosmetics, 26, 30, 36, 37, 38, 53*n13*; financial structure, 7; global development of, 7, 99–100

Baez, Joan, 238
Baldwin, James, 202, 213
Ballard, Martha, 41, 42, 43, 46, 47
Bargh, John, 239
Belenky, Mary Field, 103
Bemiller, Michelle, 60, 109–118, 130, 140*fig*, 173, 174, 175, 176, 178, 233, 239
Benedict, Ruth, 185
The Blacker the Berry: A Novel of Negro Life (Morgan), 202
Black Feminist Thought (Collins), 35
Board of Lady Managers (Chicago), 47
Book clubs, African American, 3, 198–208, 236, 237; book selection, 205–206, 211–214; commitment to, 215–216; connection to culture and community, 206–207; cultural legacies and, 204–208; exchange of

advice and assistance at, 215; feminist epistemology of, 200; involvement in, 211; literacy rates and, 198; literary canon and, 202; literary societies among, 199–201; Oprah Book Club, 200; political activism and, 209; politics and power of, 208–216; preservation of Black culture through, 199; relating books to personal/professional experience, 206; as safe environments for discussion, 207; sister friends and, 203–204; slave narratives and, 200; sociality and, 214–215; storytelling and, 198, 204; as venue of empowerment, 207–208; writings of African Americans in, 202–203
Brazil, 13, 58, 62, 86–92, 237
Bromley, Dorothy Dunbar, 51, 52
Brown, Elsa Barkley, 201
Buffet, Warren, 100

Capitalism: defining, 165*n4*; dependence on consumers (women), 105; domestic labor in, 42; exploitation of party plan work, 64; exploitation of women's labor in, 110; failures of, 10–11; free-market, 92; global, 157; ideological influence on women, 136; interface with patriarchy, 171; manipulation of women's relationships by, 130; new markets for, 11; patriarchal, 111–112, 132*n32*, 187; removal of production from

About the Book

Do Tupperware parties and Mary Kay sales empower individual women, or do they exploit personal relationships for corporate gain? Looking through the overlapping lenses of gender, work, and culture, Susan Williams and Michelle Bemiller critically explore the world of party plan sales.

The authors investigate this $30-billion-a-year enterprise through a wide range of case studies that unpack its personal and professional results for women. Closely examining the promises of multilevel marketing programs, their book challenges the way we see women's participation in the party plan economy.

L. Susan Williams is associate professor of sociology at Kansas State University. **Michelle Bemiller** is assistant professor of sociology at Kansas State University.